CLARENDON LAW SERIES

Edited by

TONY HONORÉ AND JOSEPH RAZ

CLARENDON LAW SERIES

PRECEDENT IN ENGLISH LAW

by

RUPERT CROSS and J. W. HARRIS

FOURTH EDITION

CLARENDON PRESS · OXFORD

Oxford University Press, Great Clarendon Street, Oxford OX2 6DP
Oxford New York
Auckland Bankok Buenos Aires Cape Town Chenna
Dar es Salaam Delhi Hong Kong Istanbul Karachi Kolkata
Kuala Lumpur Madrid Melbourne Mexico City Mumbai
Nairobi São Paulo Shanghai Taipei Tokyo Toronto

Oxford is a trade mark of Oxford University Press

Published in the United States
by Oxford University Press, New York

British Library Cataloguing in Publication Data
(data available)

Library of Congress Cataloging in Publication Data
Cross, Rupert, Sir, 1912–
Precedent in English law / Rupert Cross.—4th ed. / edited by
J.W. Harris.
(Clarendon law series)
Includes bibliographical references and index.
1. Stare decisis—Great Britain. I. Harris, J. W. II. Title.
III. Series   KD695.C76 1991   347.42—dc20   [344.207]   90–26514
ISBN 0–19–876162–7
ISBN 0–19–876163–5 (pbk.)

4 6 5 3

Typset by Hope Services (Abingdon) Ltd.
Printed in Great Britain by
Selwood Printing Ltd,
Burgess Hill, West Sussex

PREFACE

THE three editions of this book, written by the late Sir Rupert Cross, have been the basic textbook on the subject of precedent in English Law for students and practitioners alike. He brought to the subject his characteristic combination of scholarship and practical common sense. It is with awe that I have undertaken the updating of the work for this fourth edition. I am grateful to Lady Cross and to the editors of the Clarendon Law Series for the honour of doing so. All Sir Rupert's colleagues and former pupils cherish his memory and mourn his loss. I first met him more than thirty years ago when he came to speak at his and my old school on the challenges and pitfalls of a career in the law. He was then, and continued to be, a source of inspiration to me and many others. I offer this fourth edition as an all too modest tribute to his memory.

The aim of the book continues to be a comprehensive statement of the current doctrine of precedent in England, set in the wider context of the jurisprudential problems which any treatment of this topic involves. Such problems include the nature of the *ratio decidendi* of a precedent and of its binding force, the significance of precedents alongside other sources of law, their role in legal reasoning, and the account which must be taken of them by any general theory of law. In all these matters, Sir Rupert Cross expounded, with clarity, a fairly traditional practitioners' view. This approach is preserved in the present edition, although references are included in Chapters II, V, VI, and VII to competing answers, taking into account developments in the literature since the third edition.

The principal alterations concern case-law. The main justification for producing this new edition is that much has changed since 1976 so that the book could not continue to fulfil its role as a work of reference unless it were updated. We have now much more experience as to the exercise by the House of Lords of its power, assumed in 1966, to overrule its own decisions. Other developments in *stare decisis* have been ambivalent. On the one hand, the decision in *Davis* v. *Johnson* (1979) AC 264 has, for the time being, settled the rule that the Court of Appeal is generally bound

by its own decisions. On the other hand, the exceptions to that rule
have been given a wider interpretation, and further putative
exceptions to *stare decisis* as a whole have been developed—
especially in relation to decisions without argument and 'obsolete'
decisions. All these topics have required a considerable rewriting
of Chapters III and IV. At many other points, recent illustrations
have also been inserted.

Another development, omitted from the previous edition,
concerns the possible implications for the doctrine of precedent of
the impact of European Community law. Additional material has
been incorporated in Chapters I and V to take account of this. I
wish to express my great indebtedness to Professor Eric Barendt of
University College, London, for his invaluable advice on this
subject. I also acknowledge with thanks help received from
Ms Anne De Moor of Somerville College, Oxford and Dr
Christine Gray of St Hilda's College in connection, respectively,
with French and public international law.

J. W. H.

Keble College, Oxford
July 1990

CONTENTS

LIST OF ABBREVIATIONS

ALJ	*Australian Law Journal*
ASSAL	*Annual Survey of South African Law*
CJQ	*Civil Justice Quarterly*
CLJ	*Cambridge Law Journal*
Col. LR	*Columbia Law Review*
Cr. LR	*Criminal Law Review*
HLR	*Harvard Law Review*
Int. and Comp. LQ	*International and Comparative Law Quarterly*
Isr. LR	*Israel Law Review*
LQR	*Law Quarterly Review*
LS	*Legal Studies*
MLR	*Modern Law Review*
Minn. LR	*Minnesota Law Review*
OJLS	*Oxford Journal of Legal Studies*
SLR	*Stanford Law Review*
Vand. LR	*Vanderbilt Law Review*
Yale LJ	*Yale Law Journal*

BIBLIOGRAPHY

A valuable collection of essays on precedent is contained in *Precedent in Law*, edited by LAURENCE GOLDSTEIN.

The leading contemporary work on the sources of law is *Law in the Making* (7th edn.), by SIR CARLETON ALLEN.

The Nature and Sources of the Law, by J. C. GRAY (2nd edn.) is a classic written primarily from the point of view of the United States.

The Science of Legal Judgment, by JAMES RAM, contains much valuable information about precedent in English law in the early part of the nineteenth century.

Another important study is *Precedent in English and Continental Law*, an inaugural lecture by DR A. L. GOODHART.

There are valuable chapters on precedent and the other sources of law in *A Textbook of Jurisprudence* (4th edn.), by G. W. PATON, *Jurisprudence*, by SIR JOHN SALMOND (12th edn.), edited by P. J. FITZGERALD, and *Jurisprudence* by R. W. M. DIAS (5th edn.).

For the *ratio decidendi* of a case, reference should be made to *Essays in Jurisprudence and the Common Law*, by DR A. L. GOODHART.

Legal reasoning is discussed in *The Nature of Legal Argument* by O. C. JENSEN; *An Introduction to Legal Reasoning*, by EDWARD H. LEVI; *Legal Reasoning and Legal Theory*, by NEIL MacCORMICK; *Justice, Law and Argument*, by CHAIM PERELMAN; *Precedent and Law*, by JULIUS STONE; and *A Theory of Legal Argumentation*, by ROBERT ALEXY.

The French Legal System, by DAVID and DE VREES, contains a helpful account of the sources of French law; for precedent in Scotland reference should be made to *Precedent in Scots Law*, by T. B. SMITH.

American works dealing with many of the subjects mentioned in this book are: *The Nature of the Judicial Process*, by BENJAMIN CARDOZO; *Law and the Modern Mind*, by JEROME FRANK, *The Bramble Bush*, and *The Common Law Tradition*, by K. LLEWELLYN. Precedent is treated from a philosophical point of view in R. A. WASSERSTROM, *The Judicial Decision*, and D. H. HODGSON, *Consequences of Utilitarianism*.

INTRODUCTION

PRECEDENT is usually discussed in books on jurisprudence. Jurisprudence may be roughly described as the study of a lawyer's fundamental assumptions. Bentham spoke of it as 'the art of being methodically ignorant of what everybody knows'. If for 'everybody' we substitute 'every lawyer', we arrive at the conception of jurisprudence to which the following pages seek to give effect. Every lawyer, whether he is a practitioner or a legal writer, usually takes for granted the meaning of such statements as 'that is a rule of law', 'this was the *ratio decidendi* of the case', 'the decision is binding on the Court of Appeal, but not on the House of Lords', and 'X has a legal right to be paid £100 by Y'. One of the purposes of jurisprudence is to elucidate these statements. It is not, or at least need not be, the only purpose of jurisprudence. A consideration of the ethical or social merits of legal rules also forms part of that subject. When the elucidation of legal concepts is the primary object of investigation, the undertaking is often spoken of as 'analytical jurisprudence'; this book may be described as an essay in analytical jurisprudence because it is primarily concerned with the elucidation of the rules of precedent and of some other problems raised by case-law.

The study of jurisprudence is often divided into three parts— legal theory, the sources of law, and the analysis of legal concepts. Legal theory is mainly concerned with the nature and definition of law, the sources of law are the agencies through which law is made, while the analysis of legal concepts entails an examination of such matters as ownership, possession, and legal personality. In England, the major sources of law are Parliament and the judges of the superior courts. If an English lawyer wants to know what the law is, his first enquiry will be whether the point is governed by statute, in which case he will wish to consult the relevant enactments, since the judges are bound to give effect to Acts of Parliament under the doctrine of the sovereignty of Parliament. According to this doctrine, it is, in legal theory, possible for Parliament to make or unmake any law, although its powers are subject to a number of practical limitations. The English lawyer's second enquiry would relate to the activity of the judges. He would want to know whether there were any reported cases on the point, because, under the doctrine of precedent, much English law is derived from the decisions and observations of judges which are to be found in the different series of law reports. As this book is mainly concerned with the doctrine of precedent, it is a work on one aspect of the topic of the sources of law.

Another division of jurisprudence is into particular and general. Particular jurisprudence is concerned with the fundamental assumptions of one legal system, whereas general jurisprudence covers a wider field. According to Austin (1790–1859), general jurisprudence is the study of the 'principles, notions and distinctions' common to the maturer systems of law. This book is confined to the operation of precedent in English law. It may therefore be called a work on particular jurisprudence, although several questions of a general nature are raised.

The operation of precedent in England is compared with its operation elsewhere in Chapter I. Chapters II, III, and IV deal with different aspects of the English doctrine of precedent. In Chapter V case-law is related to the other sources of English law. Chapter VI touches on the subject of legal reasoning upon which case-law has had its influence, while Chapter VII is concerned with the bearing of the doctrine of precedent on such questions of legal theory as the definition of law and the distinction between law, fact, and discretion. These divisions are not watertight. Problems of legal theory are mentioned before Chapter VII is reached, and, all through the book, attention is drawn to the merits and demerits of various points in the English doctrine of precedent.

Much of the book, like the whole of this introduction will no doubt seem to the trained lawyer to be unduly simple. Before he condemns it on this score the reader may perhaps be asked to bear in mind the following words of Austin:

The elements of a science are precisely the parts of it which are explained least easily. Terms that are the largest, and, therefore, the simplest of a series, are without equivalent expressions into which we can resolve them concisely. And when we endeavour to define them, or to translate them into terms which we suppose are better understood, we are forced upon awkward and tedious circumlocutions.

I
THE ENGLISH DOCTRINE OF PRECEDENT

1. PRELIMINARY STATEMENT

It is a basic principle of the administration of justice that like cases should be decided alike.[1] This is enough to account for the fact that, in almost every jurisdiction, a judge tends to decide a case in the same way as that in which a similar case has been decided by another judge. The strength of this tendency varies greatly. It may be little more than an inclination to do as others have done before, or it may be the outcome of a positive obligation to follow a previous decision in the absence of justification for departing from it. Judicial precedent has some persuasive effect almost everywhere because *stare decisis* (keep to what has been decided previously) is a maxim of practically universal application. The peculiar feature of the English doctrine of precedent is its strongly coercive nature. English judges are sometimes obliged to follow a previous case although they have what would otherwise be good reasons for not doing so.

Case-law

The strongly coercive nature of the English doctrine of precedent is due to rules of practice, called 'rules of precedent', which are designed to give effect to the far more fundamental rule that English law is to a large extent based on case-law. 'Case-law' consists of the rules and principles stated and acted upon by judges in giving decisions.[2] In a system based on case-law, a judge in a subsequent case *must* have regard to these matters; they are not, as in some other legal systems, merely material which he *may* take

---

[1] For philosophical discussion of this principle in the context of precedents see David Lyons, 'Formal Justice and Judicial Precedent', *Vand. LR* 38 (1985), 495; Theodore Benditt, 'The Rule of Precedent', in Laurence Goldstein (ed.), *Precedent in Law*, ch. 4.

[2] For the extent to which advisory opinions can constitute sources of law see Joseph Jaconelli, *LQR* 101 (1985), 586.

into consideration in coming to his decision. The fact that English law is largely a system of case-law means that the judge's decision in a particular case constitutes a 'precedent'. If we place ourselves in the position of a judge in a later case, there may be said to be many different kinds of precedent. The judge may simply be obliged to consider the former decision as part of the material on which his present decision could be based, or he may be obliged to decide the case before him in the same way as that in which the previous case was decided unless he can give a good reason for not doing so. Finally, the judge in the instant case may be obliged to decide it in the same way as that in which the previous case was decided, even if he can give a good reason for not doing so. In the last-mentioned situation the precedent is said to be 'binding' or of 'coercive effect' as contrasted with its merely 'persuasive' effect in the other situations in which the degree of persuasiveness may vary considerably.

Some branches of our law are almost entirely the product of the decisions of the judges whose reasoned judgments have been reported in various types of law report for close on 700 years. Other branches of our law are based on statutes, but, in many instances, case-law has played an important part in the interpretation of those statutes. As the sovereignty of Parliament is more complete in England than practically anywhere else in the world, it might be thought that the rigidity of the doctrine of precedent in this country is of no particular importance because any unsatisfactory results of case-law can be swept away by legislation, but the promotion of a statute on matters of this nature is often slow and difficult. There are many instances in which the recommendations of Royal Commissions and Law Revision Committees, designed to ameliorate the situation produced by case-law have been ignored, apparently for no other reason than pressure on parliamentary time.

Perhaps the number of such instances will be reduced in the future because there are now in existence several very important law-reforming agencies, notably the Law Reform Committee dealing with the reform of the civil law on matters referred to it by the Lord Chancellor, the Criminal Law Revision Committee dealing with the reform of the criminal law on matters referred to it by the Home Secretary, and, most important of all, the Law Commission. The Commission was set up by statute in 1965, and it is charged with the task of reviewing the law with a view to systematic development and reform, including, in particular, codification. When the work of the Law Commission results, as it probably will do, in codes of the more important branches of English law, the role of case-law will, *pro tanto*, be diminished.

Rules of precedent

The rules of precedent are dependent on the practice of the courts, which has varied considerably. As recently as 1948 it was possible for Dr Goodhart, one of the leading contemporary writers on precedent, to say: 'The English doctrine of precedent is more rigid today than it ever was in the past.'[3]

Since then, however, there have been pronounced signs of relaxation, and they culminated in 1966 in a very important Practice Statement, set out in full on p. 104, in which the Lord Chancellor said that, while, in general, the House of Lords would continue to treat its past decisions as binding on it, it would modify its then present practice by departing from a past decision when it thought right to do so. Under the practice prevailing between 1898 and 1966, the House considered itself absolutely bound by its past decisions, and there had been pronounced tendencies in this direction throughout the nineteenth century.

At present the English doctrine of precedent is to some extent in a state of flux, but there appear to be three constant features. These are the respect paid to a single decision of a superior court, the fact that a decision of such a court is a persuasive precedent even so far as courts above that from which it emanates are concerned, and the fact that a single decision is always a binding precedent as regards courts below that from which it emanated. These points will be better understood in the light of a brief account of the hierarchy of the English courts.

The hierarchy of the courts

It will be convenient to begin with the civil courts. At the bottom of the hierarchy there are the County and Magistrates' Courts with a limited jurisdiction over cases of first instance. Next comes the High Court whose judges exercise an unlimited jurisdiction over such cases. The Divisional Courts, which are part of the High Court, enjoy a limited appellate jurisdiction in addition to hearing certain special applications in the first instance. Next in the

---

[3] 64 *LQR* 40.

hierarchy of civil courts comes the Court of Appeal (Civil Division) which hears appeals from the County Courts and the High Court. Finally, there is the House of Lords which hears appeals from the English Court of Appeal, the Court of Sessions in Scotland, and the Court of Appeal in Northern Ireland.

So far as the criminal courts are concerned, the Magistrates' Courts exercise an important summary jurisdiction over cases of first instance. A convicted person has a right of appeal to the Crown Court in a summary case, but the most important appellate and supervisory work in relation to summary jurisdiction is done by the Divisional Courts of the Queen's Bench Division of the High Court. Trials on indictment take place in the Crown Court. A person convicted on indictment may appeal to the Court of Appeal (Criminal Division) whence an appeal lies to the House of Lords.

Preliminary statement of the English doctrine of precedent

The Practice Statement in the House of Lords shows how easily the rules of precedent can be changed, but the following preliminary statement represents the practice current at the end of July 1990. Every court is bound to follow any case decided by a court above it in the hierarchy, and appellate courts (other than the House of Lords) are bound by their previous decisions.

There is room for debate over certain matters of detail, and it cannot be denied that this statement is inaccurate in one respect, although a trivial one. The inaccuracy concerns the effect of a decision of the Crown Court on an appeal from a Magistrates' Court. Such a decision is probably not binding for the future on a Magistrates' Court or the Crown Court itself. The inaccuracy is trivial because the doctrine of precedent is primarily of importance in relation to courts whose decisions on questions of law are regularly reported. The decisions of the Crown Court in the exercise of its appellate jurisdiction are not included in any series of law reports in daily use, and, in the absence of reports, the doctrine of *stare decisis* is liable to be ineffective. There are, however, some serious reasons why the above preliminary formulation of the English doctrine of precedent is too concise and dogmatic. It does not indicate that only certain aspects of a previous case, called the *ratio decidendi*, are binding, and it does not refer to the existence of important exceptions to the rule of *stare decisis*. These matters are discussed in subsequent chapters but it must not be forgotten that the rules of precedent are subsidiary to, and far less important than, the obligation of judges to consider case-law. On two recent occasions the Court of Appeal has declined to follow decisions of the House of Lords and the House has reacted in an appropriately admonitory manner, but the common law is intact. A judge who repudiated his obligation to have regard to case-law would be treated very differently, and, if such a repudiation were ever to be generally accepted, the English legal system would have undergone a revolution of the highest magnitude.

After they have been illustrated, the modern English rules of precedent will be contrasted with the rules of precedent as applied in other countries today, and in England at other times.

2. ILLUSTRATIONS

The first of the features of the English doctrine of precedent mentioned above, the respect paid to a single decision of a superior court,[4] may be illustrated by the treatment of *R. v. Millis* in *Beamish v. Beamish*. In *R. v. Millis*,[5] for doubtful historical reasons, and without much previous authority, the House of Lords adopted the rule that the presence of an episcopally ordained priest is essential, at common law, to a valid marriage in England or Ireland with the result that an Irish Presbyterian marriage was held void. Though greatly modified by statute and, to some extent, by later decisions, the case has caused much trouble. It is rendered all the more impressive as an illustration of the effectiveness of a single decision by the fact that the members of the House of Lords who voted whether to accept the advice of the judges were evenly divided. The decision of the Irish Appellate Court, which was against the validity of the marriage, was accordingly only affirmed on the principle *praesumitur pro negante*. A motion had been proposed, and as it had not been carried, it was deemed to have been defeated.

In *Beamish v. Beamish*[6] the House of Lords decided that the fact that the bridegroom was in Holy Orders did not prevent the rule in *R. v. Millis* from applying. In order that the marriage

---

[4] i.e. the House of Lords, Court of Appeal, High Court, and, when it acts as a court of first instance, the Crown Court.

[5] (1844) 10 Cl. & F. 534.

[6] (1861) 9 HLC 274, see specially *per* Lord Campbell at 338.

should be valid, the priest had to be present as a celebrant not as a party to the ceremony. Lord Campbell had disapproved of the view which prevailed in the previous case; but, in *Beamish* v. *Beamish*, he said:

If it were competent to me, I would now ask your Lordships to reconsider the doctrine laid down in *R.* v. *Millis*, particularly as the judges who were then consulted complained of being hurried into giving an opinion without due time for deliberation, and the members of this House who heard the argument, and voted on the question, 'that the judgment appealed against be reversed', were equally divided; so that the judgment which decided the marriage by a Presbyterian clergyman of a man and woman, who both belonged to his religious persuasion, who both believed that they were contracting lawful matrimony, who had lived together as husband and wife, and who had procreated children while so living together as husband and wife, to be a nullity, was only pronounced on the technical rule of your Lordships' House, that where, upon a division, the numbers are equal, *semper praesumitur pro negante*. But it is my duty to say that your Lordships are bound by this decision as much as if it had been pronounced *nemine dissentiente*, and that the rule of law which your Lordships lay down as the ground of your judgment, sitting judicially, as the last and supreme Court of Appeal for this Empire, must be taken for law till altered by an act of Parliament, agreed to by the Commons and the Crown, as well as by your Lordships. The law laid down as your *ratio decidendi*, being clearly binding on all inferior tribunals, and on all the rest of the Queen's subjects, if it were not considered as equally binding upon your Lordships, this House would be arrogating to itself the right of altering the law, and legislating by its own separate authority.

It is to be noted that Lord Campbell referred to a rule laid down by the House when sitting as the supreme court of appeal. In the highly unusual context of the House of Lords instituting contempt proceedings of its own motion, where an appellate committee of the House sits as both a tribunal of first instance and a tribunal of last resort, it was said to be open to question whether its ruling on any question of law raised in the proceedings would constitute a binding authority.[7]

The second feature of the English doctrine of precedent mentioned on p. 5, the fact that a decision of a superior court is treated as persuasive by courts above that court in the hierarchy, may be illustrated by the treatment of *Simonin* v. *Mallac*[8] by the House of Lords in *Ross-Smith* v. *Ross-Smith*.[9]

[7] *Re Lonrho plc* (1990), 2 AC 154, 201.
[8] (1860) 2 Sw. & Tr. 67.   [9] [1963] AC 280.

Simonin v. *Mallac* was a decision of the full court of Divorce and Matrimonial Causes which slightly antedated the modern hierarchy; its decisions were and are in no way binding on the House of Lords. It was held that the English courts had jurisdiction to hear a petition for nullity of marriage on the ground that the marriage was void *ab initio* because of a defect in the ceremony if it was celebrated in England although the parties were domiciled in France (i.e. had their permanent home there), and the husband was temporarily resident in Naples. The ground of the decision was that, 'The parties by professing to enter into a contract in England mutually gave to each other the right to have the force and effect of that contract determined by an English tribunal.'[10]

Ross-Smith v. *Ross-Smith* was considered by seven members of the House of Lords, one of whom died before he could deliver his speech, although he had prepared it. The speech was read, but the case must presumably be regarded as having been decided by six members of the House. None of them accepted the *ratio decidendi* of *Simonin* v. *Mallac* which has just been quoted; but a precedent may be a persuasive authority although it does not persuade, especially if it has been followed, as *Simonin* v. *Mallac* had been followed, on a number of occasions. Lord Reid said:

Before holding that the decision should be overruled I must be convinced not only that the *ratio decidendi* is wrong but that there is no other possible ground on which the decision can be supported.[11]

Being unable to find any such ground, Lord Reid and two of his colleagues were prepared to overrule *Simonin* v. *Mallac* but, as the House was evenly divided on this point, they ultimately based their conclusion, as did two other members of the House, on the ground that the decision in *Simonin* v. *Mallac* must be confined to marriages alleged to be void; the sixth member of the House dissented, and would have extended *Simonin* v. *Mallac* to the case before him.

The issue in *Ross-Smith* v. *Ross-Smith* was whether the English courts had jurisdiction to annul a marriage on the ground that it was voidable on account of wilful refusal or incapacity to consummate, if the marriage was celebrated in England, though the parties were domiciled elsewhere and the husband resided abroad. By a majority of five to one, the House of Lords gave a negative answer.

[10] 2 Sw. & Tr. 67, at 75.   [11] [1963] AC at 294.

Whether a decision of the full court of Divorce and Matrimonial Causes is binding on a judge of first instance is perhaps a somewhat knotty point, but the fact that *Simonin* v. *Mallac* had been impliedly treated as good law by the Court of Appeal and the treatment accorded to it in the House of Lords in *Ross-Smith* v. *Ross-Smith* were enough to induce Sir Jocelyn Simon P to treat himself as bound by it in *Padolecchia* v. *Padolecchia*.[12] We thus have an illustration of the third feature of the English doctrine of precedent mentioned on p. 5. However anomalous a decision of a superior court may be (and the treatment accorded to *Simonin* v. *Mallac* was judicially described as 'the perpetuation of error'),[13] once it has received the blessing of an appellate court, it binds all courts below that court in the hierarchy.

Until recently it was widely supposed that the mere refusal by an appeal committee of the House of Lords of leave to appeal rendered a decision more authoritative. The House emphatically corrected this 'erroneous impression' in *Wilson* v. *Colchester Justices*.[14] There were many reasons why leave might be refused other than approval of the decision. Grant or refusal of leave is in no way to be taken as implying disapproval or approval of the decision and judgments of the court below.

3. COMPARISON WITH FRANCE

Although there are important differences between them, the French legal system may be taken as typical of those of western Europe for the purposes of the present discussion.

From the standpoint of strict legal theory, French law is not based on case-law (*la jurisprudence*) at all. The Civil and Penal Codes are theoretically complete in the sense that they (and other statutory provisions) are supposed to cover every situation with which the ordinary courts are concerned. It can still be argued that, strictly speaking, case-law is not a source of law in France because a judge is not obliged to consider it when coming to a decision. Art. 5 of the Civil Code forbids his laying down general rules when stating a decision, and it would be possible for a French appellate court to set aside a ruling founded exclusively on a past decision on the ground that the ruling lacked an adequate legal

---

[12] [1967] 3 All ER 863.
[13] *Garthwaite* v. *Garthwaite* [1964] P 356 at 391 *per* Diplock LJ.
[14] (1985) AC 750.

basis.[15] None the less, there is a substantial body of case-law dealing with the construction of the Codes and the solution of problems on which they are in fact silent. Moreover, there is no code governing the *droit administratif* of the Counseil d'État, which is not numbered among the ordinary courts, and it is mainly based on case-law.

From the practical point of view one of the most significant differences between English and French case-law lies in the fact that the French judge does not regard himself as absolutely bound by the decision of any court in a single previous instance. He endeavours to ascertain the trend of recent decisions on a particular point. To quote a distinguished French legal writer: 'The practice of the courts does not become a source of law until it is definitely fixed by the repetition of precedents which are in agreement on a single point.'[16] Although it has been suggested that statements of this nature do something less than justice to the influence of an occasional single decision on the development of French law,[17] there can be little doubt that a French judge would not have shared Lord Campbell's inhibitions about differing from *R. v. Millis*.

Three of the principal reasons for the difference between the French and English approaches to the doctrine of precedent are that the need for certainty in the law was formerly felt more keenly by the English judge than most of the judges on the Continent, the highly centralized nature of the hierarchy of the English courts, and the difference in the position of the judges in the two countries.

The need for certainty

The first point has been stressed by Dr Goodhart. The continental judge has no doubt always wanted the law to be certain as much as the English judge, but he has felt the need less keenly because of

[15] David and De Vrees, *The French Legal System*, 115.

[16] Lambert, 'Case-method in Canada', 39 *Yale LJ* 1 at 14. A helpful account of the operation of precedent in France together with examples of the judgments of French courts is given by Lawson, 'Negligence in Civil Law', 231–5. See also Esmein, *Revue trimestrielle de droit civile* (1902), i. 5; *Encyclopédie Dalloz*, iii. 17; 'Le Droit privé français', by Ripert, i. 9; O. Kahn-Freund, C. Lévy, and B. Rudden, *A Source-book of French Law* (2nd edn.), pt. 1. In Spain it seems that 2 decisions of the Supreme Court constitute a 'doctrina' binding on inferior courts, though the Supreme Court may later alter the 'doctrina' (Neville Brown, 'The Sources of Spanish Law', 5 *Inst. Comp. LQ* (1956), 367.)

[17] Gutteridge, *Comparative Law*, 90.

the background of rules provided first by Roman law and codified custom, and later by the codes of the Napoleonic era. These resulted in a large measure of certainty in European law. Roman law was never 'received' in England, and we have never had a code in the sense of a written statement of the entirety of the law. 'English justice, if it were not to remain fluid and unstable, required a strong cement. This was found in the common-law doctrine of precedent with its essential and peculiar emphasis on rigidity and certainty.'[18]

The hierarchy of the courts

The French judicial system is based on the division of the country into districts. So far as civil cases are concerned, each district has a court of first instance and a court of appeal. The district courts of first instance are not bound by their own previous decisions or those of any other district court of first instance, nor are such courts of first instance bound by the previous decisions of their own appellate court or that of any other district. The district appellate courts are not bound by their own past decisions or those of any other district court of appeal. There is a right of appeal on points of law from the district appellate court to the *Cour de Cassation* in Paris. In theory, this body is not bound by any previous decision of its own, and the district courts are not bound to follow an individual decision of the *Cour de Cassation* in a previous case. So far as the actual litigation under consideration by the *Cour de Cassation* is concerned, that court may remit it for re-hearing by an appellate court of a district near to that from which the appeal came. If the case should be brought before the *Cour de Cassation* again, it is only since 1967 that the Court has had power finally to dispose of the case instead of remitting it to yet another district court of appeal with a binding direction concerning the manner in which it was to be decided.

The more serious criminal cases are tried by a district assize court from which there is no appeal apart from the possibility of an application to the *Cour de Cassation* on a question of law which may result in an order for a new trial.

With a system of courts as decentralized as that which has just been sketched, it would have been difficult for France to have evolved a doctrine of precedent as rigid in every respect as our

---

[18] 'Precedent in English and Continental Law', *LQR* 50 (1934), 40 at 62.

own. Even if the *Cour de Cassation* had come to treat itself and the district courts as absolutely bound by each of its past decisions, there would almost inevitably have been considerable flexibility at the level of the district courts of appeal. It would have been too much to expect anything approximating to the uniformity of decision demanded of the English judges. French law owes its uniformity to the various codes in which it is declared and to *la doctrine*—the opinions of jurists—rather than to *la jurisprudence*.

The different position of the judges

The French judge occupies a very different position from that of his English counterpart. In the first place, there are fewer judges of our superior courts than there are members of the French judiciary. Secondly, the French judiciary is not, like ours, recruited from the Bar but from the civil service, and thirdly, many French judges are relatively young and inexperienced men. They go into the Ministry of Justice with the intention of taking up a judicial career and become junior judges in small district courts after what is little more than a period of training. The result is that the judiciary tends to be considered as less important in France than in England, and, although it is difficult to assess the significance of these matters, it is generally, and probably rightly, assumed that they help to explain the greater regard which is paid to case-law in this country than that which is paid to it on the Continent. Still more important is the fact that the judges have been the architects of English law.

The common law is a monument to the judicial activity of the common law judge. He, not the legislator or the scholar, created the common law. He still enjoys the prestige of that accomplishment.[19]

Further reasons for the difference

Allowance must also be made for the difference in the structure of the judgments of English and French courts to be mentioned on p. 49 and for the vast number of cases decided by the *Cour de Cassation*. A rule that a single precedent should be binding would be unlikely to develop when it was difficult to discover a precise *ratio decidendi* and it is not always easy to extract a precise *ratio* from a French judgment. A rule that one single decision of an appellate court should suffice to constitute a binding precedent is

---

[19] von Mehren, *The Civil Law System*, 839.

hardly likely to develop in a jurisdiction in which there are numerous appeals. The House of Lords only hears some 30 appeals from the English courts each year, but some 10,000 cases are dealt with annually by the different chambers of the *Cour de Cassation*.

Notwithstanding the great theoretical difference between the English and French approaches to case-law, and the total absence of rules of precedent in France, the two systems have more in common than might be supposed. In the first place, French judges and writers pay the greatest respect to the past decisions of the *Cour de Cassation*.[20]

Secondly, the manner in which the English judges interpret the *ratio decidendi* of a case tends to assimilate their attitude towards a legal problem to that of their French counterparts. In *Wells* v. *Hopwood*,[21] for example, the Court of King's Bench had to decide whether a vessel had been 'stranded' within the meaning of a charter party. A number of previous decisions had some bearing on this point, and Lord Tenterden CJ dealt with them in the following terms:

Several of the cases hitherto decided on this subject are very near to each other, and not easily distinguishable. But it appears to me that a general principle and rule of law may, although perhaps not explicitly laid down in any of them, be fairly collected from the greater number.[22]

Lord Tenterden proceeded to formulate a principle on the basis of which he solved the problem before him. This is a common type of judicial reasoning in England, and further reference will be made to it in due course. It means that several cases dealing with the same point may have to be read together in order to determine the proposition of law for which any one is authoritative at a given time. It would be wrong to say that, in deciding case *D*, an English High Court judge of first instance considers cases *A* and *B*, decided by the Court of Appeal, together with case *C*, decided by another High Court judge of first instance, in order to see whether

[20] 'On peut dire sans paradoxe que la cour de cassation a plus de respect pour les arrêts de ses chambres réunies que pour la loi elle-même, car s'il lui arrive d'altérer ou de modifier la loi sous couleur de l'interpréter, elle n'abandonne jamais la jurisprudence créée par un arrêt des chambres réunies': *Encyclopédie Dalloz*, iii. 22, para. 26. Since 1967 the description of a full session of all the chambers of the *Cour de Cassation* has been 'Assemblée Plénère'.
[21] (1832) 3 B. & Ald. 20.
[22] At 34. For a modern example, see *Unit Construction Company Ltd.* v. *Bullock* [1960] AC 351 at 368 *per* Lord Radcliffe.

the law has become 'definitely fixed by the repetition of precedents which are in agreement on a single point'. However, his attitude towards the *ratio decidendi* of case *A* might be profoundly affected by the observations of the judges in cases *B* and *C*. English case-law is not the same as *la jurisprudence*, but it is a mistake to suppose that our judges permanently inhabit a wilderness of single instances. If, for the time being, we ignore the difference in the form in which the English and French judges express their conclusions, it seems that the divergence between the two systems is most noticeable when there is only one important decision on the point before the court, as was the case in *Beamish* v. *Beamish*. It is quite possible that a French judge of first instance would have felt himself as much bound to follow *Simonin* v. *Mallac* as did Sir Jocelyn Simon in *Padolecchia* v. *Padolecchia*, although this would be on account of the fact that *Simonin* v. *Mallac* had been followed on numerous occasions rather than on account of the fact that the decision had received the blessing of appellate courts on relatively few occasions. A further respect in which the two systems of case-law differ profoundly is due to Art. 5 of the Civil Code which prohibits a judge from laying down general rules. It is not uncommon for the judgments of English appellate courts to lay down rules, concerning the quantum of damages for example, to be followed by lower courts in the future. This could hardly happen in France. On the other hand, whilst, as we shall see, the *ratio decidendi* of a binding English case may be narrowed by subsequent distinguishing so that the rule for which it comes to be seen as authority is not as broad as its original formulation, this does not happen to the statements of the *Cour de Cassation*. The latter may, in practice, harden into rules of law as strongly tied to their formulation as statutory rules. Paradoxically, then, although Art. 5 denies the status of 'formal' sources of law to the decisions of the court, as 'material' or 'historical' sources they may, through constant repetition, acquire greater legislative effect even than decisions of the House of Lords.

4. COMPARISON WITH THE EUROPEAN COURT OF JUSTICE

Since 1 January 1973 directly applicable law of the European communities has constituted a source of English law. The implications of this development for English rules of precedent are considered at the end of Chapter V. At this stage something will be said, for comparative purposes, about the attitude adopted by the European Court of Justice in Luxemburg to its own previous decisions.[23] The jurisprudence established by these decisions has become an increasingly important part of European Community law and, consequently, of increasing significance for lawyers in all member states.

The style of the judgments of the European Court resembles that of French superior courts considered in the last section, and, to some extent, French understanding of the status, as sources of law, of judicial rulings has been carried over. Thus, although, when a reference is made under Art. 177 of the Treaty of Rome by the court of a member state for a preliminary ruling on a point of Community law, the ruling handed down by the European Court is binding on the referring court for the case at hand, it has never been explicitly stated that such rulings are binding in other cases. Nevertheless, the view that they are so binding is implicit in some of the Court's judgments.[24]

Furthermore, under the jurisprudence of the European Court, a national court is always free to ask the European Court to reconsider its previous rulings. This was originally decided in the *Da Costa* case.[25] There a Dutch court referred to the European Court of Justice the same question of treaty interpretation it had put in an earlier case. The European Court held that it could consider the question, but in the absence of new factors simply referred the Dutch court to its earlier ruling.

It follows that the European Court of Justice does not regard itself as bound by its own previous decisions. Advocate-General Lagrange submitted that it could reconsider them in the light of new facts and arguments or simply because it thought a different conclusion appropriate.[26] The Court has exercised this freedom in a number of cases, most strikingly when it removed a much

---

[23] See N. Brown and F. G. Jacobs, *The Court of Justice of the European Communities* (3rd edn.), 311–18.

[24] See e.g. 66/80 *International Chemical Corporation SpA* v. *Amministrazione delle Finanze dello Stato* [1981] ECR 1191 and 112/83 *Société des Produits des Mais SA* v. *Administration des Douanes et Droits Indirects* [1988] 1 CMLR 459, both holding that an Art. 177 ruling that a Community measure is invalid is sufficient reason for all national courts to so regard it.

[25] 28–30/62 *Da Costa en Schaake NV* v. *Nederlandse Belasting Administratie* [1963] ECR 31.

[26] Ibid. 42–3.

criticized jurisdictional hurdle it had erected as a barrier to actions for non-contractual wrongs.[27]

The practice of the European Court of Justice

Nevertheless, in practice the European Court of Justice generally adheres to precedent. It frequently repeats paragraphs from earlier cases, referring to them by name, albeit sometimes with slight changes in the wording. It is often hard to know whether such changes are accidental or are designed to indicate a shift of emphasis. Although the Court often explicitly follows one of its previous rulings, it does not discuss them in an analytical way. Nor does it make any attempt to distinguish them or explain why it is not following them, where an English court in comparable circumstances would think that course appropriate. However, there is almost always a full discussion of the relevant precedents in the Advocate-General's opinion given before the Court considers its judgment. (The Court further gives no explanation when, as is often the case, it does not follow the Advocate-General's opinion.)

It almost goes without saying that the European Court does not draw the distinction, essential to the English doctrine of precedent, between *ratio* and *obiter dictum*. The distinction has, however, been drawn by Advocate-General Warner,[28] and one judge of the Court writing extrajudicially has argued that the European Court has adopted it in practice.[29] It is most improbable that the Court would draw the distinction explicitly. For to do that would be to accept the doctrine of *stare decisis* at a theoretical level, and that, as we have seen in the case of France, is foreign to civil law jurisdictions. Further, the style of the Court's rulings does not lend itself to the articulation of the distinction. They tend to be short, certainly compared with the judgments of English appellate courts, and dogmatic in tone—with much discussion of abstract principle and less detailed examination of the facts. Another difference from English decisions is the absence of separate

[27] See 4/69 *Lütticke GmbH* v. *Commission of the EEC* [1971] ECR 325, in effect overruling on this point 25/62 *Plaumann and Co.* v. *Commission of the EEC* [1963] ECR 95.

[28] 112/76 *Manzoni* v. *Fonds National de Retraite des Ouvriets Mineurs* [1977] ECR 1647, 1662.

[29] T. Koopmans, 'Stare Decisis in European Law', in D. O'Keefe and H. G. Schermers (eds.), *Essays in European Law and Integration* (Amsterdam, 1982), 11, 22–3.

concurring and dissenting judgments. This feature of English (and United States) judicial practice often makes it extremely hard to determine the *ratio* of appellate rulings. This difficulty does not exist in the interpretation of the European Court's rulings. On the other hand, the absence of any discussion of precedent and the abstract style of the Court's judgments frequently makes for compensating problems of interpretation.

Reasons for the differences

In practice it may be that the European Court's attitude to precedent is similar to that of some superior Commonwealth and United States Courts. On the other hand, it is probably more prepared to depart from its case-law than is the House of Lords. Moreover, when it does so, the Court does not seem to consider itself under any obligation to explain its change of mind. An obvious reason for the differences is that the European Court of Justice is primarily a court in the civil law tradition. The vast majority of its thirteen members have been educated and have practised in civil law jurisdictions, where the notion of binding case-law and the *ratio obiter* distinction are unknown. Continental, and particularly French, modes of legal thought have prevailed since the period before Britain and Ireland joined the Community. The discussion in the last few pages of the French judicial system is therefore pertinent in this context.

It should also be stressed that the Court of Justice is as much a constitutional as an administrative (or other type of) court. For example, it decides disputes between the political institutions of the Community and has formulated various principles governing the relationship of the community and national legal systems. Just as the United States Supreme Court has been prepared freely to overrule its own previous decisions, so the European Court is ready to extend or (some would say) disregard precedent, when it considers this constitutionally opportune. There are some good general arguments for allowing constitutional courts (or courts like the European Court which exercise constitutional functions) more freedom to disregard precedent than ordinary private or common law courts. In the European Community context, it can also be said that the difficulties of Treaty amendment make it imperative for its provisions to be interpreted in a flexible way, which may make it right to overrule outdated decisions. Secondly, the Court's own errors cannot easily be put right. The EEC legislative process is cumbersome and ill-suited to correcting judicial mistakes. Furthermore, in many areas of constitutional importance, for example in its development of the doctrine of direct effect, the European Court has often behaved quite unlike the English courts: it prefers to interpret Treaty provisions in the light of their spirit rather than their text, and appears equally prepared to treat its precedents in the same way.[30]

5. CONTRAST WITH USA

Although the North American practice of giving judgment in the form of elaborate discussions of previous cases is more like the English than the continental, the United States' Supreme Court and the appellate courts in the different states do not regard themselves as absolutely bound by their past decisions. There are many instances, some American lawyers would say too many, in which the Supreme Court has overruled a previous decision.

Thanks to the change of practice in the House of Lords, the English rules of precedent may come to approximate more closely to the North American, but two reasons why the North American rules should remain more lax suggest themselves. These are the number of separate State jurisdictions in the former country and the comparative frequency with which the North American courts have to deal with momentous constitutional issues.

Numerous jurisdictions

A multiplicity of jurisdictions produces a multiplicity of law reports which has, in its turn, influenced the teaching of law and led to the production of 'restatements' on various topics. The 'case method' of instruction which, in one form or another, prevails in most North American law schools aims at finding the best solution of a problem on the footing of examples from many jurisdictions, and few schools confine their instruction to the law of any one State. The restatements are concise formulations and illustrations of legal principles based on the case-law of the entire United States and, from time to time, model codes and sets of uniform rules relating to various branches of the law are produced in a form fit for immediate adoption by the legislature. Judges who have been trained by the case method and who are familiar with the

---

[30] See Lord Diplock in *R. v. Henn & Darby* [1982] AC 850 for a discussion of the different approaches of the ECJ and English courts to interpretation.

restatements and kindred documents will tend to concentrate on recent trends after the fashion of the French courts.

Constitutional issues

When a court is construing a written constitution the terms of that document are the governing factor and the case-law on the meaning of those terms is only a secondary consideration. This point was put very clearly by Frankfurter J when he was giving judgment in the Supreme Court. He said:

The ultimate touchstone of constitutionality is the Constitution itself, and not what we do about it.[31]

A further reason why North American courts in general, and the United States' Supreme Court in particular, should not apply our rule of the absolutely binding effect of a single decision to constitutional matters is provided by the momentous nature of the issues involved in such cases. To quote Lord Wright:

It seems clear that, generally speaking, a rigid method of precedent is inappropriate to the construction of a constitution which has to be applied to changing conditions of national life and public policy. An application of words which might be reasonable and just at some time, might be wrong and mischievous at another time.[32]

When the difficulty of amending the Constitution of the United States is borne in mind, it is scarcely surprising that the Supreme Court has become less and less rigorous in its adherence to the principle of *stare decisis*.[33]

6. CONTRAST WITH SCOTLAND

The following remarks made by a Scottish court as recently as 1950 certainly suggest that the Scottish doctrine of precedent is less strict than our own.

[31] *Graves* v. *New York*, 306 US 466 at 491 (1939). The importance of the fact that the United States' Supreme Court is frequently concerned with constitutional problems is stressed by Goodhart in 'Case Law in England and America', in *Essays in Jurisprudence and the Common Law*. See also Goodhart, 'Some American Interpretations of Law', in *Modern Theories of Law*, 1.
[32] 'Precedents', 8 *CLJ* 118 at 135.
[33] Most strikingly when it overruled its decision in *Minersville School District* v. *Gobilitis*, 310 US 586 (1940) only 3 years later in *West Virginia State Board of Education* v. *Barnette*, 319 US 624 (1943) (holding it contrary to the First Amendment for schoolchildren to be required to salute the flag).

If it is manifest that the *ratio decidendi* upon which a previous decision has rested has been superseded and invalidated by subsequent legislation or from other like cause, that *ratio decidendi* ceases to be binding.[34]

No doubt it would be quite incorrect to represent the English judiciary as a body which pays no attention to the maxim *cessante ratione cessat lex ipsa,* but the House of Lords considers that it should be treated as a ground for creating an exception to a binding rule when that is possible, not as a ground for disregarding it. The maxim also indicates a fact to be taken into account by an English court when deciding whether to overrule a case which it has power to overrule.[35]

The collegiate nature of the Court of Session, the superior civil court in Scotland, may account for such differences as there are in the application of the doctrine of precedent north and south of the Tweed. The Lords Ordinary hear cases of first instance in the Outer House of the Court of Session, and an appeal lies to the Inner House. The Lords Ordinary are bound to follow the past decisions of the Inner House. The Inner House sits in divisions, and it appears to be a moot point whether the divisions are absolutely bound by each other's decisions. Provision may be made for the hearing of a case by the whole Court of Session, and although it seems clear that the divisions of the Inner House as well as the individual Lords Ordinary are bound by the decisions of the whole court, it also seems to be a moot point whether the decisions of the whole court are binding on subsequent sessions of that body. The Lords Ordinary are not bound by each other's decisions, and, in theory at least, their decisions do not bind the Sheriffs whose courts are lower in the Scottish judicial hierarchy.

The more serious criminal cases come before the High Court of Justiciary. The judges sit singly and in quorums. A single judge is not bound to follow the decisions of other single judges, but he must follow the previous decisions of a quorum. The quorums are bound by the previous decisions of other quorums of an equal or greater number. A full bench may be assembled for a difficult case. It is not clear whether the decisions of a full bench bind a similar tribunal convened for a later case.

---

[34] *Beith's Trustees* v. *Beith* [1950] SC 66 at 70; see also *Douglas-Hamilton* v. *Duke and Duchess of Hamilton's ante-nuptial marriage contract trustees* [1961] SLT 305 at 309. For the operation of precedent in Scotland see *Precedent in Scots Law,* by T. B. Smith.
[35] *Miliangos* v. *George Frank (Textiles) Ltd.* (1976) AC 443 at 472–6.

An appeal lies to the House of Lords in civil cases only. The decisions of the House on a Scottish appeal bind the courts of Scotland. In practice, if not according to strict legal theory, they also bind the English courts below the House of Lords on points on which the law of the two countries is the same.[36]

7. CONTRAST WITH PARTS OF THE COMMONWEALTH

The Judicial Committee of the Privy Council used to be the final court of appeal for all Commonwealth countries outside the United Kingdom. The Judicial Committee has never considered itself to be absolutely bound by its own previous decisions on any appeal. The form in which the decisions are expressed is often said to militate against the adoption of a rigid rule of precedent, for the judgment of the Committee consists of advice tendered to the Sovereign together with the reasons upon which such advice is based. Another factor which makes for a less strict rule of *stare decisis* is the comparative frequency upon which the Privy Council is called upon to deal with appeals on questions of constitutional law, but there are several cases which were not concerned with constitutional law in which the Committee has dissented from the advice which it gave on a former occasion.[37] The Judicial Committee is, however, strongly disposed to adhere to its previous decisions.[38] The decisions of the Privy Council are only of strong persuasive authority in the English courts.

The right of appeal to the Privy Council has been abolished in some Commonwealth countries, including Canada and Australia. In the days when there was still an appeal to the Privy Council, the Supreme Court of Canada regarded itself as bound by its own past decisions although there was a saving clause relating to 'exceptional circumstances'.[39] Since the abolition of the right of appeal to the Privy Council, the Supreme Court of Canada has claimed the power of declining to follow its own past decisions as it is the successor to the final appellate jurisdiction of the Privy

[36] *Glasgow Corporation* v. *Central Land Board* [1956] SC (HL) 1.
[37] e.g. *Mercantile Bank of India* v. *Central Bank of India* [1938] AC 287 and *Gideon Nkambule* v. *R.* [1950] AC 379.
[38] *Fatuma Binti Mohamed Bin Salim and Another* v. *Mohamed Bin Salim* [1952] AC 1.
[39] *Stewart* v. *Bank of Montreal* (1909) 41 SCR 522 at 535. See Andrew Joanes, 'Stare Decisis in the Supreme Court of Canada', *Canadian Bar Review*, 36 (1958), 174.

Council which is not bound by its own past decisions.[40] The High Court of Australia has never regarded itself as absolutely bound by its own past decisions,[41] although, even on constitutional questions, it will not depart from an earlier decision where all the arguments presently canvassed were considered on the former occasion and nothing has changed except the composition of the court.[42]

As long ago as 1879 it was said to be of the utmost importance that in all parts of the Empire where English law prevails, the interpretation of that law by the courts should be as nearly as possible the same.[43] It is for this reason that, in the absence of some special local consideration to justify a deviation, the Australian and Canadian courts would be loath to differ from decisions of the House of Lords, but there does not appear to be any question of the decisions of the House being binding in either country. The High Court of Australia in fact stated that a leading decision on the English criminal law (since largely overruled by an English statute) was to be treated as no authority in Australia,[44] and the Judicial Committee of the Privy Council has held in a civil case that the Australian High Court was right not to follow a decision of the House of Lords on exemplary damages.[45] On the other hand, the High Court will accept that a decision of the House of Lords which cannot be shown to have misapplied prior authorities must be taken to have laid down a rule of the common law applicable in Australia.[46]

In recent years the Privy Council has been loath to recognize divergencies. In *De Lasala* v. *De Lasala*,[47] it was held that where recent legislation was common to England and a colony, there could be no question of development along different lines and the Privy Council would follow decisions of the House of Lords, but that a different approach was appropriate as regards decisions of the House on rules of common law. However, in *Hart* v. *O'Connor*,[48] the Privy Council insisted that the common law of

[40] *Re Farm Products, Marketing Act* (1957), 7 DLR (2nd) 257 at 271.
[41] *Australian Agricultural Co.* v. *Federated Engine Drivers and Firemens' Association of Australasia* (1913) 17 CLR 261.
[42] *Queensland* v. *The Commonwealth* (1978) 139 CLR 585. See Harris, *OJLS* 10 (1990), 135.
[43] *Trimble* v. *Hill*, 5 App. Cas. 342 at 345.
[44] *Parker* v. *R.* [1963] 111 CLR 610.
[45] *Australian Consolidated Press Ltd.* v. *Uren* [1969] 1 AC 590.
[46] *State Government Insurance Commission* v. *Trigwell* (1979) 142 CLR 617.
[47] (1980) AC 546.   [48] (1985) AC 1000.

New Zealand must be identical with that of England and Australia; and in *Tai Hing Cotton Mill Ltd.* v. *Liu Chong Hing Bank Ltd.*,[49] the Board held that, once it was accepted that the applicable law was 'English law' (whether statutory or case law), it would regard itself as bound by any House of Lords decision, it being in no position to invoke the 1966 Practice Statement under which the House has assumed the power to depart from its own decisions. Nevertheless, even where the common law is taken to be one and indivisible, the Privy Council may, in an exceptional case, find that a decision of the House of Lords constituted an erroneous statement of the common law so that it ought not to be followed.[50]

The desirability of having the same common law throughout the Commonwealth is not as self-evident as it is sometimes made to appear. Much depends on the branch of the law concerned. In commercial matters, for example, where members of the different Commonwealth countries are liable to be affected by the same rule, there is much to be said for uniformity; but the demand for uniformity in other spheres may militate against useful developments. For historical reasons, Australian and Canadian judges may, *faute de mieux*, have to start their thinking with English law, but there is no obvious merit in their binding themselves to adopt the English solution. The first answer to a legal problem is not necessarily the right one and each of two answers may be equally meritorious.[51]

8. HISTORY

The upshot of the foregoing summary of the operation of the doctrine of precedent in other countries is that it is more difficult to get rid of an awkward decision in England than almost everywhere else in the world. The English doctrine of precedent was not always as strict as it is today. The importance of case-law has been emphasized since the days of the year books, and there are signs that the system was becoming rigid in the eighteenth century, but the strict rules summarized on p. 6 are the creature of the nineteenth and twentieth centuries. They could only come into being when law reporting had reached its present high standard, when the hierarchy of courts assumed something like its present

[49] (1986) AC 80.   [50] *Frankland* v. *R.* (1987) AC 576.
[51] See J. W. Harris, 'The Privy Council and the Common Law', *LQR* 106 (1990) 574.

shape, and when the judicial functions of the House of Lords were placed in the hands of eminent lawyers as they are today. The standard of law reporting was high at the beginning of the nineteenth century, but the hierarchy of courts and the judicial functions of the House of Lords did not assume their present form until after 1850.[52]

As late as 1869 a judge of first instance seems to have had no compunction in delivering a judgment in which he did no more than say that a decision of the Lord Chancellor hearing Chancery appeals was clearly mistaken and that he must therefore decline to follow it.[53] In spite of the clear manner in which it was stated by Lord Campbell in *Beamish* v. *Beamish*,[54] the former rule that the House of Lords was absolutely bound by its past decisions was not completely settled until the end of the nineteenth century.[55] As late as 1852 Lord St Leonards had used the following words when addressing the House of Lords:

You are not bound by any rule of law which you may lay down, if upon a subsequent occasion you should find reason to differ from that rule; that is, that this House, like every court of justice, possesses an inherent power to correct an error into which it may have fallen.[56]

The rule that the Court of Appeal is, in general, absolutely bound by its past decisions is the product of this century.[57] As late as 1903 the Court acted on the contrary view[58] and that view was repeated in the course of a judgment in the Court of Appeal as recently as 1938.[59] It is only in the present century that the Divisional Courts have come to apply the principle of *stare decisis* in its full rigour to their own past decisions.

No historical account would be complete without a reference to two further features of English case-law. These are the judges' practice of reasoning by analogy and what has been described as 'the declaratory theory' hallowed by Coke, Hale, and Blackstone. According to this theory, the decisions of the judges never make law, they merely constitute evidence of what the law is. The

---

[52] See Jim Evans, 'Change in the Doctrine of Precedent During the Nineteenth Century', in Goldstein (ed.), *Precedent in Law*, ch. 2.
[53] *Collins* v. *Lewis*, LR 8 Eq. 708.   [54] p. 7 *supra*.
[55] *London Tramways* v. *LCC* [1898] AC 735.
[56] *Bright* v. *Hutton*, 3 HLC 343 at 388.
[57] *Young* v. *Bristol Aeroplane Co. Ltd.* [1944] KB 718.
[58] *Wynne-Finch* v. *Chaytor* [1903] 2 KB 475.
[59] *Re Shoesmith* [1938] 2 KB 637 at 644.

practice of reasoning by analogy is the same today as it has been for a long time, but the declaratory theory no longer holds sway.

Reasoning by analogy

It is possible to quote passages from the time of Bracton onwards as evidence that reasoning by analogy is a commonplace of English judicial procedure. Writing in the thirteenth century Bracton said:

If any new and unwonted circumstances shall arise, then, if anything analogous has happened before, let the case be adjudged in like manner, proceeding *a similibus ad similia*.[60]

Six hundred years later Parke B spoke in substantially the same terms in *Mirehouse* v. *Rennell*[61] when he said:

Our common law system consists in the applying to new combinations of circumstances those rules of law which we derive from legal principles and judicial precedents; and for the sake of obtaining uniformity, consistency and certainty, we must apply those rules where they are not plainly unreasonable and inconvenient, to all cases which arise; and we are not at liberty to reject them, and to abandon all analogy to them, in those to which they have not yet been judicially applied, because we think that the rules are not as convenient and reasonable as we ourselves could have devised.

The rule of *stare decisis* causes the judges to reason by analogy because the principle that like cases must be decided alike involves the analogical extension of the decision in an earlier case. Allowance must also be made for the converse principle that dissimilar cases should be decided differently. It is only necessary to open a contemporary English law report in order to find a judge of our own day stating that there is not a material distinction between a previous case and the case before him. It is this approach to legal problems by proceeding from case to case which marks one of the main differences between the judicial process in common-law countries (including the United States) and the judicial process on the Continent. The principle of *stare decisis* may be applied so laxly in the United States that the American judge appears to be nearly as little fettered by past cases as his French counterpart, but the appearance is superficial. A French critic would say that the English and American judges were equally victims of *la superstition du cas*.

---

[60] *De Legibus*, fo. 1 (*b*).   [61] (1833) 1 Cl. & F. 527 at 546.

The similarities and differences in the reasoning with regard to precedent which is commonly employed by the English and American judges are strikingly revealed by the following passage in a book by an American legal writer of the twentieth century. He says the question before the judge is:

> Grant that there are differences between the cited precedent and the case at Bar, and assuming that the decision in the earlier case was a desirable one, is it desirable to attach legal weight to any of the factual differences between the instant case and the earlier case?[62]

The author of these words was writing of the United States. The first question for the English judge would concern the authority of the earlier decision. If it was that of a court whose decisions were binding upon him, he would follow it unless he thought that a reasonable distinction existed between it and the case before him and regarded the distinction as one upon which he should act. If the earlier decision was of merely persuasive authority, the English judge would follow it unless he was able to give cogent reasons for not doing so. (In this context, a 'reasonable' distinction means one which a lawyer might reasonably consider to be relevant having regard to the existing state of the law.) There is, of course, a difference between following a previous decision because of the absence of a convincing distinction between it and the instant case, and following a previous decision because a reasonable distinction which exists between it and the instant case is not regarded as one which should be acted upon.[63] In the latter situation the previous decision is 'applied' rather than 'followed', and the difference between the two procedures is often, though not invariably, recognized in English legal terminology.

The declaratory theory of judicial decision[64]

Sir Matthew Hale, writing in the seventeenth century, stated the declaratory theory by asserting that the decisions of courts cannot

make a law properly so called, for that only the King and Parliament can do; yet they have a great weight and authority in expounding, declaring, and publishing what the law of this Kingdom is, especially when such

[62] F. S. Cohen, *Ethical Systems and Legal Ideals*, 38.
[63] See the judgment of Roxburgh J in *Re House Property & Investment Co. Ltd.* [1954] Ch. 576 at 601.
[64] See Gerald Postema, 'Roots of our Notion of Precedent', in Goldstein (ed.), *Precedent in Law*, ch. 1; also Peter Wesley-Smith, 'Theories of Adjudication and the Status of *Stare Decisis*', ibid., ch. 3.

decisions hold a consonancy and congruity with resolutions and decisions of former times, and though such decisions are less than a law, yet they are a greater evidence thereof than the opinion of any private persons, as such whatsoever.[65]

In the eighteenth century Blackstone said 'the decisions of courts of justice are the evidence of what is common law'.[66] As late as 1892 Lord Esher said:

There is in fact no such thing as judge-made law, for the judges do not make the law though they frequently have to apply existing law to circumstances as to which it has not previously been authoritatively laid down that such law is applicable.[67]

The doctrine of Hale and Blackstone appears to have been that the common law consists of the usages and customary rules by which Englishmen have been governed since time immemorial supplemented by general principles of private justice and public convenience, and liable to be varied by Act of Parliament. This was the characteristic approach of the eighteenth-century judge towards the situation which was not covered by case-law. Thus, Willes J said:

Private justice, moral fitness and public convenience, when applied to a new subject, make common law without precedent, much more when received and approved by usage.[68]

It is difficult to be a great deal more explicit in the twentieth century about the basis of judicial reasoning when there is no precedent, but, when there is a precedent, orthodox theory has ceased to maintain that the precedent is no more than evidence of the moral fitness, public convenience, or conformity to usage of a rule derived from a previous decision or series of decisions. Such a rule is law 'properly so called' and law because it was made by the judges, not because it originated in common usage, or the judges' idea of justice and public convenience. Holdsworth once wrote in a manner suggesting that the views of Hale and Blackstone represent twentieth-century judicial doctrine,[69] but it is difficult not to share the scepticism of Dr Goodhart who asked in 'reply whether it would be possible today for counsel to argue that a

---

[65] *History of the Common Law* (6th edn.), 90.
[66] *Commentaries* (13th edn.), i. 88–9.
[67] *Willis v. Baddeley* [1892] 2 QB 324 at 326.
[68] *Millar v. Taylor* (1769) 4 Burr. 2303 at 2312.
[69] 'Case-Law', *LQR* 50 (1934), 180.

judgment of the House of Lords is not law because it conflicts with the settled principles of the common law.[70]

So far as Lord Esher's statement is concerned, the application of existing law to new circumstances can never be clearly distinguished from the creation of a new rule of law. Moreover, if there is no such thing as judge-made law, it is impossible to account for the evolution of much legal doctrine. For example, it is a matter of common knowledge among legal historians that the requirement of consideration in the law of contract is based on a series of decisions which can be cited by name. The effect of the requirement is that a promise, which is not contained in a deed, is legally void unless the promisee suffered some detriment in return for the promise when it was made. The doctrine has nothing to do with the ancient usages of Englishmen, and it is no part of the common stock of morality or justice; in fact, it is frequently criticized because it occasionally fosters immorality and promotes injustice by permitting the promisor to break his promise with impunity. One result of the requirement of consideration is that A may write to B offering to sell his house to him, promising to keep the offer open for a fortnight, and, seven days later, when B is about to accept the offer, tell him that he cannot do so because the house has been sold to C.

No one has ever denied that the rules of equity laid down by the Court of Chancery owe their authority to the fact that they are judge made. Sir George Jessel said:

It must not be forgotten that the rules of courts of equity are not, like the rules of the common law, supposed to have been established from time immemorial. It is perfectly well known that they have been established from time to time—altered, improved, and refined from time to time. In many cases we know the names of the chancellors who invented them.[71]

Most modern lawyers would repudiate the remarks of Lord Esher and consider that Mellish LJ came nearer to the truth when he said:

The whole of the rules of equity and nine-tenths of the common law have in fact been made by judges.[72]

From the historical point of view there is a slight element of truth in the declaratory theory because medieval judges sometimes

---

[70] Ibid. 196.   [71] *Re Hallett's Estate* (1880) 13 Ch. D. 696 at 710.
[72] *Allen* v. *Jackson* (1875) 1 Ch. D. 399 at 405; see also Sir Kenneth Diplock, *Courts as Legislators*, 2.

did regard themselves as charged with the duty of ascertaining, and declaring, and enforcing contemporary customs and usages. From the analytical point of view, on the other hand, the theory is inconsistent with current rules of precedent. A judge is bound to follow a previous decision, and appellate courts may overrule the previous decisions of courts beneath them in the hierarchy, provided they are not precluded from doing so by a decision which is binding upon them or by an Act of Parliament. If a previous decision is only evidence of what the law is, no judge could ever be absolutely bound to follow it, and it could never be effectively overruled because a subsequent judge might always treat it as having some evidential value.

There are, however, at least three good reasons why the declaratory theory should have persisted for some time after the modern English doctrine had begun to take shape. In the first place, it appealed to believers in the separation of powers, to whom anything in the nature of judicial legislation would have been anathema. Secondly, it concealed a fact which Bentham was anxious to expose, namely, that judge-made law is retrospective in its effect. If in December a court adjudges that someone is liable, in consequence of his conduct during the previous January, it would certainly appear to be legislating retrospectively, unless the liability is based on an earlier Act of Parliament, or unless the court is simply following a previous decision. A way of disguising the retrospective character of such a judgment would be to maintain the doctrine that the court really was doing no more than state a rule which anyone could have deduced from well-known principles or common usage, for the conduct in question would then have been prohibited by the law as it stood in January. The third reason for the persistence of the declaratory theory may be thought to justify its retention in a revised form today. When confronted with a novel point, judges always tend to speak as though the answer is provided by the common law.

So far as the first reason is concerned, it is only necessary to observe that the fact that our judges can and do make law is now universally recognized by writers on the British Constitution. Indeed, they use that fact as one of several illustrations of the impossibility of accepting the doctrine of the separation of powers in a rigid form.

The second reason must be discussed at slightly greater length. One of Bentham's comments on judge-made law is particularly famous. He said, 'it is the judges who make the common law', and continued:

Do you know how they make it? Just as a man makes law for his dog. When your dog does anything you want to break him of, you wait till he does it and then beat him. This is the way you make laws for your dog, and this is the way the judges make law for you and me.[73]

The merits of this criticism of judge-made law may be considered in the light of a famous case of the 1930s, which was thought by a number of contemporary lawyers to have effected a considerable change in the law. In *Donoghue* v. *Stevenson*,[74] a decision reached by a majority of 3 to 2 in the House of Lords on the hearing of a Scots appeal in 1932; a woman and her friend visited a café in Paisley where the friend ordered for her some ice-cream and a bottle of ginger beer. These were supplied by the shopkeeper, who opened the ginger-beer bottle and poured some of the contents over the ice-cream which was contained in a tumbler. The woman drank part of the mixture, and the friend then proceeded to pour the remaining contents of the bottle into the tumbler. As she was doing so, a decomposed snail floated out of the ginger beer. In consequence of having drunk part of the contaminated contents of the bottle, the woman alleged that she contracted a serious illness. The bottle was stated to have been of dark opaque glass, so that the condition of the contents could not have been ascertained by inspection. The shopkeeper was merely the retailer of the ginger beer and the question before the courts was whether the woman could recover damages as compensation for her illness from the manufacturers, assuming that she could prove that they, or their servants, were negligent in permitting, or failing to guard against, the presence of the snail in the bottle. Cast into the terminology of the English law which was said to be the same as the law of Scotland on the point under consideration, the problem was whether the manufacturer owed a duty of care to the ultimate consumer. Before 1932 most lawyers would have answered this question in the negative. On the authority of a number of earlier cases, they would have said that the manufacturers had broken their contract with the wholesaler or retailer who bought the ginger beer from them, but that did not entitle the consumer to sue them in tort. Had she bought the drink from the shopkeeper she would have been able to recover damages for breach of contract

[73] *Works*, v. 235.   [74] [1932] AC 562.

from him, but, as things were, the majority of contemporary lawyers would have said that she had no legal remedy. The majority of the House of Lords came to the opposite conclusion. They were not bound to follow the earlier cases, and they explained away or condemned a number of *dicta* in them. Most lawyers of today would agree that the decision of the majority placed the law on a rational basis, but the fact remains that most lawyers of 1932 would have advised the manufacturers that they were not legally liable. The manufacturers won in the Court of Session, and, when sitting as a court, the House of Lords legislated retrospectively by overruling *dicta*, if not decisions, by which the Court of Session considered itself bound. Blackstone would have said that the House declared that a decision or dictum overruled by it was not bad law, 'but that it was not law, that is, that it is not the established custom of the realm as has been erroneously determined'.[75]

Nothing is to be gained by concealing the truth in this way, and it is better to admit that, in situations such as that with which *Donoghue* v. *Stevenson* was concerned, the courts make new law with retrospective effect. Such an admission does not imply a whole-hearted acceptance of Bentham's condemnation of judge-made law. Retrospective legislation is only pernicious if it entails liability for conduct which might well have been different if the agent had known of the terms of the subsequent law. This is not the case with much new law which is made by judges. It is difficult to believe, for instance, that the manufacturers in *Donoghue* v. *Stevenson* would have conducted themselves differently had they known that the law was what the House of Lords later declared it to be.[76] Hardships may arise where contracts held to be valid by an earlier decision are declared void by an appellate court in a later case. The justification for the decision of the appellate court is that the social hardship of continuing an unsatisfactory rule is greater than the individual hardship suffered by those who may have made contracts on the faith of the earlier decision. In any event, retrospective judicial legislation must surely be a necessary evil once it is granted that we have not got, and cannot have, an unambiguous and all-embracing legal code, and that not all possible legal issues are covered by past decisions. Judges must

[75] *Commentaries* (13th edn.), i. 87.
[76] If the manufacturers were insured against claims, it would have been an odd policy under which that of the plaintiff would have been excluded.

decide cases as they arise: when the facts are not clearly covered by a statute, when there is room for two views concerning the meaning of statutory words, and when no past decision is clearly in point. The possibility that past cases should only be overruled prospectively is examined in Chapter VIII but, subject to this, what can our judges do but make new law and how can they prevent it from having retrospective effect?

The third reason for the persistence of the declaratory theory, the judges' tendency to speak as though the common law has an answer to every question that comes before them when the matter is not covered by legislation, is attributable to the fact that our courts are obliged to consider a far greater quantity of material than the contents of statutes and the *rationes decidendi* of cases binding upon them. The statutes and *rationes decidendi* have to be *followed*, but persuasive precedents, *obiter dicta* and the general principles or standards which have guided judges in the past, have to be *considered*. The result is that, although it is absurd to regard such rules as that simple contracts require consideration as the product of the customs of the English, it is facile to speak, as Austin did, of

The childish fiction employed by our judges that judiciary or common law is not made by them, but is a miraculous something, made by nobody, existing, I suppose, from eternity, and merely declared from time to time by the judges.[77]

Not everybody would agree with the contention of some of the writings of Professor Dworkin that there is in theory a legally correct answer, based on the principles underlying the pre-existing law, to every claim brought before a modern judge,[78] but most lawyers would probably endorse the following words of Professor Geldart written as long ago as 1911:

In the absence of clear precedents which might govern a question, we find judges relying on such considerations as the opinions of legal writers, the practice of conveyancers, the law of other modern countries, the Roman law, principles of 'natural justice', or public policy. The proper application of these may be a matter of dispute and difficulty but in any case the judge is applying a standard; he shows that he is not free, as a

---

[77] *Jurisprudence* (5th edn.), ii. 655.
[78] See e.g. 'Is There Really No Right Answer in Hard Cases?', *A Matter of Principle*, ch. 5.

legislator would be, to decide as he pleases; he is bound to decide according to principle.[79]

Limitations of judicial legislation

It has been said to be 'merely misleading' to speak of judicial legislation,[80] and it must be admitted that to do so is to use highly metaphorical language. There is no equivalent to the authoritative text of a statute, and, even when they are not bound by a statute or indistinguishable precedent, the judges' power to innovate is limited by what they cannot consider as well as by what they must consider. They cannot conduct those extensive examinations of empirical data and considerations of social policy which precede, or should precede, much legislation. In *Morgans* v. *Launchbury*,[81] for example, the House of Lords declined to hold that the owner of the 'family car' (in this instance the wife) was liable to passengers injured by the negligence of a friend of the husband when driving the car, at the request of the husband, on a pub crawl. The wife, unlike the driver, was insured against risks to passengers, but it would have involved a drastic change in the law to hold her liable simply by virtue of her ownership of the 'family car'. Lord Wilberforce said:

Liability and insurance are so intermixed that judicially to alter the basis of liability without adequate knowledge (which we have not the means to obtain) as to the impact which this might make on the insurance system would be dangerous and . . . irresponsible.[82]

The modern English judge is at a disadvantage as a lawmaker when contrasted with the legislature because he cannot unmake law which has been effectively declared by statute, or, in spheres in which there is no statute, by decisions which are binding upon him. He is subject to the even greater restriction that he can only make law on such specific issues as happen to be litigated before him. Considerations of this nature led Holmes J, one of the greatest American judges, to say:

I recognise without hesitation that judges do and must legislate, but they can do so only interstitially; they are confined from molar to molecular

[79] *Elements of English Law* (1st edn.), 23. The passage is unchanged in the current 7th edn.

[80] A. W. B. Simpson, in *Oxford Essays in Jurisprudence*, second series, 86.

[81] [1973] AC 127.

[82] At 137. For similar reasons the House of Lords refused to make a radical reappraisal of the law relating to damages for personal injuries in *Lim Poh Choo* v. *Camden and Islington Area Health Authority* [1980] AC 174.

motion. A common law judge could not say, I think the doctrine of consideration a bit of historical nonsense and shall not enforce it in my court.[83]

The declaratory theory was beneficial in at least one respect. It provided a court with an excellent reason not to follow or apply a case of which it strongly disapproved. While the doctrine was in force, it appeared natural to say that if the common law consists of principles, of reason, justice, and convenience, a previous decision may be rejected on the ground that it is unreasonable, unjust, or inconvenient. In *Mirehouse* v. *Rennell*[84] Parke B, believed by some to have been 'the greatest legal pedant that ever existed',[85] appears to have recognized that rules derived from precedent might be ignored if they were plainly unreasonable and inconvenient. It is possible to point to a number of instances at the beginning of the nineteenth century in which judges declined to follow a previous decision because it was 'absurd',[86] because it 'cannot be supported in principle',[87] or because it 'does not convince'.[88] In 1802 Lord Eldon said of a previous decision:

I feel it to be my duty to understand the principle of the case before I confirm it, or to decide against it upon a principle stated from this place so clear that there can be no doubt upon it.[89]

These words were echoed by Sir George Jessel as late as 1880 when he said:

The only thing in a Judge's decision binding as an authority upon a subsequent Judge is the principle upon which the case was decided, but it is not sufficient that the case should have been decided on a principle if that principle is not itself a right principle, or one not applicable to the case; and it is for a subsequent Judge to say whether or not it is a right principle, and, if not, he may himself lay down the true principle. In that case the prior decision ceases to be a binding authority or guide for any subsequent Judge, for the second Judge who lays down the true principle in effect reverses the decision.[90]

[83] *South Pacific Co.* v. *Jensen* (1917) 244 US 205 at 221.
[84] p. 26 *supra.*
[85] Letter quoted in Lord Hanworth's *Life of Pollock, C.B.*, 190.
[86] *Vere* v. *Cawdor and King* (1890) 11 East. 568.
[87] *Wickes* v. *Gordon* (1819) 2 B. & Ald. 235.
[88] *R.* v. *St Mary's, Leicester* (1818) 1 B. & Ald. 327.
[89] *Aldrich* v. *Cooper*, 8 Ves. 382 at 388.
[90] *Osborne to Rowlett*, 13 Ch. D. 774 at 785.

Today no one would doubt that it is only the principle upon which the case was decided which binds a subsequent judge, and no one would doubt that the principle must be applicable to the case before him if the subsequent judge is to be bound by it, but, assuming that the principle derived from the first case is applicable to the case before the subsequent judge, the extent to which he can refuse to act upon it, because it is not a right principle, is greatly limited by the doctrine of precedent. Once it is recognized that a rule laid down by a judicial decision is law because it is so laid down, the source of the judicial decision, whether it be another decision, a dictum in a previous judgment, or a principle of justice and convenience, ceases to be relevant from the point of view of binding authority. All that matters is the precedent and this must be followed if, according to our doctrine of precedent, it is binding, although it is not regarded as a right principle by the judge who is considering the matter. We shall see that there are exceptions to the rule of *stare decisis* today, but, unlike the exceptions of the nineteenth century, they are not based on the declaratory theory. Even if it was a childish fiction, that theory unified the exceptions to *stare decisis* that were recognized in the eighteenth century and throughout much of the nineteenth century. The current exceptions to the doctrine are as miscellaneous as they are ill defined.

9. JUDICIAL REGRETS

Although the English doctrine of precedent has not lacked encomia, it has also been the subject of judicial regrets. Speaking in the days when the House of Lords held itself absolutely bound by its past decisions, Lord Reid said in *Nash* v. *Tamplin & Sons Brewery Brighton Ltd.*:[91]

It matters not how difficult it is to find the *ratio decidendi* of a previous case, that *ratio* must be found. It matters not how difficult it is to reconcile that *ratio* when found with statutory provisions or general principles, that *ratio* must be applied to any later case which is not reasonably distinguishable.[92]

In *Radcliffe* v. *Ribble Motor Services Ltd.*[93] the House of Lords declared itself unable to depart from the doctrine of common

---

[91] [1952] AC 231.   [92] [1952] AC at 250.   [93] [1939] AC 215.

employment on account of previous decisions of the House. The doctrine in question was that under which a servant injured by the negligence of his fellow servant was disabled from claiming damages from his master at common law although the injury was sustained in circumstances in which a stranger could have successfully sued the master if he had been injured by the negligence of one of that master's servants. The doctrine had troubled the courts for the better part of a century, and everyone connected with *Radcliffe's* case would have agreed that it was unjust and ill suited to modern conditions. Lord Atkin even went so far as to say that the decision on which the common employment rule was based.

proceeded on a fallacious proposition from first to last—namely, that the doctrine of *respondeat superior* only applies to strangers.[94]

The House was incapacitated from overruling the doctrine by the practice concerning the absolutely binding effect of its previous decisions; even today it is open to question whether the House of Lords would be prepared to overrule any doctrine that had been as thoroughly established by case-law. The doctrine of common employment was held to be inapplicable to the facts of *Radcliffe's* case but continued to plague the courts until it was abolished by statute in 1948.

The lot of judges of the Court of Appeal may be harder since they are still bound by their own decisions as well as by those of the House of Lords. In one recent case, the Court held that it was bound by a previous decision of its own to hold that a majority verdict was void because, although the foreman had stated in open court that the number of jurors who concurred was ten, he had not stated the arithmetically obvious corollary that the number of those who dissented was two.[95] The rule was 'bordering on the absurd', but since the case was indistinguishable it had to be followed. In another recent case, the Court of Appeal was constrained by an indistinguishable decision of the House of Lords to give an interpretation to a taxing statute which it regarded as unfair and oppressive and not an inevitable reading of the act.[96] It

[94] At 228.
[95] *R. v. Pigg* (1982) 74 Cr. App. Rep. 352. The decision was reversed by the House of Lords, but the House indicated that the Court of Appeal were right to hold themselves bound: (1982) 75 Cr. App. Rep. 79.
[96] *Bird v. Inland Revenue Commissioners* (1987) STC 168. The decision of the Court of Appeal was varied on appeal to the House of Lords: (1989) AC 300.

reached its decision with the 'utmost distaste'.[97] For all the exceptions and qualification discussed later in this book, the English doctrine of *stare decisis* retains its coercive edge.

[97] (1987) STC 168, 181 Sir Nicholas Browne-Wilkinson VC.

II

RATIO DECIDENDI AND *OBITER DICTUM*

1. *RATIO DECIDENDI* AND THE STRUCTURE OF JUDGMENTS

According to the preliminary statement of the English rules of precedent contained in the last chapter, every court is bound to follow any case decided by a court above it in the hierarchy, and appellate courts (other than the House of Lords) are bound by their previous decisions. This statement is too concise because it does not indicate that the only part of a previous case which is binding is the *ratio decidendi* (reason for deciding). The principal object of the present chapter is to consider what is meant by the *ratio decidendi* of a case when the phrase is used by judges and other lawyers and by what methods it may be determined. This will show what is entailed by 'following' or 'applying' a case and by being 'bound' by a previous decision, although these matters are not discussed until the beginning of the next chapter.

The *ratio decidendi* is best approached by a consideration of the structure of a typical judgment. The contemporary English judge almost invariably gives reasons for his decision in a civil case. Assuming that the trial is by a judge alone without a jury, he generally summarizes the evidence, announces his findings of fact, and reviews the arguments that have been addressed to him by counsel for each of the parties. If a point of law has been raised, he often discusses a number of previous decisions. Nowadays it is comparatively seldom that a civil case is tried by a judge and jury. When there is a jury, the judge sums the evidence up to them and bases his judgment on their findings of fact. In criminal cases tried on indictment, the all-important feature from the point of view of a lawyer is the summing up to the jury. The form of the judgments in appellate courts is similar to that of a judge who tries a civil case without a jury. It consists of a review of facts and arguments and a discussion of relevant questions of law. Several opinions are frequently delivered in appellate courts because appeals are always heard by more than one judge.

It is not everything said by a judge when giving judgment that constitutes a precedent. In the first place, this status is reserved for his pronouncements on the law, and no disputed point of law is involved in the vast majority of cases that are tried in any year. The dispute is solely concerned with the facts. For example, the issue may be whether a particular motorist was driving carelessly by failing to keep a proper look-out or travelling at an excessive speed. No one doubts that a motorist owes a legal duty to drive carefully and, very frequently, the only question is whether he was in breach of that duty when he caused damage to a pedestrian or another motorist. Cases in which the only issues are questions of fact are usually not reported in any series of law reports, but it is not always easy to distinguish law from fact and the reasons which led a judge of first instance or an appellate court to come to a factual conclusion are sometimes reported at length. For example, an employer is under a legal duty to provide his employees with a reasonably safe system of working. The question whether that duty has been broken is essentially one of fact, but the law reports contain a number of cases in which judges have expressed their views concerning the precautions which an employer should have taken in particular instances. When an injury would not have occurred if a workman had been wearing protective clothing it has been said that his employer ought to have insisted that such clothing should have been worn instead of merely rendering it available for those who desired to wear it, but the House of Lords has insisted that observations of this nature are not general propositions of law necessarily applicable to future cases and the decisions based upon them do not constitute a precedent.[1] There is no point in endeavouring to ascertain the *ratio decidendi* of such cases.

The second reason why it is not everything said by a judge in the course of his judgment that constitutes a precedent is that, among the propositions of law enunciated by him, only those which he appears to consider necessary for his decision are said to form part of the *ratio decidendi* and thus to amount to more than an *obiter dictum*. If the judge in a later case is bound by the precedent according to the English doctrine of *stare decisis*, he must apply the earlier *ratio decidendi* however much he disapproved of it, unless, to use the words of Lord Reid, he considers that the two cases are

---

[1] *Qualcast (Wolverhampton) Ltd.* v. *Haynes* [1959] AC 743.

'reasonably distinguishable'.[2] Dicta in earlier cases are, of course, frequently followed or applied, but dicta are never of more than persuasive authority. There is no question of any judge being bound to follow them. Even when the *ratio decidendi* of a previous case is merely a persuasive authority, it must be followed in later cases unless the judge has good reason to disapprove of it.[3] It constitutes a precedent, and the difference between a persuasive precedent and an *obiter dictum* is only slightly less significant than that between binding and persuasive precedents. If, for example, a High Court judge of first instance comes to the conclusion that a proposition of law contained in a previous opinion of another High Court judge of first instance is *ratio*, he will be a great deal more reluctant to differ from it than would be the case if he was satisfied that it was merely a *dictum*, although a judge of first instance is not bound to follow the decision of another judge of first instance.

The distinction between *ratio decidendi* and *obiter dictum* is an old one. As long ago as 1673 Vaughan CJ said:

An opinion given in court, if not necessary to the judgment given of record, but that it might have been as well given if no such, or a contrary had been broach'd, is no judicial opinion; but a mere *gratis dictum*.[4]

Nowadays an *obiter dictum* would normally be spoken of as a judicial opinion, but the contrary practice prevailed long after 1673. Thus Austin, lecturing between 1828 and 1832, said:

Such general propositions, occurring in the course of a decision, as have not this implication with the specific peculiarities of the case, are commonly styled extra judicial, and commonly have no authority.[5]

There are undoubtedly good grounds for the importance attached to the distinction between *ratio decidendi* and *obiter dictum*. In this context an *obiter dictum* means a statement by the way, and the probabilities are that such a statement has received less serious consideration than that devoted to a proposition of law put forward as a reason for the decision. It is not even every proposition of this nature that forms part of the *ratio decidendi*. To quote Devlin J, as he then was:

It is well established that if a judge gives two reasons for his decision, both are binding. It is not permissible to pick out one as being supposedly the

[2] p. 36 *supra*.
[3] See Richard Bronaugh, 'Persuasive Precedent', in Goldstein (ed.), *Precedent in Law*, ch. 8.   [4] *Bole* v. *Horton*, Vaughan 360 at 382.
[5] *Jurisprudence* (5th edn.), ii. 622.

better reason and ignore the other one; nor does it matter for this purpose which comes first and which comes second. But the practice of making judicial observations *obiter* is also well established. A judge may often give additional reasons for his decisions without wishing to make them part of the *ratio decidendi*; he may not be sufficiently convinced of their cogency as to want them to have the full authority of precedent, and yet may wish to state them so that those who later may have the duty of investigating the same point will start with some guidance. This is a matter which the judge himself is alone capable of deciding, and any judge who comes after him must ascertain which course has been adopted from the language used and not by consulting his own preferences.[6]

One thing which a judge cannot do is to prevent his decision on a point of law from constituting a precedent.[7]

The above remarks of Lord Devlin represent orthodox judicial theory, and, at first sight, the power they concede to those who decide a case may seem somewhat surprising. If a judge has this amount of freedom to determine which of his observations is *ratio decidendi* and which *obiter dictum*, is there not a grave danger that he will exercise an undue influence on the future development of the law? He only has to state twenty propositions and say that he bases his decision on each of them to have created twenty new legal rules. It is true that the majority of the judges of former times would have denied that they possessed any power to make new law, but we are primarily concerned with the contemporary situation in which the declaratory theory of judicial decision no longer holds sway. It is also true that the last thing any modern English judge would wish to do is to fetter his successors by laying down a multitude of superfluous rules. But just now we are concerned with legal theory. The answer to the question raised is that there are several considerations which may be said to redress the balance in favour of the judges who come afterwards. No doubt the *ratio decidendi* of a previous case has to be gathered from the language of the judge who decided that case, but it is trite learning that the interpreter has nearly as much to say as the speaker so far as the meaning of words is concerned. Of even greater significance is the existence of certain rules of judicial practice concerning the construction to be placed by a future judge upon past decisions. By stressing the necessity of having regard to

---

[6] *Behrens* v. *Bertram Mills Circus Ltd.* [1957] 2 QB 1 at 25.
[7] *In re Showerings, Vine Products and Whiteways Ltd.'s application* [1968], 1 WLR at 1384 *per* Megarry J.

the facts of the previous case and the language of prior or subsequent judgments, these rules greatly curtail the influence that can be exercised on legal development by means of the reasons which a particular judge sees fit to give for his decisions. Indeed, the significance of these limitations is so great that it will be convenient to illustrate them by reference to some of the cases that are usually mentioned in discussions concerning the *ratio decidendi*.

Judgements must be read in the light of the facts of the cases in which they are delivered

There would be no point in setting out many of the remarks of judges insisting on the importance of paying the most scrupulous attention to the facts of the previous cases cited to them. The number of such remarks is legion. The requirement goes to the root of the doctrine of precedent according to which like cases must be decided alike. Only so is it possible to ensure that the court bound by a previous case decides the new case in the same way as the other court would have decided it. Of course, it is all a question of probabilities, but the probability that a court will decide a new case in the same way as would the court which decided one of the cases cited becomes less and less as the differences between the facts of the two cases increase.[8] A further reason for the rule of judicial practice now under consideration was stated by Lord Halsbury at the beginning of a famous passage in his judgment in *Quinn* v. *Leathem*.[9] Lord Halsbury said:

Every judgment must be read as applicable to the particular facts proved or assumed to be proved, since the generality of the expressions which may be found there are not intended to be expositions of the whole law but govern and are qualified by the particular facts of the case in which such expressions are to be found.

The way in which the practice works may be illustrated by a further reference to *Donoghue* v. *Stevenson*.[10] That was the case in which the House of Lords was concerned with the civil liability of the manufacturer of a bottle of ginger beer to the ultimate

---

[8] 'Although the courts below will not impugn your lordships' judgments in cases *ad idem*, yet they do not hold that they are bound by them beyond the point actually decided. The courts below truly say, "We cannot know that the House of Lords would carry this determination further than they have carried it" ', *per* Best CJ in *Fletcher* v. *Lord Sondes* (1826) 3 Bing. 501 at 560.
[9] [1901] AC 495 at 506.   [10] [1932] AC 562, p. 31 *supra*.

consumer with whom he has made no contract. If the consumer becomes ill in consequence of the presence of a decomposed snail in the bottle, can he recover damages from the manufacturer if he can prove that the manufacturer or his servant was negligent? It will be recollected that the House of Lords answered this question in the affirmative by a majority of 3 to 2. Elaborate judgments were delivered, but there has been a high degree of unanimity among subsequent judges and writers in regarding the following passage with which Lord Atkin concluded his speech as containing the *ratio decidendi* of the case:

If your Lordships accept the view that this pleading discloses a relevant cause of action you will be affirming the proposition that by Scots and English law alike a manufacturer of products, which he sells in such a form as to show that he intends them to reach the ultimate consumer in the form in which they left him with no reasonable possibility of intermediate examination, and with the knowledge that the absence of reasonable care in the preparation or putting up of the products will result in an injury to the consumer's life or property, owes a duty to the consumer to take that reasonable care.[11]

At an earlier stage in his speech Lord Atkin made some famous generalizations concerning the law of negligence expressing what has come to be known as 'the neighbour principle'. He said:

At present I content myself with pointing out that in English law there must be and is some general conception of relations giving rise to a duty of care of which the particular cases found in the books are but instances. The liability for negligence, whether you style it such or treat it as in other systems as a species of 'culpa', is no doubt based upon a general public sentiment of moral wrong-doing for which the offender must pay. But acts or omissions which any moral code would censure cannot in a practical world be treated so as to give a right to every person injured by them to demand relief. In this way rules of law arise which limit the range of complainants and the extent of their remedy. The rule that you are to love your neighbour becomes in law, you must not injure your neighbour, and the question, who is my neighbour? receives a restricted reply. You must take reasonable care to avoid acts or omissions which you can reasonably foresee would be likely to injure your neighbour. Who then in law is my neighbour? The answer seems to be persons who are so closely and directly affected by my act that I ought reasonably to have them in contemplation as being so affected when I am directing my mind to the acts or omissions which are called in question.[12]

[11] At 599.   [12] At 580.

This statement of the neighbour principle has been pivotal in the subsequent development of the law of negligence. On one view, there is a prima-facie duty of care where damage is within reasonable contemplation, which may be negatived by considerations of public policy.[13] On another view, which is prevalent in recent decisions, there are distinct categories of duty-situations which cannot be encapsulated within a single principle.[14] On neither view, it would seem, does the neighbour principle constitute part of the *ratio decidendi* of *Donoghue* v. *Stevenson*. No judge is required by the ruling in that case to hold that a defendant is liable in damages merely because he could reasonably foresee that an act or omission of his might cause loss to some other person.

Every judgment must be read in the light of judgments in other cases

A good illustration of the necessity of interpreting the *ratio decidendi* of a case in the light of the judgments in prior and subsequent cases is provided by the treatment of *Barwick* v. *The English Joint Stock Bank*[15] in *Lloyd* v. *Grace, Smith & Co.*[16] When the first of these cases came before the Exchequer Chamber (the predecessor of the Court of Appeal) in the middle of the nineteenth century, doubts had been expressed on the question whether a master was civilly liable to the victim of a fraud perpetrated by his servant when acting in the course of his employment. One of the Bank's managers fraudulently induced the plaintiff to accept a worthless guarantee on the strength of which he supplied goods on credit to a third party. The third party was thus enabled to pay off his overdraft with the Bank. Judgment had been entered for the defendants at first instance and the Exchequer Chamber ordered a new trial. When stating that Court's reasons for doing so, Willes J said:

But with respect to the question whether a principal is answerable for the act of his agent in the course of his master's business, *and for his master's benefit*, no sensible distinction can be drawn between the case of fraud and the case of any other wrong. The general rule is that the master is answerable for every such wrong of the servant or agent as is committed in

---

[13] *Anns* v. *Merton London Borough Council* (1977) AC 728, 751–2 Lord Wilberforce.
[14] See the speech of Lord Bridge in *Caparo Industries plc* v. *Dickman* (1990) 2 AC 605.
[15] (1866) LR 2 Ex. 259.   [16] [1912] AC 716.

the course of the service *and for the master's benefit* though no express command or privity of the master be proved.[17]

There was no doubt that the Bank had benefited in consequence of the manager's fraud on the facts of the particular case, but were the words in italics part of the *ratio decidendi*? Is the case authority for the broad proposition that a master is answerable for the fraud of his servant committed in the course of the service, or for the narrower proposition that the master is only liable for such a fraud if he benefits from it? On the latter view, *Barwick*'s case could be used as the basis of an argument against the master's liability in a case in which he had not benefited from the servant's fraud. If the Court of Exchequer Chamber considered that the employer's benefit was an essential prerequisite of their liability, the requirement would be part of the *ratio decidendi*.

This is exactly how counsel for the defendant did use *Barwick* v. *The English Joint Stock Bank* in *Lloyd* v. *Grace, Smith & Co.* The managing clerk of a firm of solicitors fraudulently induced the plaintiff to convey two cottages and transfer a mortgage to him. He sold the cottages, called in the mortgage, and absconded with the proceeds with the result that his employer derived no benefit from his fraud. The employer was, none the less, held liable in the court of first instance. He successfully appealed to the Court of Appeal, but the plaintiff's appeal to the House of Lords succeeded. Accordingly it is now settled law that a master is liable for frauds committed by his servant acting in the course of his employment. The House of Lords took the view that the reference by Willes J in *Barwick*'s case to the master's benefit was a mere incidental allusion to the facts before him and not, as the Court of Appeal and some earlier judges had concluded, an essential part of the *ratio decidendi*. In the House of Lords, Lord Loreburn appears to have reached his decision on the construction of Willes J's judgment in *Barwick*'s case when read as a whole, but Lord Halsbury laid special stress on a statement made by Holt at the beginning of the eighteenth century, while Lord Macnaghten based his interpretation of the language of Willes J on statements made by other members of the court in *Barwick* v. *The English Joint Stock Bank* when giving judgment in later cases.

It seems to follow that, whatever a judge may say, expressly or by implication, concerning the proposition of law on which he

[17] LR 2 Ex. 265, with italics added.

bases his decision, that proposition must be construed in the light of the existing case-law at the time when the proposition falls to be considered by a later judge or by anyone else who may be concerned with the question. Further support for this view may be obtained from the words of Lord Tenterden in *Wells* v. *Hopwood*[18] which have already been quoted. This rule of judicial practice, like that which stresses the significance of the facts before the court, cannot be formulated precisely, but any discussion of the *ratio decidendi* of a case which fails to take account of both practices is liable to become highly unrealistic.

Decisions without reasons

A minor complication in discussions concerning the *ratio decidendi* is due to the fact that in some cases no reasons are given for the decision. The report merely contains a statement of the facts, with or without an account of the arguments of counsel, and concludes with some such remark as 'judgment for the plaintiff'. Reasons for judgment are generally given in our superior courts nowadays, and, when this is not done, the case is hardly ever reported, but some of the earlier reports contain elaborate accounts of decisions for which no grounds are stated. It would be a mistake to assume that such decisions necessarily lack a *ratio decidendi* which enables them to be cited as a precedent, for a proposition of law on which they must have been based may be inferred with more or less confidence from the facts coupled with the conclusion. The derivation of a proposition of law from the facts of a case coupled with the order made by the court after taking account of those facts is an important feature of discussions concerning the *ratio decidendi*. For this purpose the order of the court must be treated as the conclusion of a syllogism of which the facts on which that order was based constitute the minor premiss and the proposition alleged to be the *ratio decidendi* is the major premiss.

In general, however, the authority of a decision for which no reasons are given is very weak, because it is so hard to tell which facts were regarded as material and which were thought to be immaterial. Suppose, for example, that no reasons had been given for the decision in *Donoghue* v. *Stevenson*. It would be going a little too far to say that the case would only have been authority for the proposition that a manufacturer of ginger beer owes a duty to

---

[18] (1832) 3 B. & Ad. 20 at 34, p. 14 *supra*.

Scots women by whom that beverage is lawfully consumed in Paisley, to take care that snails do not get into the opaque bottles in which it is contained,[19] but we would have lacked the guidance which is provided by the terms of the speeches in the House of Lords on the extent to which some of the above peculiarities of the particular case can be ignored in determining its *ratio decidendi*. Even if we had no such assistance, we would have been justified in concluding that the facts that the consumer was Scots and that the consumption took place in Paisley rather than any other Scots town were immaterial. But, thanks to Lord Atkin's reference to 'products' in the passage quoted on p. 44, we can tell that the principle of *Donoghue* v. *Stevenson* is not confined to the liability of manufacturers of beverages. Four years after the case was decided it was argued that the principle was confined to articles of food and drink, but the argument was unsuccessful and *Donoghue* v. *Stevenson* was applied against the manufacturers of underpants who carelessly allowed an excessive quantity of sulphur to get into their wares and thus caused a purchaser to suffer from dermatitis.[20]

Diversity of forms of judgment

To revert to cases in which reasons are given for the decision, every English law student is familiar with the difficulty of differentiating those parts of the leading judgments that are *ratio* from those that are mere *dicta*, and disagreements over the distinction lie at the root of a number of legal controversies. These difficulties and disagreements are largely, if not entirely, due to the elaborate and varied forms in which English judgments are delivered. The judgments may consist of nothing but findings of fact in cases in which the law is not in dispute, they may take the form of a summing up of the evidence with a direction to a jury on the law, a conclusion with regard to the law may be held to render a decision on some of the facts unnecessary, numerous legal rules or authorities may be canvassed and, in appellate courts, the different opinions may contain a variety of conflicting reasons for reaching the same conclusion. To make matters worse for those who are concerned to discover the principle on which a case was decided, it is comparatively seldom that a judge expressly indicates the proposition on which he relies as *ratio decidendi*, yet legal theory demands that there should be a *ratio decidendi* in all cases

[19] Cf. 20 *MLR* 6 and references there cited.
[20] *Grant* v. *Australian Knitting Mills* [1936] AC 85.

in which the judgment contains more than factual statements or reasoning on the facts. The main problem of this chapter can be stated quite simply. Is it possible to do appreciably more than say that propositions of law which a judge appears to consider necessary for his decision are *ratio* and all other legal propositions that emerge from his judgment are *dicta*? It will be submitted that it is not possible to do appreciably more than this, although some valiant attempts have been made to go further. The importance of these attempts is, of course, enhanced by the fact that it is not only a judge in a later case who is concerned to know what proportions of a previous judgment ought to be regarded as *ratio*. The identical problem confronts a lawyer advising his client and a legal writer called on to expound the existing law.

The search for the *ratio decidendi* is largely a peculiarity of the judicial processes of England, Scotland, and those countries whose legal system derives from ours. In the *Cour de Cassation* in France, the reasons for a decision are stated very succinctly and anything in the nature of a general discourse is prohibited so far as all French civil courts are concerned.[21] The result is that continental discussions on the subject of judicial decisions do not share the preoccupation of writers on Anglo-American jurisprudence with the method of distinguishing *ratio decidendi* from *obiter dictum*. According to Dr Goodhart it is the doctrine of the binding precedent which may be said to furnish the fundamental distinction between English and continental legal methods;[22] but it is open to question whether the difference between the forms in which the more important judgments are delivered is not equally fundamental.

Le style actuel des décisions, notamment de la *Cour de Cassation*, est un peu la messe en latin. C'est le prolongement d'une tradition infiniment respectable. Mais c'est aussi la répétition de formules que beaucoup ne comprennent pas et qui permettent à l'esprit de s'orienter où il veut.[23]

2. THE AMERICAN REALISTS

Before proceeding any further with our endeavour to elucidate the distinction between *ratio decidendi* and *obiter dictum*, account must be taken of an opinion held in some quarters that any attempt of this nature is nothing more than a wild goose chase.

[21] Code Civil. art. 5.   [22] 50 *LQR* 42.
[23] Touffait and Tunc, *Revue trimestrielle de droit civil* (1974), 507.

This is, in substance, the opinion of a body of American writers, among whom the late Judge Jerome Frank was prominent, and who are often spoken of as realists. By way of contrast with the stress placed by orthodox English judicial theory on the freedom of the judge who decides the case in the matter of its *ratio decidendi*, they emphasize the liberty which a later judge enjoys of disregarding what his predecessors said in the cases cited to him. The realists maintain that it is a mistake to pay too great a regard to the vocal as opposed to the non-vocal behaviour of judges. 'Don't worry so much about what the courts say, consider what they do', is one of the chief cries of this school. Its members appear to take seriously a joke made to a Lord of Appeal in ordinary (Lord Asquith) by 'one of our greatest judicial luminaries'. When asked about the distinction between *ratio decidendi* and *obiter dictum*, he replied:

The rule is quite simple, if you agree with the other bloke you say it is part of the *ratio*; if you don't you say it is *obiter dictum*, with the implication that he is a congenital idiot.[24]

The authors of an English textbook on jurisprudence once went so far as to describe the distinction between *ratio* and *dicta* as a mere 'device employed by subsequent courts for the adoption or rejection of doctrine expressed in previous cases according to the inclinations of the subsequent courts'.[25]

In the United States, the mantle of the realists has, during the past decade, fallen on a new school, the critical legal studies movement. Its members draw much more radical political inferences from the allegedly spurious 'formalism' which they detect whenever judges claim to be constrained by authority. They see in such assertions sinister attempts to disguise the contradictions and oppressive social hierarchies inherent in liberal societies.[26] In American legal literature 'formalism' has become the boo word of the day.

Judges are human, and, as Lord Asquith observed, the joke made to him 'may well, as a matter of pure psychological fact, have more underlying truth than we know or care to avow'. Moreover, there can be little doubt that conclusions are often

[24] *Journal of the Society of Public Teachers of Law*, NS 1 (1950), 359.
[25] Dias and Hughes, *Jurisprudence*, 81.
[26] R. M. Unger, 'The Critical Legal Studies Movement', *HLR* 96 (1983), 561. See Harris, 'Unger's Critique of Formalism', *MLR* 52 (1989), 42.

reached before the authorities against them are considered. In the words of Lord Wright:

Sometimes a judge seems to move almost instinctively to the heart of the problem and its solution, though the detailed explanation and justification of what the problem is and how the solution is justified may require some elaborate reasoning and citation of authorities.[27]

Although he was at the time a Lord of Appeal in Ordinary, Lord Wright was writing extra-judicially, but the law reports abound in similar observations.

When confronted with a case in which the defendants and third party, respectively the landlord and tenant of a public house, who were seeking to put the blame for injuries sustained by one Heap on account of a defective cellar flap on to each other, or else to shift it on to a superior landlord who was not a party to the proceedings, McKinnon LJ said:

So far as I am concerned I freely avow that, inasmuch as in common sense and decency Heap ought to be able to recover against somebody, and, in the circumstances of this case, and having regard to the correspondence which has taken place, in all common sense and decency he is able to recover against these defendants if the law allows it, my only concern is to see whether, upon the cases, the law does allow him so to recover. I think that it does.[28]

McKinnon LJ then discussed the cases and showed how they supported the view that Heap was entitled to judgment. Procedure such as this does not warrant the conclusion that, when the authorities do come to be examined, any resort to the distinction between *ratio decidendi* and *obiter dictum* is in the nature of a façade behind which decisions are made on grounds which have little to do with the previous cases. The significance of a piece of reasoning by analogy is not greatly affected by the fact that it succeeds the conclusion which it justifies. From the point of view of the validity of the orthodox theory of the judicial process, the important thing is that a judge should be prepared to alter any provisional decision at which he may have arrived when he considers a case, the *ratio decidendi* of which is binding upon him and which supports a contrary view, and there is no evidence that this is not the current judicial practice in England.

[27] 8 *CLJ* 138.
[28] *Heap* v. *Ind Coope and Allsopp Ltd.* [1940] 2 KB 476 at 483.

The extreme realist position can in fact only be supported on the assumption that our judges are capable of the grossest hypocrisy. Why should the judicial regrets to which reference was made at the end of the last chapter not be taken seriously? Why do not judges situated, as Lord Campbell was in *Beamish* v. *Beamish*,[29] avail themselves of minute factual differences in order to distinguish a decision of which they disapprove? When a case appears to have two *rationes decidendi* why do subsequent judges generally concede coercive effect to both instead of following the one they prefer? We can safely assume that whatever the position in the United States may be, the distinction between *ratio decidendi* and *obiter dictum* is not entirely chimerical so far as the English courts are concerned, and proceed to consider the important suggestions with regard to the distinctions that have been made in the last century by Wambaugh and in this century by Dr Goodhart.

3. WAMBAUGH'S TEST

Starting with the assumption that the *ratio decidendi* is a general rule without which a case must have been decided otherwise, Wambaugh propounded his famous test of inversion for determining whether a given proposition is *ratio*. Addressing himself to the student he stated the test in the following words:

First frame carefully the supposed proposition of law. Let him then insert in the proposition a word reversing its meaning. Let him then inquire whether, if the court had conceived this new proposition to be good, and had had it in mind, the decision could have been the same. If the answer be affirmative, then, however excellent the original proposition may be, the case is not a precedent for that proposition, but if the answer be negative the case is a precedent for the original proposition and possibly for other propositions also. In short, when a case turns only on one point the proposition or doctrine of the case, the reason for the decision, the *ratio decidendi*, must be a general rule without which the case must have been decided otherwise.[30]

A proposition of law which is not *ratio decidendi* under the above test must, according to Wambaugh, constitute a mere *dictum*.

The exhortation to frame carefully the supposed proposition of law and the restriction of the test to cases turning on only one

---

[29] (1861) 9 HLC 274, p. 8 *supra*.
[30] *Study of Cases* (2nd edn.), 17–18. This book appeared in the United States as long ago as 1894 but is still of great value even to an English reader.

point rob it of most of its value as a means of determining what was the *ratio decidendi* of a case, although it has its uses as a means of ascertaining what was not *ratio*.

Framing the supposed proposition of law

It is not enough to select *any* proposition of law formulated by the judge in the course of his judgment, even though that proposition was sufficient to justify his decision. This can be made clear by a further reference to *Donoghue* v. *Stevenson*. We have already mentioned two propositions of law in the speech of Lord Atkin:[31]

(1) A manufacturer of products, which he sells in such a form as to show that he intends them to reach the ultimate consumer in the form in which they left him with no reasonable possibility of intermediate examination, and with the knowledge that the absence of reasonable care in the preparation or putting up of the products will result in an injury to the consumer's life or property, owes a duty to the consumer to take that reasonable care.

(2) A party must take reasonable care to avoid acts or omissions which he can reasonably foresee would be likely to injure persons who are so closely and directly affected by his act that he ought reasonably to have them in contemplation as being so affected when he is directing his mind to the acts or omissions which are called in question.

The insertion of the word 'no' after the word 'owes' at the end of the first proposition, and the insertion of the words 'need not' in lieu of 'must' at the beginning of the second proposition lead, on Wambaugh's test, to the conclusion that both propositions were the *ratio decidendi*. The first alone is entitled to be so described because it is more closely related to the facts of the case; but, if the admonition to frame carefully the supposed proposition of law means that due regard must be paid to the facts of the case, the student is entitled to ask what facts, all the facts, all the material facts, whatever that may mean, or facts regarded as material by the judge? We shall see that these are the very questions raised in discussions concerning the definition and determination of the *ratio decidendi* of a case.

Cases turning on only one point

Wambaugh's test was cited in argument before the House of Lords in *Jacobs* v. *London County Council*. Speaking of cases with two *rationes decidendi* Lord Simonds said:

[31] p. 44 *supra*.

There is in my opinion no justification for regarding as *obiter dictum* a reason given by a judge for his decision because he has given another reason also. If it were a proper test to ask whether his decision would have been the same apart from the proposition alleged to be *obiter*, then a case which *ex facie* decided two things would decide none.[32]

It would be unfair to treat these remarks as a refutation of Wambaugh's test because it is restricted to cases turning on one point, but the restriction is of considerable importance. This is not because the number of cases with two *ratios* is particularly high, but because Wambaugh's words 'when a case turns only on one point, . . . the *ratio decidendi* must be a general rule without which the case must have been decided otherwise' must be taken to refer to cases which the court treated as turning on but one point. Were this not so, very few cases could be said to turn on only one point, simply because very many decisions could have been reached by some route other than that chosen by the judge. To establish this fact it is only necessary to refer to the numerous cases in which significant facts are treated as immaterial, or simply ignored, or assumed to exist by the court. An example of each is given in the following paragraphs.

Rylands v. *Fletcher*[33] is a leading instance of a case in which a significant fact was treated as immaterial with the result that its *ratio decidendi* was greatly broadened. The plaintiff and defendant occupied adjacent land. The defendant employed an engineer to construct a reservoir and, owing to the negligence of the engineer, the reservoir overflowed from the defendant's land to the plaintiff's. Two points were mentioned in the special case brought before the Exchequer Chamber. First, it was said that the defendant was liable to keep the water in at his peril, and secondly it was said that the defendant was liable for the negligence of the engineer, his independent contractor. The Court decided for the plaintiff on the first point, and did not consider the second. There thus came into being an important rule imposing civil liability without fault:

The person who for his own purposes brings on his land and collects and keeps there anything likely to do mischief if it escapes, must keep it in at his peril, and if he does not do so is *prima facie* answerable for all the damage that is the natural consequence of the escape.

[32] [1950] AC at 369.

[33] (1868) LR 3 HL 330. The statement of the rule in the text is that of Blackburn J in the Exchequer Chamber (1865), 1 Ex. 265 at 279.

This statement can only be regarded as a general rule without which the case must have been decided otherwise if the negligence of the engineer is left out of account for the defendant could well have been held liable for that negligence.

In *South Staffordshire Water Co.* v. *Sharman*[34] the plaintiff was the owner and occupier of land covered by a pool. The defendant was a workman employed to clean the pool out. While doing so he found two valuable rings embedded in some mud at the bottom of the pool. No one knew who was the owner of the rings and the plaintiff sued the defendant for them. A Divisional Court gave judgment for the plaintiff because

> The possession of land carries with it in general, by our law, possession of everything that is attached to or under that land, and, in the absence of a better title elsewhere, the right to possess it also.

The fact that the defendant was an employee of the plaintiff was ignored; had it been taken into account, judgment for the plaintiff might have been given on the basis of another general rule, viz. that the finder of the goods is entitled to possession of them against all but the true owner, an employee's finding in the course of his employment being treated as that of his employer.[35]

In *Farrugia* v. *Great Western Railway*[36] the defendants were negligent in sending out an overloaded lorry and the plaintiff sustained injuries in consequence of the spilling of part of the load while the lorry was being driven under a bridge. The plaintiff was a little boy who had been running after the lorry picking up sugar which was falling from it. The only point of law taken by the defendants was that they owed no duty of care to the plaintiff because he was not a lawful user of the highway as he was using it for the unlawful purpose of taking someone else's sugar, not for the lawful purpose of transit. According to the defendants, the plaintiff was a trespasser on the road. The Court of Appeal gave judgment for the plaintiff without deciding this point, Lord Greene MR saying that the defendants were liable

> even if it be the fact—and I am not saying that it is—that, when the plaintiff was running along the road he was doing something in respect of

[34] [1896] 2 QB 44.
[35] Cf. *Newman* v. *Bourne and Hollingsworth* (1915), 31 TLR 209. It is not clear whether the finder was a servant or an independent contractor in *Sharman*'s case.
[36] [1947] 2 All ER 568.

56   *RATIO DECIDENDI* AND *OBITER DICTUM*

which the owner of the soil of the highway could have maintained an action for trespass against him.

This decision appears to have been based on the proposition that those who send out lorries owe a duty of care with regard to the loading to all users of the highway including trespassers, but it is only if we bear in mind that the fact that the plaintiff was a trespasser was assumed by the Court that we can describe the general proposition as *ratio*. The case could have been decided in favour of the plaintiff by a finding that he was not a trespasser.

Negative value of Wambaugh's test

In short, Wambaugh's test assumes that the *ratio decidendi* is a proposition of law considered by the court to be necessary for its decision. We shall see that there is much to be said for this as a description of what lawyers mean by *ratio decidendi*, but the test is not of much assistance in the search for ways and means of determining what proposition of law was considered necessary by the court for its decision. The merit of Wambaugh's test is that it provides what may be an infallible means of ascertaining what is *not ratio decidendi*. It accords with the generally accepted view that a ruling can only be treated as *ratio* if it supports the ultimate order of the court.

A recent illustration, in a context in which the distinction between *ratio decidendi* and *obiter dicta* is important, is provided by the decision of the Court of Appeal in *Re State of Norway's Application (no. 2)*.[37] As we shall see in the next chapter, the Court of Appeal generally regards itself as bound by its own prior decisions. But this binding force attaches only to propositions which formed part of the *ratio* in the earlier case. A Norwegian court issued Letters of Request addressed to the High Court in England requesting the Court to summon two witnesses to attend before an examiner in London to give oral evidence relevant to issues in a revenue suit in Norway. A Queen's Bench master made an order granting the application in purported exercise of jurisdiction conferred by the Evidence (Proceedings in Other Jurisdictions) Act 1975, and his decision was upheld at first instance in the High Court. The witnesses appealed to the Court of Appeal. In *Re State of Norway's Application (no. 1)*,[38] the Court of Appeal was principally concerned with two issues. First, were

[37] (1990) AC 723, 732.   [38] (1987) QB 433.

the proceedings 'civil proceedings' within the 1975 Act so as to confer jurisdiction on English courts to grant the application? Second, if there was jurisdiction, were the terms of the request so wide as to constitute a 'fishing expedition', which would entail that the application ought not to be granted? The first question was considered at length and it was ruled that the proceedings did indeed come within the 1975 Act; but the Court of Appeal found for the witnesses on the 'fishing' question and allowed the appeal on this ground, indicating that a request giving more details of the specific questions to be put to the witnesses would be acceptable. The Norwegian court accepted this invitation and made a further request containing specific questions. In *Re State of Norway's Application (no. 2)*, a differently constituted Court of Appeal held that the Court of Appeal's construction of the 1975 Act had been erroneous and that the witnesses' appeal would be allowed on the ground that the proceedings were not 'civil proceedings' within the Act so that there was no jurisdiction. They found that the construction given in the first case was not part of the *ratio decidendi* because it had not affected the final outcome. (On appeal from both decisions, the House of Lords held that the first Court of Appeal's construction of the Act was the correct one and allowed the applicants' appeal, but without comment on the question of what was the *ratio* in the first case.)[39] ·

4. LORD HALSBURY IN *QUINN V. LEATHEM*

Before discussing Dr Goodhart's method of determining the *ratio decidendi* of a case, it will be convenient to consider the views expressed by Lord Halsbury in *Quinn* v. *Leathem*.[40] After stressing the necessity of reading every judgment as applicable to the facts proved or assumed to be proved,[41] Lord Halsbury continued:

A case is only authority for what it actually decides. I entirely deny that it can be quoted for a proposition that may seem to flow logically from it.

The first sentence is, to say the least, slightly cryptic, for, taken *au pied de la lettre*, it confuses precedent with *res judicata*. All that a case actually decides is an *inter partes* question—that there shall be judgment for the plaintiff or defendant, or that the accused be convicted or acquitted. But it is clear from the context of his

---

[39] (1990) AC 723.   [40] [1901] AC 459 at 506.   [41] p. 43 *supra*.

speech that Lord Halsbury was thinking in terms of the proposition for which a decision may be quoted as authority in subsequent litigation in which different parties are concerned. He seems to have meant that a case can only be cited as authority for the proposition that the same order should be made if there is no legally relevant difference between the fact with which it was concerned and those proved, assumed or admitted in the later case. On this view the proposition of law for which a case is authority cannot be derived from all the facts, because no two cases ever have completely identical facts. At the very least, there are bound to be differences between the persons involved and the time of relevant events. The basis of Lord Halsbury's pronouncement seems to have been that every case has certain facts which every lawyer would agree to be irrelevant. On the view under consideration, in order to arrive at the proposition of law for which a case is authority, it is only necessary to eliminate facts which are indisputably irrelevant as the basis of a valid legal distinction between the case in question and other fact situations. Such facts are often called 'immaterial', and the words 'material' and 'immaterial' are used accordingly in this section.[42] There may not be as many facts of this nature as Lord Halsbury supposes, but the conception is by no means incomprehensible and lies at the root of what some American realists deem to be the *ratio decidendi* of a case,[43] and of the narrow interpretation of *stare decisis* discussed in Chapter IV.

It is only necessary to mention the remarks of Devlin J, which have already been quoted as typical of current English judicial practice,[44] in order to see that the definition of the *ratio decidendi*, or the proposition of law for which a case is authoritative, as the principle to be derived from all the material facts of a case has not found favour in this country. According to Devlin J the *ratio decidendi* consists of the reason or reasons for a decision which the judge who gives it wishes to have the full authority of precedent. A

[42] The conception of material facts is a difficult one. In *Donoghue* v. *Stevenson* [1932] AC 562, for instance, the fact that the plaintiff was a woman was immaterial because every lawyer would recognize that sex is irrelevant in the context. The fact that there was a snail in the bottle was material because a snail is a species of noxious matter, but in fact was also immaterial in the sense that, assuming the same damage to have occurred, it would have made no difference that a slug instead of a snail had been in the bottle.

[43] G. Oliphant, 'A Return to *Stare Decisis*', *American Bar Association Journal*, 14 (1927), 61.

[44] p. 41 *supra*.

reference to two cases which have already been cited in this chapter will show that Lord Halsbury's views concerning the authority of a past decision are too narrow. In *Rylands* v. *Fletcher*[45] the negligence of the defendant's engineer might well have been treated as a material fact. But the court did not consider the point, having decided that the defendant was liable on a broader principle. Similarly, the fact that the defendant in *South Staffordshire Water Co.* v. *Sharman*[46] was a workman employed by the plaintiffs to clean out the pond could easily have been made the basis of the decision, but the court decided the case on a totally different principle. In each of the above instances a literal adherence to Lord Halsbury's view would lead to the quoting of cases as authorities for propositions which, by common consent, are not part of the *ratio decidendi*.

Cases which are only authority for what they actually decide

There are, however, certain situations in which it is necessary to have recourse to the view that a case is only authority for what 'it actually decides', i.e. for the proposition to be derived from the order of the court plus the material facts. One of these situations has already been mentioned, namely, the rare case in which no reasons are given for the judgment,[47] and there is nothing more to be said about it. Examples of two other situations of this nature are provided by cases in which the judgment or judgments delivered by the court are unclear, and by cases which have been much distinguished in subsequent judgments. The first of these situations may be illustrated by the treatment of *River Wear Commissioners* v. *Adamson*[48] in *The Mostyn*[49] and the second by the fate of *Hillyer* v. *St Bartholomew's Hospital*.[50]

River Wear Commissioners v. *Adamson* turned on the construction of s. 74 of the Harbours, Docks and Piers Clauses Act 1847, which provides that the owner of a ship damaging a pier is liable for that damage. The wording suggests that the owner is liable without proof of fault on his part or on the part of those for whom he is responsible. But, in *Adamson*'s case, where the defendant's wreck struck a pier after being abandoned by the crew the defendant was held not liable in the absence of evidence of negligence against the crew. In *The Mostyn* the defendant's ship

---

[45] (1868) LR 3 HL 330, p. 54 *supra*.
[47] p. 47 *supra*.
[49] [1928] AC 57.
[46] [1896] 2 QB 44, p. 55 *supra*.
[48] (1877) 2 App. Cas. 743.
[50] [1909] 2 KB 820.

struck a pier while the crew was still on board and the defendants were held liable although there was no evidence of negligence on the part of anyone for whom they were responsible. The judgments in *Adamson's* case were curiously unclear as is shown by the following observation of Atkin LJ when *The Mostyn* was before the Court of Appeal. Speaking of Lord Hatherley's speech he said:

Whether he was concurring in the appeal being allowed, or the appeal being dismissed, or whether he was concurring in the opinion of Lord Cairns I do not know.[51]

Considerations of this nature led Lord Dunedin to say in *The Mostyn*:

When any tribunal is bound by the judgment of another court either superior or coordinate . . . it is of course bound by the judgment itself. And, if from the opinions delivered it is clear—as it is in most instances, what the *ratio decidendi* was which led to the judgment, then that *ratio decidendi* is also binding. But if it is not clear, then I do not think it is part of the tribunal's duty to spell out with great difficulty a *ratio decidendi* in order to be bound by it.[52]

The distinction between a court's being bound by a judgment and being bound by a *ratio decidendi* is reminiscent of Lord Halsbury's apparent confusion of precedent with *res judicata* in *Quinn* v. *Leathem*. Like Lord Halsbury when he said that a case is only authority for what it actually decides, Lord Dunedin probably meant that a court bound by a judgment, as distinct from a *ratio decidendi*, is bound to make a similar order to that made in the previous case when all the material facts are similar.

In *Hillyer* v. *St Bartholomew's Hospital*, the plaintiff entered the Hospital to be examined by Lockwood, a doctor of his own choosing who was not under a contract of service with the Hospital. The plaintiff was examined under an anaesthetic in the operating theatre where nurses and porters were in attendance. The plaintiff sustained burns in respect of which he claimed damages for negligence from the Hospital. The Court of Appeal was unanimously of the opinion that the action failed. Kennedy LJ reached his conclusion on the broad ground that the only duty owed by the defendants to the plaintiff was to use reasonable care in the selection of nurses and porters and there was no evidence

[51] [1927] P. at 37–8.   [52] [1928] AC at 73.

that this duty had been broken. Farwell LJ concurred in the dismissal of the action (i) because the damage occurred in the operating theatre and, when in that theatre, the nurses and porters ceased to be the servants of the Hospital and became the servants of Lockwood, (ii) because, even if the nurses and porters were the servants of the Hospital, it was not proved whether they or Lockwood were the negligent party, and Lockwood was certainly not the servant of the Hospital. Cozens-Hardy MR concurred with both Kennedy and Farwell LJJ. In *Gold* v. *Essex County Council* Kennedy LJ's reasoning was held not to be binding on the Court of Appeal, Lord Greene saying:

> In a case where two members of the court base their judgments, the one on a narrow ground confined to the necessities of the decision, and the other on wide propositions which go far beyond those necessities, and the third member of the court expresses his concurrence in the reasoning of both, I think it right to treat the narrow ground as the real *ratio decidendi*.[53]

In *Cassidy* v. *Minister of Health*,[54] Denning LJ expressed the view that no reliance could be placed on the first reason for the decision in *Hillyer*'s case given by Farwell LJ after *Mersey Docks & Harbour Board* v. *Coggins & Griffith*.[55] He therefore concluded that

> the result is that Hillyer's case can now only be supported on the narrow ground on which Farwell L.J. explained it in *Smith* v. *Martin*[56] that the hospital authorities were not liable for the negligence of the consulting surgeon because he was not employed by them and that no case of negligence had been proved against the nurses and carriers.[57]

In other words, *Hillyer*'s case only obliges a court bound by it to give judgment for the defendants on facts that are similar in all material respects. In consequence of a remarkable piece of interpretation, a case which could have been cited as authority for some broad propositions is now only authority for what it actually decided. A court bound by it could not give judgment for the plaintiff if he went into hospital in order to be operated on by a doctor of his own choosing who was not the servant of the hospital, and sustained injuries which might just as well have been due to the doctor's negligence as to that of the nurses and porters, each of whom must now be regarded as the servants of the hospital. That is all that is left of *Hillyer*'s case.

[53] [1942] 1 KB 293 at 298.
[55] [1947] AC 1.   [56] [1911] 2 KB 775.
[54] [1951] 2 KB 343.
[57] [1951] 2 KB at 362.

There are other situations in which a case can only be cited as authority for what 'it actually decides' in the sense in which that expression seems to have been used by Lord Halsbury in *Quinn* v. *Leathem*. One such situation may occur when the different members of an appellate court give different reasons for coming to the same conclusion. This situation is considered later in this chapter and, in Chapter V, we shall see that, according to one school of thought, the *ratio decidendi* of a case turning on the interpretation of a statute must always be derived from every material fact, regardless of what the judge may have said in the course of his judgment.

Lord Halsbury's denial that a case can be quoted for a proposition that may seem to flow logically from it will be considered in Chapter VI, but the context of the statement is material to the present discussion. In *Quinn* v. *Leathem* Lord Halsbury was concerned with the extent of the earlier decision of the House of Lords in *Allen* v. *Flood*.[58] That case had had a somewhat chequered career on its way through the various courts, for it started life as a claim for damages for civil conspiracy, but the existence of the conspiracy could not be proved. On the state of facts assumed by the House of Lords in *Allen* v. *Flood* a trade-union official who was found by the jury to have been actuated by malice had warned the plaintiffs' employer that union members would be called out on strike if the plaintiffs were not dismissed, and the plaintiffs had been dismissed in consequence of this warning. A majority of the House of Lords ultimately gave judgment for the defendant, the trade-union official. In *Quinn* v. *Leathem*, the facts were similar, but the defendants were two trade-union officials acting in concert, and they had caused one of the plaintiff's customers to terminate a contract with him by conduct which amounted to a threat rather than a warning. The defendants were found by the jury to have been actuated by malice. In the course of the speeches in *Allen* v. *Flood*, statements were made which could easily have formed the major premiss of a syllogism with the conclusion that there should be judgment for the defendants in *Quinn* v. *Leathem*, the material facts of that case being the minor premiss. Lord Halsbury was anxious to concur in the result reached by the House of Lords in *Quinn* v. *Leathem*, namely, that there should be judgment for the plaintiff. He

[58] [1898] AC 1.

accordingly stressed the significance on each of the major factual distinctions between *Allen* v. *Flood* and *Quinn* v. *Leathem*. These were the presence of a conspiracy and threats as opposed to individual action and mere warnings in *Quinn* v. *Leathem*. Yet it may be doubted whether the insistence on taking all material facts into account in determining the *ratio decidendi* of *Allen* v. *Flood* proved beneficial to the development of English law, for it led to a prolonged controversy concerning the true distinction between *Allen* v. *Flood* and *Quinn* v. *Leathem*. Was it the threats or the conspiracy or both? This controversy was probably inevitable because no single principle can be extracted from the totality of the judgments in *Allen* v. *Flood*, but a contributory cause of the controversy seems to have been Lord Halsbury's refusal either to seek for a principle underlying the decision in *Allen* v. *Flood* or to formulate a principle as the basis of the decision in *Quinn* v. *Leathem*.

5. DR GOODHART'S METHOD OF DETERMINING THE *RATIO DECIDENDI*

According to Dr Goodhart the *ratio decidendi* of a case is determined by ascertaining the facts treated as material by the judge. It is the principle to be derived from the judge's decision on the basis of those facts. Any court bound by the case must come to a similar conclusion unless there is a further fact in the case before it which it is prepared to treat as material, or unless some fact treated as material in the previous case is absent. This method of determining the *ratio decidendi* has the great merit of paying more regard to the facts as seen by the judge than is provided for by Wambaugh's test, while it is less narrow and therefore more calculated to produce the proposition of law regarded by the judge as necessary for his decision than the suggestions to be derived from Lord Halsbury's views in *Quinn* v. *Leathem*. It will be convenient to summarize Dr Goodhart's views by referring to six of the most important propositions contained in his essay on 'Determining the *Ratio Decidendi* of a Case',[59] and to defer comment until after this has been done. Dr Goodhart speaks more frequently of the 'principle of a case' than of the *ratio decidendi*,

---

[59] *Essays in Jurisprudence and the Common Law*, 1. The quotations in the text are from this essay.

but there can be little doubt that the two expressions are generally intended to be synonymous.

(i) The principle of a case is not found in the reasons given in the opinion. Dr Goodhart considers the phrase *ratio decidendi* something of a misnomer 'for the reason which the judge gives for his decision is never the binding part of the precedent'. The reasons may be demonstrably false while the decision continues to be authoritative. One of Dr Goodhart's examples is *Priestley* v. *Fowler*.[60] That was the case in which the doctrine of common employment is usually said to have been propounded for the first time. As long as that doctrine remained part of our law, a servant could not succeed against a master for damages due to injuries occasioned by the negligence of a fellow servant in a common employment. The judgment in *Priestley* v. *Fowler* was based on the grounds that any other rule would be absurd, and that a servant impliedly consents to run the risk of having negligent fellow servants. Neither reason will bear scrutiny, but this did not prevent *Priestley* v. *Fowler* from becoming an important authority.

(ii) The principle is not found in the rule of law set forth in the opinion. According to Halsbury's *Laws of England*,[61] the general rule is that the part alone of a decision is binding which consists of the enunciation of the reason or principle upon which the question before the court has really been determined. According to Professor Morgan[62] those portions of the opinion setting forth the rules of law applied by the court, the application of which was required for the determination of the issues presented, are to be considered as decision and as primary authority in later cases in the same jurisdiction. Dr Goodhart considered that these statements are misleading

for it is not the rule of law *set forth* by the court, or the rule *enunciated* as Halsbury puts it, which necessarily constitutes the principle of the case. There may be no rule of law set forth in the opinion, or the rule when stated may be too wide or too narrow. In appellate courts, the rules of law set forth by the different judges may have no relation to each other. Nevertheless each of these cases contains a principle which can be discovered on proper analysis.

---

[60] (1837) 3 M and W 1. The ground that any other conclusion would be absurd is easily deducible from the judgment. It is not so clear that the judgment was also based on the ground that the servant impliedly undertakes the risk of his fellow servant's negligence.

[61] (1st edn.), xviii. 210.   [62] *The Study of Law* (1st edn.), 109.

We have already mentioned Dr Goodhart's example of a case in which the rule was too narrow, namely, *Barwick* v. *English Joint Stock Bank*,[63] a case in which the bank was held liable for its manager's fraud, and, it will be recollected, Willes J said:

> The general rule is, that the master is answerable for every such wrong of the servant or agent as is committed in the course of the service and for the master's benefit, though no express command or privity of the master be proved.

(iii) The principle is not necessarily found by a consideration of all the ascertainable facts of the case and the judge's decision. Dr Goodhart refers to the realist doctrine of Professor Oliphant which was popular at the time when the essay under consideration was written. According to that doctrine it is not the judges' opinions, but the way they decide cases which should be the dominant subject-matter of any truly scientific study of law. This is reminiscent of Lord Halsbury's views which have already been considered, and, as Dr Goodhart observes, the outcome of the doctrine should be that the judges' opinions need never be consulted in order to find the proposition of law for which a case is authority. Dr Goodhart also points out that the fallacy underlying Professor Oliphant's doctrine is the supposition that the facts of a case are a constant factor—that the judge's conclusion is based upon the fixed premiss of a given set of facts. The crucial question is—What facts are we talking about?

(iv) The principle of a case is found by taking account (*a*) of the facts treated by the judge as material, and (*b*) his decision as based on them. According to Dr Goodhart the answer to the question posed at the end of the last paragraph is that, when discussing the *ratio decidendi* of a case, we ought to have in mind the facts as the judge sees them, for it is on these that he bases his judgment and not on any others.

It follows that our task in analysing a case is not to state the facts and the conclusion, but to state the material facts as seen by the judge and his conclusion based on them. It is by his choice of the material facts that the judge creates law.

There are thus two steps involved in the ascertainment of the *ratio decidendi* according to Dr Goodhart's method. First, it is

---

[63] (1866) LR 2 Ex. 259. Dr Goodhart cites *R.* v. *Fenton* (1830) 1 Lew. 179 as a case in which the rule was stated too widely. See *R.* v. *Franklin* (1883) 15 Cox CC 163 which is, however, probably in conflict with *R.* v. *Fenton*.

necessary to determine all the facts of the case as seen by the judge; secondly, it is necessary to discover which of those facts were treated as material by the judge.

Dr Goodhart illustrates his telling remark that it is by his choice of the material facts that the judge creates law by referring to *Rylands* v. *Fletcher*.[64] It will be recollected that in that case the defendant employed an engineer to make a reservoir on his land. Owing to the engineer's negligence some water escaped and flooded the plaintiff's land. Dr Goodhart analyses the case in the following manner: facts of the case, fact (1), D had a reservoir built on his land. Fact (2), the contractor who built it was negligent. Fact (3), water escaped and injured P. Material facts as seen by the court: fact (1), D had a reservoir built on his land. Fact (2), water escaped and injured P. Conclusion: D is liable to P. By the omission of fact (2) the doctrine of absolute liability was established.

(v) A judge may expressly or impliedly treat certain facts as material or immaterial. It is comparatively seldom that a judge expressly indicates which facts he considers material or immaterial. Dr Goodhart accordingly suggests various tests for determining which facts must be assumed to have been treated as material or immaterial by the judge. Thus the facts of person, time, place, kind, and amount are presumably immaterial unless stated to be material. The different reports of a case and the arguments of counsel may also have to be considered and

the reasons given by the judge in his opinion, or his statement of the rule of law which he is following, are of peculiar importance, for they may furnish us with a guide for determining which facts he considered material and which immaterial. His reason may be incorrect and his statement of the law too wide but they will indicate to us on what facts he reached his conclusion.

(vi) A conclusion based on a hypothetical fact is a *dictum*. Dr Goodhart evidently considers that a *ratio decidendi* cannot be based on assumed facts.

A conclusion based on a fact, the existence of which has not been determined by the court, cannot establish a principle.

He recognizes that a case may have two *rationes decidendi* based on separate sets of judicially determined facts, as in *National*

[64] (1868) LR 3 HL 330.

Sailors' and Firemen's Union v. *Read*[65] where trade-union action was held to be invalid both because it was in furtherance of the general strike of 1926 which Astbury J held to be illegal, and because it involved an infringement of the union's rules.

The first set of facts included the fact of the general strike. The second set excluded the general strike, but included the fact that the internal rules of the union were violated.

Since writing the essay which has just been summarized, Dr Goodhart has said that he was merely trying to give a guide to the method which he believed most English courts follow when attempting to determine the *ratio decidendi* of a doubtful case,[66] and there can be no doubt that he has performed a most useful service because any attempt to ascertain the *ratio decidendi* without paying due regard to the facts treated as material by the judge is completely unrealistic. What may be more open to question is whether Dr Goodhart does not expose himself to a charge of lack of realism on account of his almost exclusive emphasis on those facts, and of his scanty regard to the way in which the case was argued and pleaded, the process of reasoning adopted by the judge and the relation of the case to other decisions. The extent, if any, to which this charge is justified can best be appreciated in the light of a few points which may be made concerning the first, second, fifth, and sixth of the propositions which have been mentioned above.

The first proposition does not call for much consideration. Up to a point it is undoubtedly true to say that the principle of a case is not found in the reasons given in the opinion. By common consent, the *ratio decidendi* is a proposition of law, and statements to the effect that any conclusion, other than that adopted by the court, would be absurd, plainly do not fall within this category. Many of the judge's reasons for arriving at the proposition of law upon which he bases his decision are not part of the *ratio decidendi* in its technical sense. To borrow one of the phrases used by Professor Stone,[67] it is essential to distinguish between the descriptive and prescriptive meanings of *ratio decidendi*.

Turning to the second proposition, Dr Goodhart's criticism of views such as those of Professor Morgan is a little difficult to follow. Professor Morgan said:

[65] [1926] Ch. 536.   [66] 22 *MLR* 123–4.
[67] See an article entitled 'The *Ratio* of the *Ratio Decidendi*', 22 *MLR* 597.

Those portions of the opinion setting forth the rules of law applied by the court, the application of which was required for the determination of the issues presented, are to be considered as decision.

According to Dr Goodhart, the rule of law set forth by the court does not necessarily constitute the principle of the case. This is, of course, a truism when no rule of law is set forth in the opinion, but Professor Morgan was concerned with cases in which rules of law are set forth in the opinion and applied by the court, the application being required for the determination of the issues presented. It seems that rules of law of this nature do 'necessarily constitute' the principle of the case. Moreover, if the court considered them to be 'required for the determination of the issues presented', they must, it seems, be principles which are found by taking account of the facts treated by the judge as material and his decision as based on those facts. For example, Dr Goodhart cites *Barwick* v. *English Joint Stock Bank*[68] as an instance in which the rule of law set forth in the opinion was stated too narrowly to constitute the principle of the case, but we arrive at that very rule if we seek to ascertain the *ratio decidendi* according to the tests proposed in the essay under consideration. The facts of *Barwick*'s case were (i) the defendant's manager fraudulently induced the plaintiff to accept a worthless guarantee, (ii) the manager was the defendant's servant, (iii) the manager was acting in the course of his employment, and (iv) the defendant benefited in consequence of the manager's fraud. The conclusion was that the Bank was liable to pay damages for deceit to the plaintiff. Dr Goodhart says that

if the opinion does not distinguish between material and immaterial facts, then all the facts set forth in the opinion must be considered material with the exception of those that on their face are immaterial.

Willes J did not clearly indicate whether he considered the fact that the defendant benefited from the fraud as material or immaterial, and it is certainly not *ex facie* immaterial. Therefore, it must be treated as material according to Dr Goodhart with the result that the *ratio* would be that 'the master is answerable for every such wrong of the servant or agent as is committed in the course of the service and for the master's benefit'.

---

[68] (1866) LR 2 Ex. 259. Similar observations to those made in this paragraph are applicable to Dr Goodhart's treatment of *R.* v. *Fenton* (1830) 1 Lew. 179 and *R.* v. *Franklin* (1883) 15 Cox CC 163.

There appear to be two plausible explanations of the position with regard to *Barwick* v. *English Joint Stock Bank*. First, it may be said that the statement concerning the master's benefit formed part of the *ratio decidendi* and in *Lloyd* v. *Grace, Smith & Co.*[69] the House of Lords simply decided that it was a mistake to suppose that, by treating the master's benefit as a material fact, Willes J had intended to imply that a master was not liable for fraud committed by his servants in the course of their employment in cases in which he derived no benefit from the fraud. On this view the House of Lords simply extended the *ratio* of *Barwick*'s case. Secondly, it may be said that a consideration of other cases enabled the House of Lords to conclude, in *Lloyd* v. *Grace, Smith & Co.*, that Willes J did not intend to suggest that the fact that the English Joint Stock Bank benefited from its manager's fraud was material to his decision. On this view the remarks concerning the master's benefit did not form part of the *ratio decidendi*. The other cases included cases subsequent to *Barwick*'s in which judges who had participated in that decision made no reference to the requirement concerning the master's benefit in their formulations of the principle of vicarious liability. The second explanation is, in the main, supported by the speeches in the House of Lords in *Lloyd* v. *Grace, Smith & Co.*, and it suggests that a consideration of other decisions should have been mentioned by Dr Goodhart as one of the methods to which recourse must sometimes be had in order to determine which facts of a case were treated as material by the court which decided it. If the other decisions are earlier than the instant case, they are relevant to the pre-existing law which may well have affected the judge's view of the facts. If the other decisions occurred after the instant case, they may have a peculiar importance if made by judges who were members of the court in that case.

Turning to the fifth of the propositions stated above, it is difficult to find fault with Dr Goodhart's proposals for determining which facts were impliedly treated as material or immaterial. Moreover, it cannot be too strongly emphasized that it is a mistake to suppose that there is any suggestion in the essay we are examining that the reasons given by the judge in his opinion or his statement of the rule of law which he is following can be ignored in the quest for the *ratio decidendi*. In fact we are told that they are

[69] [1912] AC 716, p. 45 *supra*.

of peculiar importance as they may furnish us with a guide for determining which facts the judge considered material and which immaterial. But this is not the only ground on which the reasons given by a judge in his opinion or his statement of the rule of law are of importance, and other reasons why they are important should perhaps have been mentioned by Dr Goodhart. In some instances it is quite impossible to formulate the *ratio decidendi* merely by reference to the facts regarded as material by the court, and the decision based on those facts. It is often essential to know why certain facts were regarded as material and for this purpose it may be necessary to know what portions of the law were in the mind of the court when the selection was made.

In *Bourhill* v. *Young*,[70] for example, three members of the House of Lords considered that the following facts were material: (i) Young, a motor-cyclist, after passing a tramcar at excessive speed, collided with a motor-car and was killed by his own negligence at a distance of about 50 feet ahead of the tramcar; (ii) at the time of the accident the tramcar was at a stopping place and Mrs Bourhill was alighting; (iii) Mrs Bourhill heard the collision and saw blood on the road after the accident; (iv) Mrs Bourhill suffered a nervous shock; (v) Mrs Bourhill was outside that which Young ought reasonably to have contemplated as the area of potential danger which would arise from his careless driving. The decision was that Mrs Bourhill's action for damages against Young's estate should be dismissed. If no further attention were paid to the speeches in the House of Lords, the *ratio decidendi* would have to be stated somewhat as follows. 'A driver of a motor vehicle is not liable for nervous shock suffered in consequence of his careless driving by someone outside the area of potential danger which ought reasonably to have been contemplated as the result of his negligence.' This conclusion might be based on either of two views of the law, (i) that the driver owes no duty of care in respect of his driving to persons outside the area of reasonably foreseeable danger, or (ii) though the driver owes a duty of care to such persons, damages flowing from nervous shock are too remote a consequence of the breach of duty to be recoverable. On the second view, but not on the first, the person suffering the shock might be able to recover damages for bodily injury if, by some curious chance, such injury had resulted from the driver's breach

[70] [1943] AC 92.

of duty. Further perusal of the speeches of three of the Law Lords makes it plain that they based their conclusions on the first view. We thus arrive at what is, by common consent, the *ratio decidendi* of *Bourhill* v. *Young* according to these Law Lords:

A driver of a motor vehicle owes no duty of care in respect of his driving to persons outside the area of potential danger which ought reasonably to have been contemplated as the result of his negligence.

So far as the sixth of the above propositions is concerned, a conclusion based on a fact the existence of which has not been determined by the court sometimes does establish a precedent although the proposition seems to affirm that this cannot be the case. One instance is provided by cases decided on a *demurrer*, an old pleading device according to which the defendant contended that, even if all the facts alleged by the plaintiff were true, the plaintiff would still have no cause of action.[71] *Donoghue* v. *Stevenson* was a case of this type, for the truth of the allegations concerning the snail in the bottle was never determined judicially as the House of Lords merely decided that the consumer of the beverage had a good cause of action provided her allegations of fact could be substantiated. Indeed, it was once commonly believed that the Scots courts decided that there never was a snail in the bottle, but the case was in fact settled without further litigation after the decision of the point of law by the House of Lords. Another instance is provided by a decision after legal argument concerning the manner in which a jury should be directed, and every summing up to a jury which contains a pronouncement on the law provides a further example of a *ratio decidendi* based on assumed facts.[72]

The upshot of the foregoing commentary on Dr Goodhart's essay seems to be that, although it is always essential and sometimes sufficient in order to arrive at the *ratio decidendi* of a case to consider the facts treated as material by the court and the decision based on those facts, it is sometimes necessary to do a great deal more.

---

[71] Glanville Williams, *Learning the Law* (11th edn.), 79.
[72] See also *Farrugia* v. *Great Western Railway*, p. 55 *supra*.

6. DESCRIPTIONS OF THE *RATIO DECIDENDI*[73]

A further upshot of the foregoing discussion seems to be that it is impossible to devise formulae for determining the *ratio decidendi* of a case; but although the contrary view has been expressed,[74] this does not mean that it is impossible to give a tolerably accurate description of what lawyers mean when they use the expression. It is submitted that the following is such a description.

The *ratio decidendi* of a case is any rule of law expressly or impliedly treated by the judge as a necessary step in reaching his conclusion, having regard to the line of reasoning adopted by him,[75] or a necessary part of his direction to the jury.

Strictly speaking, as Professor MacCormick has pointed out,[76] the above formulation should speak of a 'ruling on a point of law' rather than a 'rule of law'. A statutory rule, whose interpretation is not in question, may constitute an essential step in a judge's reasoning but it will not, of course, be what is called '*ratio decidendi*'. If, however, the meaning of a statute is disputed and the judge rules, as part of the justification for his conclusion, that it has one meaning rather than another, this ruling is his *ratio decidendi*. In practice, in the present context 'rule' and 'ruling' are used interchangeably.

Professor Montrose suggested that the expression *ratio decidendi* is used in two senses: (i) 'The rule of law for which a case is binding authority', and (ii) 'The rule of law to be found in the actual opinion of the judge, forming the basis of his decision'.[77] If our description of the *ratio decidendi* is correct, there is generally no distinction between these two senses of the phrase until a decision has been interpreted in subsequent cases. Up to that moment the rule of law for which the decision is binding authority is that which is to be found in the actual opinion of the judge, forming the basis of his decision. Very often there will continue to be no distinction

---

[73] See N. H. Andrews [1985] 5 LS 205.

[74] Stone, *Legal System and Lawyer's Reasonings*, 36.

[75] The adoption of one line of reasoning by the judge is not incompatible with his adopting a further line of reasoning. Allowance must be always made for the fact that a case may have more than one *ratio decidendi*.

[76] Neil MacCormick, 'Why Cases have *Rationes* and What These Are', in Goldstein (ed.), *Precedent in Law*, at 179.

[77] *Annual Law Review of the University of Western Australia* (1953), 319. See also the discussion between Professor Montrose and A. W. B. Simpson, 20 *MLR* 123, 413, 487, and Goodhart, 22 *MLR* 117 and Stone, 22 *MLR* 597.

between the two suggested senses of the phrase *ratio decidendi* even after the decision has been interpreted in subsequent cases. No lawyer would deny that the rule of law for which *Rylands* v. *Fletcher* may be cited as authority today is that which was stated as the basis of the judgment of the Exchequer Chamber as qualified by Lord Cairns in the House of Lords. There are, however, many instances in which the rule of law forming the basis of a decision ceases to be the rule of law for which the case is binding authority because judges in later cases have followed the practice to which reference has already been made of interpreting the decision in the light of the facts of the case and other relevant judgments. The 'interpretation' of a case frequently means no more than the ascertainment of its *ratio decidendi*, but it may mean a great deal more. It may involve first, the ascertainment of the *ratio decidendi* of the case, secondly, a consideration of that *ratio decidendi* in the light of the facts of the case, thirdly, a consideration of observations with regard to the case made by judges in later cases, fourthly, the ascertainment of the *rationes decidendi* of later cases, and finally the formulation of a rule of law based on a number of cases. It may then appear that the case which is being interpreted was decided consistently with that rule, although the *ratio decidendi* of the case has ceased to be the proposition of law for which it is authoritative. If it is assumed that Willes J's remarks concerning the master's benefit formed part of the *ratio* of *Barwick* v. *English Joint Stock Bank*, that case is no longer authoritative for the proposition enunciated by Willes J, but, even after *Lloyd* v. *Grace, Smith & Co.*, *Barwick*'s case is authority for the proposition that a banker is liable for the fraud of his clerk committed in the course of his employment.

The process of interpretation is most likely to occur when the original *ratio decidendi* was a wide one for, to quote Professor Glanville Williams,[78] 'Courts do not accord to their predecessors an unlimited power of laying down wide rules.' No doubt this is especially true when the court interpreting the earlier case is not strictly bound to follow it; but broad statements by the highest tribunals are sometimes restrictively interpreted in lower courts. It is at least arguable that Lord Atkin considered the neighbour principle which he enunciated in *Donoghue* v. *Stevenson*[79] to be

---

[78] Glanville Williams, *Learning the Law* (11th edn.), 75.
[79] [1932] AC 562 at 580, p. 44 *supra*. See 20 *MLR* 7.

ratio decidendi, but it was immediately said to have been too wide in the Court of Appeal.[80]

The claim that *ratio decidendi* describes the rule first laid down by the deciding court is compatible with the recognition that subsequent courts, even those bound within the rules of precedent to follow the decision, have a residual power to restrict the scope of the rule. This power has been called by Professor Raz a power to distinguish 'in the strong sense', as distinct from the weak sense of distinguishing where a *ratio* is simply held not to apply to the facts in question;[81] and it has been called by Professor MacCormick a power to 'revise' the original *ratio*.[82] None of the above modes of interpretation to which a *ratio* may be subjected warrants the claim made by Professor Julius Stone that *ratio decidendi* describes nothing, that it is a 'category of illusory reference'.[83] In the ordinary run of cases, it is not that difficult to articulate what the *ratio* was.

The fact that a decision is liable to be subjected to a process of interpretation led Professor Glanville Williams to say that the phrase 'the *ratio decidendi*' of a case is slightly ambiguous.[84] According to him:

It may mean either (i) the rule that the judge who decided the case intended to lay down and apply to the facts, or (ii) the rule that a later court concedes him to have had the power to lay down.

But it is very doubtful whether this second sense of the term is sanctioned by judicial usage. The possible contrast to which Professor Glanville Williams rightly wished to draw attention when speaking of the two meanings of the phrase *ratio decidendi* was perhaps expressed more felicitously by Professor Llewellyn when he said:

There is a distinction between the *ratio decidendi*, the court's own version of the rule of the case, and the true rule of the case, to wit what it will be made to stand for by another later court.[85]

Whatever may be the right way of describing it, the distinction is one which does not need to be drawn in the majority of cases.

---

[80] *Farr* v. *Butters* [1932] 2 KB 606.
[81] J. Raz, *The Authority of Law*, ch. 10.
[82] MacCormick, 'Why Cases have *Rationes* and What These Are', in Goldstein (ed.), *Precedent in Law*, ch. 6.
[83] J. Stone, *Precedent and Law*, 74–5, 123–38.
[84] Glanville Williams, *Learning the Law* (11th edn.), 75.
[85] *The Bramble Bush* (1930 edn.), 52.

Judicial statements

It remains to consider some of the judicial statements which support our description of the *ratio decidendi* of a case as any rule of law expressly or impliedly treated by the judge as a necessary step in reaching his conclusion, or a necessary part of his direction to a jury. It is evident from the terms of Lord Campbell's speech in *Beamish* v. *Beamish*[86] that by *ratio decidendi* he meant 'the rule of law which your Lordships laid down as the ground of your judgment'. In *Attorney-General* v. *Dean and Canons of Windsor*,[87] the same judge spoke of 'the rule propounded and acted upon in giving judgement'. It is also clear from the terms of Lord Simonds's speech in *Jacobs* v. *London County Council*[88] that he was thinking of the *ratio decidendi* in terms of 'a reason given by a judge for his decision', and in *Korner* v. *Witkowitzer*[89] Denning LJ, as he then was, did not think it would be right to treat 'one of the links in the chain of reasoning' leading to the conclusion in a previous case as a mere *obiter dictum*. One of the fullest judicial statements concerning the meaning of *ratio decidendi* occurs in the South African case of *Pretoria City Council* v. *Levison*.[90] After discussing Dr Goodhart's essay, Schreiner JA said:

As I understand the ordinary usage in this connection, where a single judgment is in question, the reasons given in the judgment, properly interpreted, do constitute the *ratio decidendi*, originating or following a legal rule, provided (a) that they do not appear from the judgment itself to have been merely subsidiary reasons for following the main principle or principles, (b) that they were not merely a course of reasoning on the facts and (c) (this may cover (a)) that they were necessary for the decision, not in the sense that it could not have been reached along other lines, but in the sense that along the lines actually followed in the judgment the result would have been different but for the reasons.

This last quotation is of course a concise summary of a lot that has been said in this chapter with regard to the *ratio decidendi* of a case.

7. *OBITER DICTA*

Is it possible to say more with regard to an *obiter dictum* than that it is a proposition of law which does not form part of the *ratio*

---

[86] (1861) 9 HLC 274 at 338, p. 8 *supra*.
[88] [1950] AC 361 at 369, p. 53 *supra*.
[90] 1949 (3) SA 405 at 417.

[87] (1860) 8 HLC 369 at 392.
[89] [1950] 2 KB 128 at 158.

decidendi? The foregoing discussion of the *ratio decidendi* suggests that the answer to this question is 'no'. But something must be said about the definitions of *obiter dicta* offered by Professor Patterson and Dr Goodhart. When this has been done, the varying degrees of authority enjoyed by *obiter dicta* and the different kinds of *dictum* will be considered.

Patterson's definition of an obiter dictum

According to Professor Patterson an *obiter dictum* is a 'statement of law in the opinion which could not logically be a major premiss of the selected facts of the decision'.[91] This looks like the converse of Wambaugh's test for determining whether a statement is *ratio*— would the decision have been different if the meaning of the statement were reversed? The reference to the 'selected facts of the decision' gives rise to difficulty. What facts are to be selected, and who is to select them? Whatever the answer may be, it seems that it will always be possible to point to cases in which a *dictum* could logically have been treated as the major premiss of a syllogism of which the selected facts are the minor premiss and the decision is the conclusion.[92] If this is so, the suggested method of determining whether a given statement is *obiter* is no more capable of general application than are the various tests for determining the *ratio decidendi* of a case which have already been discussed.

Goodhart

It has already been shown that the same is true of Dr Goodhart's definition of a *dictum* as 'a conclusion based on a fact the existence of which has not been determined by the court'.[93] Dr Goodhart had in mind cases such as *Lynn* v. *Bamber*[94] in which McCardie J first held that concealed fraud would, as a matter of law, prevent the Statute of Limitations from running against the plaintiff, and then gave judgment for the defendant because he had not been

---

[91] *Jurisprudence*, 313. This is a current leading American textbook.

[92] See, e.g. *Lickbarrow* v. *Mason* (1780) 2 TR 63, in which the famous observation of Ashurst J that, 'wherever one of two innocent persons must suffer by the acts of a third, he who has enabled such third person to occasion the loss must sustain it' could logically have formed the major premiss of the decision, if it is ever possible to treat such a statement as a major premiss, and the decision that the defendant should have judgment .as the conclusion of any syllogism. The observation of Ashurst J was none the less a *dictum* and has been so treated ever since it was made. The *ratio decidendi* was that the right of stoppage *in transitu* is unavailable against an indorsee for value of a bill of lading.

[93] *Essays in Jurisprudence and Common Law*, 22.   [94] [1930] 2 KB 72.

guilty of concealed fraud. The initial statement of law was undoubtedly an *obiter dictum* because the judge cannot conceivably have regarded the statement as necessary to the order which he made, but there is a difference between statements based on facts the existence of which is denied by the court and statements based on a fact the existence of which has not been determined by the court. The latter class of statement may represent the *ratio decidendi* of a number of different sorts of case including cases concerned with a *demurrer* in which the court is invited to pronounce upon the rights of the parties on the assumption that the facts are as the plaintiff alleges, and cases in which the judge directs a jury concerning the law on the assumption that they subsequently find that certain facts do or do not exist.

Varying degrees of authority of dicta

It is a truism upon which there is no need to enlarge that *dicta* are of varying degrees of persuasiveness. At one end of the scale we have the considered opinion of all the members of the House of Lords who sat to hear a case. At the other end of the scale we have broad observations made on the spur of the moment such as the remark which prompted Lord Abinger to say 'It was not only an *obiter dictum*, but a very wide divaricating *dictum*'.[95] *Dicta* of the highest degree of persuasiveness may often, for all practical purposes, be indistinguishable from pronouncements which must be treated as *ratio decidendi*, and there are certain situations where this is the case which are of sufficient importance to be separately mentioned.

Independent issues

The first situation is where litigation between A and B involves two points of law a decision as to any one of which in favour of A will oblige the court to give judgment for him. If an appellate court decides one point in favour of A, and the other in favour of B, the decision on the second point is *obiter* because the *ratio decidendi* of a case must be a proposition of law upon which the order of the court was based. Yet it is difficult to believe that the decision would not have coercive effect so far as lower courts are concerned. For example, in *Perry* v. *Kendrick's Transport*,[96] the

---

[95] *Sunbolf* v. *Alford* (1838) 3 M and W 218 at 252.
[96] [1956] 1 WLR 85.

issues before the Court of Appeal were (i) whether damages for personal injuries can be recovered under the rule in *Rylands* v. *Fletcher*, and (ii) whether the defence that the damage was caused by the act of a stranger was available to the defendant. A decision in his favour on either point would have been good enough for the defendant. The court decided the first point in favour of the plaintiff, holding that damages for personal injuries can be recovered under the rule in *Rylands* v. *Fletcher*, and the court decided the second point in favour of the defendant who accordingly won the appeal. The observations on the question of personal injuries were *obiter* according to our description because the court cannot have considered them necessary for the decision of the appeal in favour of the defendant. They were also *obiter* according to Wambaugh's test because the appeal would have been decided in the same way even if the court had concluded that damages for personal injuries could not be recovered under the rule in *Rylands* v. *Fletcher*. They were also *obiter* according to Dr Goodhart's method of determining the *ratio decidendi* because the court must have regarded the fact that the injuries sustained by the plaintiff were personal and not proprietary as immaterial in concluding that the defence of the act of a stranger was available. In spite of the foregoing considerations, however, it is difficult to believe that a court of first instance would feel itself at liberty to hold that damages for personal injuries cannot be recovered under the rule in *Rylands* v. *Fletcher* although there are *dicta* in the House of Lords to this effect.[97]

Dependent issues

A situation closely resembling, but none the less differing from, that which arose in *Perry* v. *Kendrick's Transport* occurred in the House of Lords in *Minister of Health* v. *The King, ex parte Yaffé*.[98] In that case the applicant for *certiorari* to quash an order made by the Minister under the Housing Act 1925, was met by two defences, (i) that the court had no power to consider the validity of the order because it was made under a section providing that it should have the same effect as if it were contained in the statute, and (ii) that the order was in any event authorized by the Act. The House unanimously ruled against the Minister on the first point, but, by a majority of 4 to 1, decided the second point in his favour,

---

[97] *Read* v. *Lyons* [1947] AC 156.   [98] [1931] AC 494.

with the result that the applicant failed. The decision on the second point was plainly *ratio*, but what about the first point? Having regard to the view taken by the majority on the second point the House could have said 'We do not propose to consider the first defence raised by the Minister because the majority hold that the second succeeds.' However, this course was not in fact adopted, and it has been argued with great force that the decision on the first point was *ratio* because the Minister's objection went to the jurisdiction of the court and had to be disposed of before the second point could be considered. Certainly the House seems to have pursued a rational course in dealing with the question of jurisdiction first, and the answering of this question could be treated as a necessary prelude to the decision of the second point.[99]

The situation in *ex parte Yaffé* differed from that in *Perry* v. *Kendrick's Transport* because the two issues of jurisdiction and authorization were to some extent interdependent. A further instance of interdependent issues is provided by *Hedley Byrne and Partners Ltd.* v. *Heller and Partners Ltd.*[100] The plaintiffs had suffered pecuniary loss in consequence of a statement, which, for the purposes of their speeches, the members of the House of Lords assumed to have been made negligently, by the defendants who were merchant bankers. The statement was made in response to an inquiry about the solvency of a third party with whom the plaintiffs were in negotiation, and there was no contract between the plaintiffs and the defendants. The defendants had, however, disclaimed responsibility for the consequences of their statement. Were the defendants liable for pecuniary loss suffered in consequence of negligent misstatement? If so, were they protected from liability by the disclaimer? The House of Lords answered both questions in the affirmative. Their answer to the first question was flatly contradictory of that given on similar facts by the Court of Appeal in the earlier case of *Candler* v. *Crane Christmas and Co.*[101] The House of Lords could have said 'We find it unnecessary to decide whether there is a general rule that special relationships other than contractual relationships give rise to liability for negligent misstatement because, even if there is, the disclaimer is effective in this case' but this was not their approach. Their answer to the second question was treated as dependent on that given to the first. We

---

[99] Paton and Sawer, *LQR* 63 473. Cf pp. 56, 57 *supra*.
[100] [1964] AC 465.   [101] [1951] 2 KB 164.

have plainly reached a point at which the distinction between *ratio decidendi* and *obiter dictum* is meaningless in practice.

When speaking of *Hedley Byrne and Partners Ltd.* v. *Heller and Partners Ltd.* in *W. B. Anderson and Sons Ltd.* v. *Rhodes*,[102] Cairns J said:

An academic lawyer might be prepared to contend that the opinions expressed by their Lordships about liability for negligent misrepresentation were *obiter* and that *Candler* v. *Crane Christmas* is a binding decision. In my judgment that would be an unrealistic view to take. When five members of the House of Lords have all said after close examination of the authorities that a certain type of tort exists I think that a judge of first instance should proceed on the basis that it does exist without pausing to embark on an investigation whether what was said was necessary to the ultimate decision.

Criminal appeals

Another situation in which the distinction between *ratio decidendi* and *obiter dictum* is meaningless occurs on the hearing of a large number of criminal appeals. Under the proviso to s. 2 of the Criminal Appeal Act 1968,[103] the court *may*, notwithstanding that they are of opinion that the point raised in the appeal might be decided in favour of the appellant, dismiss the appeal if they consider that no miscarriage of justice has actually occurred. It is a fairly regular occurrence for appeals against conviction on indictment to be dismissed under the proviso. Whenever this is done, the only expressions of opinion essential to the order of the court—that the appeal be dismissed—are those relating to the question whether there has been a miscarriage or, in the old phraseology, a *substantial* miscarriage of justice. Yet the point that is most fully argued is usually the point of law actually raised by the appeal. Are the courts' pronouncements on this issue to be relegated to the status of *obiter dicta* simply because they were unnecessary so far as the order actually made was concerned? If so, quite a lot of our criminal law rests on a less secure basis than is commonly supposed to be the case.

There may be other situations in which the distinction between *ratio decidendi* and *obiter dictum* is meaningless in practice, but the reader must be on his guard against going to the other extreme and wrongly inferring from the fact that the distinction between *ratio*

---

[102] [1967] 2 All ER 850 at 857.
[103] Formerly the proviso to s. 4 (i) of the Criminal Appeal Act 1907

and *dictum* is sometimes devoid of practical significance that it is not an important feature of our doctrine of precedent. It is a very important feature of that doctrine, but its importance must not be exaggerated.

The different kinds of dicta

It would be possible to distinguish between different kinds of *dictum* in a great variety of ways. In the first place, there is an obvious contrast between *dicta* which are irrelevant to the case in which they occur, and those which relate to some collateral issue in that case although they do not form part of the *ratio decidendi*. The term *obiter dicta* is appropriate to the former which often consist of statements made in the course of the argument of a case, while *dicta* relevant to collateral issues are said to be 'judicial dicta'.

A mere passing remark or a statement or assumption on a matter that has not been argued is one thing, a considered judgment on a point fully argued is another, especially where, had the facts been otherwise, it would have formed part of the *ratio*. Such judicial *dicta*, standing in authority somewhere between a *ratio decidendi* and an *obiter dictum*, seem to me to have a weight nearer to the former than the latter.[104]

Professor Glanville Williams speaks of a *ratio decidendi* which, in the view of a subsequent court, is unnecessarily wide as a kind of *obiter*, although he recognizes that it may not be properly speaking an *obiter* at all.[105] This kind of *obiter*, or if the term be preferred, this kind of *ratio decidendi*, has been described as *obiter ex post facto*.[106] The terminology is not used by the judges, and it seems to be more in accordance with judicial practice to speak of 'the explanation' or 'interpretation' of the earlier case in the later case.

8. CASES WITH MORE THAN ONE *RATIO DECIDENDI*

We have already seen that a case may have more than one *ratio decidendi*. This is so whether one judgment only is delivered or whether several judgments containing the same two or more *rationes decidendi* are delivered. We have also seen that each *ratio*

---

[104] *Brunner v. Greenslade* [1971] Ch. 993 at 1002–3 *per* Megarry J.
[105] Glanville Williams, *Learning the Law* (11th edn.), 78.
[106] R. M. Gooderson, 30 *Canadian Bar Review* 894.

is binding authority according to the rules concerning the hierarchy of courts outlined in Chapter I. Views to this effect have been expressed by Lord Simonds speaking in the House of Lords,[107] by Greer LJ speaking in the Court of Appeal,[108] and by Devlin J speaking as a judge of first instance.[109] The same point was made at an earlier period by Lord Macnaghten in the Privy Council when he said:

> It is impossible to treat a proposition which the court declares to be a distinct and sufficient ground for its decision as a mere *dictum* simply because there is another ground stated upon which, standing alone, the case might have been determined.[110]

What happens in such a case is that the judge says, in effect, 'Though I could reach my conclusion on either of two grounds, I base it on both of them.'

As is the case with all questions concerning the *ratio decidendi*, the answer to the problem whether a given proposition of law is *dictum* or second *ratio* depends on the language of the judge, but the problem cannot be answered with complete certainty until another court has solved it. It would be idle to deny that there are cases in which what most lawyers would have considered a second *ratio* has been explained away as a mere *dictum* in subsequent litigation. A very strong example is provided by the treatment of *Atkinson* v. *Bettinson*[111] in *Fisher* v. *Taylors' Furnishing Stores Ltd.*[112] and subsequent cases. Under s. 30 of the Landlord and Tenant Act 1954, a landlord can resist his tenant's application for a new lease at the expiration of tenancies to which the Act applies on a number of different grounds including the facts that he intends to reconstruct a substantial part of the premises and that he requires the premises for his own occupation. The application can only be resisted on the second of these grounds if the landlord has been the owner of some interest in the premises for at least five years. But a question naturally arises concerning the case of a landlord who, although he has not been the owner of an interest in

---

[107] *Jacobs* v. *LCC* [1950] AC 361 at 369, p. 53 *supra*.
[108] *London Jewellers* v. *Attenborough* [1934] 2 KB 206 at 222. See also *Kaye* v. *Royal College of Music* [1961] 2 QB 89.
[109] *Behrens* v. *Bertram Mills Circus Ltd.* [1957] 2 QB 1 at 25, p. 42 *supra*.
[110] *Commissioner of Taxation for New South Wales* v. *Palmer* [1907] AC 179 at 184. The rule goes back at least as far as 1884, see *Crowther* v. *Thorley* (1884) 50 LT 43 at 46.
[111] [1955] 1 WLR 1126.
[112] [1956] 2 QB 78. See the notes by R.E.M. in 74 *LQR* 33 and 350.

the premises for five years, nevertheless intends both to reconstruct a substantial portion of them and to occupy them for his own purposes. *Atkinson* v. *Bettinson* was concerned with just such a problem, and it was held by the Court of Appeal that the tenant was entitled to a new lease (i) because the proposed reconstruction was a secondary purpose of the landlord whose primary object was to occupy the premises for his own requirements although he had not owned an interest in them for five years, and (ii) the landlord did not intend to reconstruct a substantial part of the premises within the meaning of the statute.

Fisher v. *Taylors' Furnishing Stores Ltd.* was another case in which the landlords resisted an application for a new tenancy on the ground that they intended to reconstruct a substantial part of the premises although they also required them for their own occupation and had not owned an interest in the premises for the required period of five years. When dealing with *Atkinson* v. *Bettinson* in the Court of Appeal, Denning LJ said that the correct ground of that decision was that the landlord did not intend to reconstruct a substantial part of the premises and Morris LJ said that *Atkinson*'s case could have been decided on this ground. Even if the primary purpose of the landlords in *Fisher*'s case was to occupy, rather than to reconstruct, the premises, their intention was to reconstruct a substantial part within the meaning of the Act of 1954. Accordingly the Court of Appeal concluded that they were not bound to decide in favour of the tenant on the authority of what might seem to have been the first *ratio* of *Atkinson* v. *Bettinson*, and they decided *Fisher* v. *Taylors' Furnishing Stores* in favour of the landlords.

Thus far there is nothing very special about the treatment of the earlier case in the later case. What most readers of the judgment would probably have taken to be the first *ratio* in *Atkinson* v. *Bettinson* was treated as a *dictum* in *Fisher* v. *Taylors' Furnishing Stores*. Practitioners are accustomed to occurrences of this sort as a kind of professional risk. But the matter was taken a good deal further by Lord Denning in *Betty's Cafés Ltd.* v. *Phillips Furnishing Stores Ltd.*[113] when he said that, in *Fisher*'s case, the Court of Appeal

virtually overruled one of the grounds of the decision in *Atkinson* v. *Bettinson* leaving that decision to rest on its other ground—a course which

[113] [1958] AC 20 at 53.

I think it was right to take, on being completely satisfied that the first ground was wrong.

Various exceptions to the rule of *stare decisis* are considered in Chapter IV. As yet there has not been numbered amongst them a case in which there are two or more *rationes decidendi*. If, in such a case, an inferior court or, assuming the decision is that of an appellate court, a court of co-ordinate jurisdiction, were to conclude that it was not bound by each *ratio*, the lot of a lawyer advising his client with regard to the effect of a decision based on two or more *rationes* would be deplorable in the extreme. A later court might consider itself bound by the first or second *ratio* alone or by both of them. According to Dr Megarry[114] for decisions based on 3, 4, or 5 grounds there seem to be respectively 7, 15, and 31 possible combinations.

Lord Denning has since expressed views concerning cases with two *rationes decidendi* similar to those expressed by him in *Betty's Cafés Ltd.* v. *Phillips Furnishing Stores Ltd.*,[115] but he has remained in a minority of one. Should it ever come to be settled practice that a court bound by a case with two *rationes* may choose which of the two it prefers, and reject the other, allowance would have to be made for a concept midway between *ratio* and *dictum*. Until the selection was made, the *rationes* would be conditionally binding. A judge bound by the case could choose between them, but he could not reject both, as he could if they were mere *dicta*.

9. THE *RATIO DECIDENDI* OF APPELLATE COURTS

Appellate courts sit with more than one judge, the usual numbers being three or five. In such cases it may be necessary to raise the question, what is the *ratio decidendi* of the court as distinct from the *rationes decidendi* to be gathered from each of the judgments? What is the proposition of law for which the case may be cited as binding authority in subsequent litigation? In some instances only one judgment is delivered and, when this happens, no particular problem arises. Neither does any special problem arise when several judgments are delivered and each judge concurs in the same *ratio* or *rationes decidendi*. But there can be very consider-

[114] 74 *LQR* 351.
[115] See his judgments in *Browning* v. *The War Office* [1963] 1 QB 750, *re Holmden's Settlement* [1966] Ch. 511, *Dixon* v. *BBC* [1979] QB 546, and *Ministry of Defence* v. *Jeremiah* [1980] 1 QB 87.

able difficulties when more than one judgment is delivered and the different judgments do not concur, although they reach the same conclusions. The *ratio decidendi* is a conception which is peculiarly appropriate to a single judgment. Accordingly it is probably impossible to avoid something in the nature of arbitrary rules to meet cases in which several judgments are delivered. The main trouble, so far as the current English practice is concerned, is that it is impossible to formulate these rules with anything like complete precision. Three situations must be distinguished in any endeavour that is made to arrive at these rules. First, there is the case in which a majority of judges allows or dismisses an appeal on one ground whereas the minority concur in the result on some other ground; then there is the case of a court which, contrary to the usual modern English practice, consists of an even number of judges and they are evenly divided as to the proper order which should be made; finally, there is the case where, though there is a majority in favour of a particular order, there is no majority in favour of a particular *ratio decidendi*. The first and third situations may be complicated by the presence of one or more judges who dissent on the question whether the appeal should be allowed or dismissed. Although dissenting judgments are often of the greatest value on account of the light which they throw upon the legal problems raised by an appeal, it is open to question whether they should ever be considered when it comes to determining the *ratio decidendi* of a case, for they inevitably consist of statements which were unnecessary for the decision of the precise question before the court.[116]

Cases in which a minority differs from the majority as to the ground of the court's order

There is a tolerably clear practice with regard to cases in which a minority sponsor one or more grounds for making the order which is in fact made by the court although there is a majority in favour of

---

[116] This, like many of the other points made in this section, was made in a note by A. M. Honoré, 71 *LQR* 196. Dissenting judgments are sometimes considered in order to clarify the statements of the majority. Thus, in *Haseldine* v. *Daw* [1941] 2 KB 343 at 375, Goddard LJ, as he then was, was assisted to the conclusion that *Donoghue* v. *Stevenson* applies to a repairer by a reference to the dissenting judgments. In *Walsh* v. *Curry* [1955] NI 112, reference was made to the dissenting speeches in *George Wimpey & Co.* v. *BOAC* [1955] AC 169 in order to ascertain whether a particular interpretation of s. 6 (1) (c) of the Law Reform (Married Women and Joint Tortfeasors) Act 1935 was adopted by a majority of the House.

reaching the same result by another route. The *ratio decidendi* concurred in by the majority is all that is strictly binding on subsequent
tribunals, although the minority views may be entitled to the weight-
iest consideration as *dicta*. To take one among several examples,
in *Amalgamated Society of Railway Servants* v. *Osborne*,[117] the
House of Lords was concerned with the validity of a trade union's
political levy compelling contributions to a political fund. The
majority considered that the appeal should be dismissed on the
ground that the levy was *ultra vires* the constitution of the union.
Lord Shaw was for dismissing the appeal on the ground that the
rule was contrary to public policy. But he expressly stated that this
could not be regarded as the *ratio decidendi* of the House.

Evenly divided courts

When an appellate court is evenly divided, the decision against
which the appeal is brought stands so far as the parties are
concerned. *R.* v. *Ashwell*[118] probably contains the most famous
example of such a result. Ashwell had been convicted of stealing.
The point of law involved was one of extreme complexity and it
was considered by no less than fourteen judges sitting in the Court
for Crown Cases Reserved. They were evenly divided on the
question of Ashwell's guilt and the conviction accordingly stood.
The problem with which we are concerned is the effect of the
decision of an evenly divided court in subsequent litigation
between different parties. Has it merely the authority of the lower
court from which the appeal is brought, or does the fact that the
appeal failed *inter partes* vest the decision with the authority of
the higher tribunal although that tribunal was evenly divided? The
answer may vary according to which appellate court is evenly
divided.

So far as the House of Lords is concerned, the decision appealed
from becomes, in the event of an equal division, the decision of the
House. This is illustrated by the treatment of *R.* v. *Millis* in
Beamish v. *Beamish* to which reference has already been made,[119]
and it is confirmed by several subsequent observations in the
House of Lords.[120] It is, of course, the *ratio* or *rationes* sponsored
by those members of the House who favour the affirmation of the
decision against which the appeal is brought that binds lower

---

[117] [1910] AC 87.   [118] (1885) 16 QBD 190.   [119] p. 7 *supra*.
[120] *Commissioners of Inland Revenue* v. *Walker* [1915] AC 519 at 522; *Ushers'
Wiltshire Brewery Ltd.* v. *Bruce* [1915] AC 433 at 444.

tribunals and the House of Lords itself in later cases. Some perplexity might be occasioned by a case in which two law lords were for dismissing an appeal while two were for allowing it and, of the two supporting the order for dismissal, one spoke in favour of *ratio* A while the other based his conclusion on *ratio* B. As there does not seem to have been any recent judical pronouncement concerning such a situation, it would be pointless to discuss it. One cannot help feeling that any court confronted with it would be justified in concluding that it was only bound to make an order similar to that confirmed by the House of Lords provided substantially similar facts were found to exist. If ever there was a case in which a court would be warranted in acting on the views expressed by Lord Dunedin in *The Mostyn*[121] this would be it.

The effect of an equal division of the Court of Appeal is somewhat doubtful so far as the authority of the decision that the appeal be dismissed is concerned. In *The Vera Cruz*[122] it was said that a subsequent Court of Appeal is not bound by a previous decision of that Court when the earlier Court was evenly divided. According to Brett MR:

There is no statute or common law rule by which one court is bound to abide by the decision of another of equal rank, it does so simply from what may be called the comity among judges. In the same way there is no common law or statutory rule to oblige a court to bow to its own decisions, again it does so on the ground of judicial comity. But when a court is equally divided, this comity does not exist, and there is no authority of the court as such, and those who follow must choose one of the two diverse opinions. . . . The case may be different with the House of Lords since it is the ultimate court of appeal, and if it is otherwise there exists an uncertainty as to the law.

Decisions of the Court of Exchequer Chamber are of co-equal authority with those of the Court of Appeal by which it was replaced and, in *Hart* v. *The Riversdale Mill Co. Ltd.*[123] Scrutton LJ treated a case in which the Exchequer Chamber was evenly divided as binding on the Court of Appeal. He does not appear to have been referred to *The Vera Cruz* and purported to act upon the rule according to which a subsequent House of Lords is bound by the decision of an earlier evenly divided House.

In *Packer* v. *Packer*[124] Denning LJ and Morris LJ took different views on the construction of s. 20 of the Matrimonial Causes Act

121 [1928] AC 57 at 71, p. 59 *supra*.   122 (1880) 9 PD 96 at 97.
123 [1928] 1 KB 176 at 188.   124 [1954] P. 14.

1950, concerning applications for the custody of children, and in *Galloway* v. *Galloway*[125] which raised the same point, the Court of Appeal did not treat *Packer* v. *Packer* as binding as it should have done on the principle stated by Scrutton LJ in *Hart* v. *The Riversdale Mill Co. Ltd.*

The only clear inference to be drawn from the cases which have just been cited is that there is no settled practice with regard to the extent to which a decision of an evenly divided Court of Appeal is authoritative. There does not seem to be any obvious reason why a decision should be elevated to the status of a decision of the Court of Appeal when that Court is evenly divided on the question of its correctness. Accordingly it would appear to be preferable to leave the decision against which the appeal was brought with its original status. The different opinions expressed in the Court of Appeal would, of course, possess great value as *dicta*, although they would inevitably counteract each other to a large extent. Brett MR spoke as though a choice must necessarily be made between the conflicting views expressed in the evenly divided Court of Appeal. Assuming that those who follow are not bound by the decision against which the appeal is brought, there is a third possibility, that neither view may seem to them to be the correct one, although one or other of the two views will, of course, have to be adopted in the vast majority of cases.

Brett MR's reason why the rule in the House of Lords might be different from that which he thought to be the right one for the Court of Appeal is not likely to convince everyone. It involves two assertions. First, it is the duty of the House of Lords to lay down the law with finality on every point brought before it, and secondly the House must be deemed to have done its duty in a case in which it was evenly divided. Some lawyers might accept the first assertion without necessarily endorsing the second. The truth of the matter is that, in such a case, the House has been prevented from fulfilling its duty of settling the law by the higher individual obligation of its members to decide a case according to what they conceive to be the law. The duty can normally be fulfilled while the obligation is carried out, but this is not necessarily so when an even number of peers sits to hear an appeal.

There is a historical reason why the House of Lords should be bound by the decision of an evenly divided House in an earlier

[125] [1954] P. 312. The problem of precedent was not considered when this case reached the House of Lords.

case. Proceedings on appeals to the House of Lords have always taken the form of the discussion of a motion—that the appeal be allowed. If a motion is proposed and the voting is even, it is lost unless there happens to be some provision for a casting vote, and there is no such provision in our parliamentary procedure so far as the House of Lords is concerned.[126] Even today proceedings on appeals to the House are parliamentary in form. The Lord Chancellor or other chairmen of the tribunal proposes a motion after the different judgments have been delivered in the form of speeches, and he declares that the motion is either won or lost. Whether it is desirable that form should be allowed to prevail over substance in this way is, of course, a wholly different question.

There is a limited class of case in which the Court of Appeal's decision is final. In these cases, according to the reasoning of Brett MR, the decision of an equally divided Court of Appeal should rank as the decision of that Court from the point of view of the doctrine of precedent.

Brett MR's statement that there is no comity obliging the Court of Appeal to follow a previous case in which it was equally divided is also open to question. Comity normally means little more than courtesy. The general rule of *stare decisis* is based on the practice of the courts, and to follow a rule because it is a practice is not necessarily the same thing as following it on account of comity. There might have been a uniform practice when *The Vera Cruz* came before the Court of Appeal according to which that Court did follow cases on which it had been evenly divided. In that case the practice would no doubt have been followed although comity did not require that this should be done.

There is nothing to be said with regard to the decision of an equally divided Criminal Division of the Court of Appeal because that court, as its predecessor was, is obliged to sit in odd numbers. The Court of Criminal Appeal was preceded by the Court for Crown Cases Reserved and, as we shall see in the next chapter, there is authority for the view that that court was bound by its own decisions as well as for the view that the Court of Criminal Appeal was bound by decisions of the Court for Crown Cases Reserved. As *R.* v. *Ashwell* shows, that court was sometimes evenly divided, but there does not appear to be any clear judicial statement on the question whether the decision of an evenly divided Court for

---

[126] Erskine May, *Parliamentary Practice* (16th edn.), 427.

Crown Cases Reserved ranks as the decision of that court from the point of view of the doctrine of precedent. The predominant opinion seems to be that the correctness of Ashwell's conviction lacks the authority of the Court for Crown Cases Reserved. If this is so, the case seems to lack all authoritative significance for the verdict of guilty was entered with the intention of obtaining the opinion of the Court for Crown Cases Reserved on the question of its correctness.

The practice of divisional courts with regard to the authority accorded to previous cases in which they were evenly divided also seems to be unsettled.[127]

The upshot of the foregoing discussion is that appellate courts should always consist of an odd number of judges. Nevertheless, owing to the pressure of business in the Civil Division of the Court of Appeal, two-judge sittings of that court have become increasingly common.

No majority in favour of a particular ratio decidendi

It sometimes happens that an appeal is heard by three Lords Justices in the Court of Appeal or five Law Lords in the House of Lords, and one Lord Justice or two Law Lords, as the case may be, allow or dismiss the appeal on ground A, while another Lord Justice or two other Law Lords do likewise on ground B. What is the position if the third Lord Justice or fifth Lord of Appeal expresses his agreement with the views of all the other members of the Court without delivering a considered judgment of his own? In such a situation it could be argued that the case has two *rationes decidendi*, a majority being in favour of each one of them; but there is authority for the view that the narrower of the two grounds should be treated as the *ratio decidendi* of the Court in the sense that it alone possesses binding force. We have seen that this course was adopted by Lord Greene MR when considering *Hillyer* v. *St Bartholomew's Hospital*[128] in *Gold* v. *Essex County Council*.[129] It is impossible to say whether this practice will always be followed in like situations. Nor is it clear that such a case will always be treated as having two binding *rationes decidendi* when one is no narrower than the other, although there is no obvious means of escape from such a conclusion.

---

[127] *Grocock* v. *Grocock* [1920] 1 KB 1 at 11 and 13
[128] [1909] 2 KB 820.   [129] [1942] 1 KB 293 at 298, p. 61 *supra*.

Another possible situation in a court consisting of three or five judges is that one, or, in the case of a five-judge court, two should be in favour of allowing the appeal on ground A while another one or two should be in favour of allowing the appeal on ground B, and the remaining judge would dismiss the appeal. This is what happened in *Hambrook* v. *Stokes Bros.*,[130] where a mother suffered nervous shock in consequence of seeing a lorry which the defendants' servant had carelessly left unattended, career down a road along which her children had just set out on their way to school. Bankes LJ based his decision in favour of the mother on the facts of the case including the fact that the shock was due to the apprehension of injury to her children. Atkin LJ was also in favour of the mother, but the ground of his decision was considerably broader. He considered that anyone to whom a duty of care was owed and broken could recover damages for nervous shock due to the apprehension of physical injury to someone else. Sargant LJ delivered a dissenting judgment. Dr Goodhart inclines to the view that the *ratio* provided by Bankes LJ should be treated as the *ratio decidendi* of the case because there is a presumption against broad principles of law.[131]

The treatment of the decision of the House of Lords in *Central Asbestos Ltd.* v. *Dodd*[132] by the Court of Appeal in *Harper* v. *National Coal Board (intended action)*[133] shows that the requirement, if there is one, that dissenting judgments should be disregarded for the purpose of ascertaining the authoritative effect of the decisions of appellate courts can produce some odd results. In the first of these cases a majority of 3 to 2 held that Dodd's writ claiming damages for negligence in consequence of which he contracted asbestosis had been issued within the relevant limitation period. Lords Reid and Morris of Borth-y-Gest reached this conclusion on the ground that time only began to run from the moment when Dodd knew that he had a cause of action. Lords Salmon and Simon of Glaisdale dissented on the ground that time had begun to run against Dodd some two years earlier when he knew that he had asbestosis sufficiently badly to cause him to leave work and was aware of the facts constituting the alleged negligence. Lord Pearson agreed with Lords Salmon and Simon on the law, but held that Dodd only became aware of the alleged

---

[130] [1925] 1 KB 141.
[131] *Essays in Jurisprudence and the Common Law*, 21.
[132] [1973] AC 518.   [133] [1974] QB 614.

negligence within the limitation period. Harper only discovered that he had a cause of action within the limitation period, but he was aware of all relevant facts before that period began. The judge of first instance refused him leave to issue a writ because three of the Lords in Dodd's case had held that, as a matter of law, time ran from the moment when Dodd knew of the facts founding his cause of action. This decision was reversed by the Court of Appeal on the ground that it was wrong to adopt a line of reasoning which led to a conclusion contrary to that finally reached by the majority of the House of Lords.

Lord Reid and Lord Morris of Borth-y-Gest took one view of the law. Lord Pearson took another. We cannot say that Lord Reid and Lord Morris of Borth-y-Gest were correct: because we know that their reasoning on the law was in conflict with the reasoning of the other three. We cannot say that Lord Pearson was correct: because we know that the reasoning which he adopted on the law led the other two (Lord Simon of Glaisdale and Lord Salmon) to a wrong conclusion. So we cannot say that any of the three in the majority was correct.[134]

The Court of Appeal therefore treated Dodd's case as one which had no discernible *ratio* and regarded itself as free to follow its own earlier decisions. Lord Simon of Glaisdale has since characterized the course taken by the Court of Appeal as a 'dexterous adherence' to a statutory construction of which the majority of the House of Lords disapproved;[135] perhaps we should not make a shibboleth of any requirement that there may be in this context that dissenting judgments should be disregarded; they may at least contain weighty *dicta*.

Lord Simonds is reported to have said that it not infrequently happens that an appeal will succeed though the majority are against the appellant on each of the individual points which the appeal raises. Suppose that five points were involved in a case coming before the House of Lords, and suppose there are five Law Lords sitting, each may be for the appellant on one point, though against him on the other four. The appellant will win, although he lost four to one on each point raised by him.[136] It is said that, according to Scots procedure, the appellant would lose in such a

---

[134] *Per* Lord Denning [1974] QB at 621–2.
[135] *Miliangos* v. *George Frank (Textiles) Ltd.* [1976] AC at 479.
[136] 66 *LQR* 298.

case because the court's opinion on each issue would be taken separately. A recent example of what Lord Simonds had in mind is provided by the decision of the House of Lords on the English appeal in *Chaplin* v. *Boys*.[137] It was heard by five Law Lords who were unanimously of the opinion that damages for personal injuries sustained in a motor accident in Malta while the plaintiff and defendant, English servicemen, were temporarily stationed there, should be assessed according to English law; but two favoured one *ratio* and two another, while the fifth Lord favoured yet another and expressly disagreed with the *ratios* of his four colleagues.

Failures of judicial technique

In an important article on *ratio decidendi* and *obiter dictum* in appellate courts, two Australian professors speak of cases in which there has been a failure of judicial technique. For the function of a court is not only to give judgment, but also to lay down a principle consistent with that judgment.[138] The article is mainly concerned with Australian cases, but they were of a type similar to the English decisions which have just been discussed—cases coming before the appellate courts in which different judgments founded on differing reasoning were delivered. It is unnecessary to cite authority for the proposition that the duty of any court, and particularly that of an appellate court, is not merely to give judgment, but to do so according to an ascertainable principle (called the *ratio decidendi*) whenever points of law are raised. If the principle on which the court acted is unascertainable there would certainly seem to have been a failure of judicial technique, and a fact which must be faced in the course of an assessment of the merits of the English system of case-law is that such failures do occur from time to time. Perhaps it would not be going too far to say that it would even have been better for English law if no considered reasons for judgment had been delivered in some cases. Although these occasions are mercifully rare, it does seem that certain changes in judicial practice might prove beneficial to the development of English law as a whole.

Single judgment in appellate courts

One such change might be an increase in the number of cases in which only one judgment is delivered in an appellate court. This is

---

[137] [1971] AC 356.   [138] G. W. Paton and G. Sawer, *LQR* 63 (1947), 461.

normal practice in the Privy Council and in the Criminal Division of the Court of Appeal.

It is of considerable advantage we think that those who have to administer the criminal law and who are bound by the decisions of the court of Criminal Appeal should have one judgment only expounding the relevant law rather than have to consider several judgments in one case and possibly have to distil out of these a ground of decision which is common to all.[139]

No doubt there are those who think this is equally true of the administration of the civil law.

There is, however, something to be said on the other side. Single judgments of multiple tribunals frequently represent compromises between conflicting views, and compromises do not always make for clarity.[140] Dissenting opinions are often very valuable and undue suppression of dissenting opinions is to be deplored. Furthermore, under the English system, one of the functions of the courts in general, and of appellate courts in particular, is to discuss and enunciate general principles as pointers to the future development of the law. This function is sometimes best fulfilled by the delivery of more than one judgment. Critics sometimes tend to give the courts the worst of both worlds in this matter.

While it is the primary duty of a court of justice to dispense justice to litigants, it is its traditional role to do so by means of an exposition of the relevant law. Clearly such a system must be somewhat flexible, with the result that in some cases judges may be criticised for diverging into expositions which could by no means be regarded as relevant to the dispute between the parties; in others other critics may regret that an opportunity has been missed for making an oracular pronouncement on some legal problem which has long vexed the profession.[141]

Lord Reid was an inveterate opponent of single judgments in appellate courts and the following extract from his speech in *Cassell and Co. Ltd. v. Broome*[142] typifies his views:

With the passage of time I have come more and more firmly to the conclusion that it is never wise to have only one speech in this House

---

[139] Report of the Interdepartmental Committee on the Court of Criminal Appeal (1965), Cmd. 2755, para. 250.
[140] *Chancery Lane Safe Deposit and Offices Co. Ltd. v. IRC* [1966] AC 85, 110 Lord Reid.
[141] *Jacobs* v. *LCC* [1950] AC 361 at 369, *per* Lord Simonds.
[142] [1972] AC at 1085.

dealing with an important question of law. My main reason is that experience has shown that those who have to apply the decision to other cases, and still more those who wish to criticise it, seem to find it difficult to avoid treating sentences and phrases in a single speech as if they were provisions in an act of Parliament. They do not seem to realise that it is not the function of noble and learned lords or indeed of any judge, to frame definitions or to lay down hard and fast rules. It is their function to enunciate principles and much that they say is intended to be illustrative and explanatory and not to be definitive. When there are two or more speeches they must be read together and then it is generally much easier to see what are the principles involved and what are merely illustrations of it.

Similar views were expressed by Lord Wilberforce and Lord Salmon in *Pickett* v. *British Rail Engineering Ltd.*[143] However, as Lord Salmon recognized, a single speech may be desirable where nothing is at stake except the semantic import of statutory words within a particular provision. In *Carter* v. *Bradbeer* Lord Diplock stated that, in this narrow field, certainty was best achieved if reasons for dissent were not elaborated. The majority in that case took the view that a bar counter was necessarily a 'bar' for the purposes of a provision of the Licensing Act 1964. He was not so sure, but he would concur with his colleagues since the word, in that context, now had the meaning that the majority said it had.[144]

Clearer indication whether cases overruled

A further possibly beneficial change of judicial practice would be the clarification of the question whether the judgments in some of the earlier cases cited and discussed still represent the law. In *Bourhill* v. *Young*[145] the speeches of all the five Law Lords who sat to hear the appeal, each of which was in favour of dismissing the appeal, referred to *Hambrook* v. *Stokes Bros.*,[146] but they did so in very varied terms. Lord Thankerton stated that certain *dicta* could be considered too wide and reserved his opinion on the correctness of the decision. Lord Russell preferred the dissenting judgment of Sargant LJ, and Lord Macmillan reserved his opinion. Lord Wright agreed with the decision in *Hambrook* v. *Stokes Bros.* 'as at present advised'. Lord Porter thought there was no duty not to cause nervous shock, unless physical injury to the plaintiff could reasonably be anticipated, but that on the facts of

---

[143] (1980) AC 136, 147, 157.
[145] [1943] AC 92, p. 70 *supra*.
[144] (1975) 3 All ER 158, 160–2.
[146] [1925] 1 KB 141, p. 91 *supra*.

Hambrook v. *Stokes Bros.* it might well have been held that a duty was owed to the mother.[147] The comment of the authors of the article mentioned in the last paragraph is that

to throw a veiled doubt on the validity of a precedent is to add to the confusion of authority. It is better to have the courage definitely to say that it is wrong or to refrain from expressing an opinion.[148]

These are strong words, and the example of *Hambrook* v. *Stokes Bros.* is possibly somewhat exceptional, but there is no doubt that unnecessary uncertainty may be occasioned by the discursive nature of the judgments in appellate courts, and those sitting in such courts should take every possible step to avoid it.

---

[147] Liability for negligently caused nervous shock has subsequently been extended by the decision of the House of Lords in *McLoughlin* v. *O'Brian* [1983] 1 AC 410, p. 218 *infra*.
[148] 63 *LQR* 477–8.

III
STARE DECISIS

1. INTRODUCTORY

According to the preliminary statement of the English doctrine of precedent in Chapter I, a court is bound to follow any case decided by a court above it, and appellate courts (other than the House of Lords) are bound by their previous decisions. What is meant by saying that a court is 'bound to follow a case' or 'bound by a decision'? In this context, according to orthodox theory, 'case' and 'decision' mean *ratio decidendi*. In other contexts they may respectively mean a particular piece of litigation, and the judgment or order of court by which that litigation is determined. 'Judgment' is also a word of many meanings. It may signify a court order as when we say that *A* got judgment for £100, it may signify everything said by a judge with regard to the grounds for making an order (the entirety of his opinion including statements of fact and *obiter dicta*), or it may be used synonymously with *ratio decidendi*. The fact that words such as 'case', 'judgment', or 'decision' may all be used to mean the *ratio decidendi* of a case sometimes leads to the confusion of *ratio decidendi* with *res judicata*, i.e. the confusion between the effect of a decision from the point of view of subsequent litigation involving different parties, and its effect on the parties to the dispute. They are generally estopped from raising the same issue at a later date.

There are some resemblances between *res judicata* and binding precedents. In the first place, if a ruling is to give rise to an issue estoppel it must, like a *ratio decidendi*, have been necessary to the decision in the earlier case. In *Re State of Norway's Application*, discussed in the last chapter,[1] the Court of Appeal held that its earlier determination that the proceedings were 'civil proceedings', even though given between the same parties as were now before the court, was not binding, for the same reason that the earlier court's construction of the 1975 Act was not part of its *ratio*

---

[1] p. 56 *supra*.

decidendi. Neither the determination of the issue, nor the ruling on the Act, was essential to the decision. Secondly, where the determination of an issue between the parties in earlier proceedings comprised a decision on a general question of construction (classifiable as a question of law), subsequent developments in case-law showing that decision to have been wrong may constitute exceptional grounds for allowing the question to be relitigated.[2] The fundamental differences concern judicial hierarchy and the range of those affected. Only *rationes decidendi* of superior courts create binding precedents, but they apply to all within their scope. A 'cause of action estoppel' or an 'issue estoppel' may be pleaded only by the parties directly affected by the earlier litigation, but it settles their rights even if the decision was made by an official with limited jurisdiction, such as the Chief Commons Commissioner,[3] or a planning inspector.[4]

A court is sometimes said to be bound by the 'judgment' in a case although it is not bound to follow the *ratio decidendi.* The House of Lords may be bound by the judgment of a judge of first instance in the sense that the House must apply the principles of *res judicata* which the judgment brings into play should subsequent litigation between the same parties involve the same issue, although there is no sense in which the House of Lords is bound by the *ratio decidendi* of a case decided by a judge of first instance. Subject to these rather obvious verbal points, the answer to the question which has been raised appears to be simple enough. When it is said that a court is bound to follow a case, or bound by a decision, what is meant is that the judge is under an obligation to apply a particular *ratio decidendi* to the facts before him in the absence of a reasonable legal distinction between those facts and the facts to which it was applied in the previous case.

But what is the nature of this obligation? It is an obligation to follow a fairly well-defined practice. Its efficacy depends on what Professor Hart terms the 'internal aspect'[5] of the rule of *stare decisis.* It is recognized by past and present holders of the judicial office who use it as a justification for their conduct.[6]

---

[2] *Arnold v. National Westminster Bank plc* (1990) 1 All ER 529 CA.

[3] *Crown Estate Commissioners v. Dorset County Council* (1990) Ch. 297 Millett J.

[4] *Thrasyvoulou v. Secretary of State for the Environment* (1990) 2 AC 273 HL.

[5] *The Concept of Law*, 86.

[6] For another view, see Stephen R. Perry, 'Judicial Obligation Precedent and the Common Law', *OJLS* 7 (1987), 215.

If a judge persistently and vociferously declined to follow cases by which he was bound according to countless statements of other judges, it is possible that steps would be taken to remove him from his office, but it would be a mistake to think in terms of such drastic sanctions for the judge's obligation to act according to the rules of precedent. Those rules are rules of practice, and, if it is thought to be desirable to speak of a sanction for the obligation to comply with them, it is sufficient to say that non-compliance might excite adverse comment from other judges. Needless to say, there are not many examples of such comment in the law reports because the obligation to follow a practice derives its force from the fact that the practice is followed with a high degree of uniformity. When confronted with the suggestion that a certain decision of the House of Lords might do no more than create an estoppel *inter partes* Lord Eldon said:

As to an observation made with respect to the case of the Feoffees of Heriot's Hospital that the judgment of this House in that case was one to be obeyed, not to be followed, I must take the liberty to say that this would be a course which, if pursued, would call for some attention. For although a court may say that, if a case varies in facts and circumstances, it is at liberty to proceed upon these different circumstances, I do not recollect that it ever fell from a judge in this country, that he would obey the judgment of this House in the particular case, but not follow it in others. That is not a doctrine to which we are accustomed.[7]

The following remarks of Lord Hailsham represent the reaction of the House of Lords to the Court of Appeal's refusal to follow a previous decision of the House on the ground that it had been reached *per incuriam*:

The fact is, and I hope that it will never be necessary to say so again, that in the hierarchical system of courts that exists in this country, it is necessary for each lower tier, including the Court of Appeal, to accept loyally the decisions of the higher tiers. Where decisions manifestly conflict, the decision in *Young* v. *The Bristol Aeroplane Co.* offers guidance to each tier in matters affecting its own decisions. It does not entitle it to question considered decisions in the upper tiers with the same freedom.[8]

These words did not deter a majority of the Court of Appeal from holding in a later case that the Court was not bound to follow a

---

[7] *Gordon* v. *Marjoribanks* (1818) 6 Dow. 87, at 112.
[8] *Cassell and Co. Ltd.* v. *Broome* [1972] AC at 1054.

decision of the House of Lords which had become obsolete under the maxim *cessante ratione cessat ipsa lex*. When the case came before the House of Lords Lord Wilberforce had this to say before supporting the majority view of the House in favour of overruling its previous decision:

> It has to be re-affirmed that the only judicial means by which decisions of this House can be reconsidered is by this House itself under the declaration of 1966.[9]

Nevertheless, as we shall see, the Court of Appeal has recently affirmed that the doctrine of obsolescence does apply to decisions of the House of Lords.[10] Nor can one be certain what the position would be if the Court of Appeal were faced with conflicting decisions of the House of Lords where the later decision had not overruled the earlier one pursuant to the 1966 Practice-Statement power. The speeches delivered in the House in *Cassell and Co. Ltd.* v. *Broome*[11] would appear to support the view that the Court of Appeal should regard itself as bound by the later decision. Some support for an alternative approach might be derived from an analogy with the practice of intermediate appellate courts which are bound by decisions of the Privy Council. In *Baker* v. *The Queen*,[12] Lord Diplock, delivering the majority judgment of the Board, stated that whilst the *Cassell* case had established that the *per incuriam* rule could not be invoked by an inferior court as regards the decisions of a superior court, the Court of Appeal for Jamaica had been entitled to choose which of two conflicting *rationes decidendi* of the Board it should follow and had acted correctly in preferring the earlier decision.[13]

Different meanings of stare decisis

The general orthodox interpretation of *stare decisis* and that which is, in general, given to it throughout this book, is *stare rationibus decidendis* ('keep to the *rationes decidendi* of past cases'), but a narrower and more literal interpretation is sometimes employed. To appreciate this narrower interpretation it is necessary to refer

---

[9] *Miliangos* v. *George Frank (Textiles) Ltd.* [1976] AC at 459.
[10] *Pittalis* v. *Grant* (1989) QB 605, p. 162 *infra*.
[11] (1972) AC 1027.   [12] (1975) AC 774.
[13] Ibid. 788. Implicit support for the view that the English Court of Appeal has a similar freedom in relation to conflicting decisions of the House of Lords may be derived from the judgment of Parker LJ in *Dobson* v. *General Accident Fire and Life Assurance Corporation plc* (1990) QB 274.

again to Lord Halsbury's assertion that a case is only authority for what it actually decides.[14] We saw that situations can arise in which all that is binding is the decision. According to Lord Reid, such a situation arises when the *ratio decidendi* of a previous case is obscure, out of accord with authority or established principle, or too broadly expressed. His speech in *Midland Silicones Ltd. v. Scruttons Ltd.*[15] makes it clear that he considered *Elder Dempster & Co. Ltd. v. Paterson Zochonis & Co.*[16] to be just such a case. He was speaking at a time when the House of Lords held itself bound by its past decisions.

The decision is binding on us, but I agree that the decision by itself will not avail the present appellants because the facts of this case are very different from those in the *Elder Dempster* case. For the appellants to succeed it would be necessary to find from the speeches in this House a *ratio decidendi* which would cover this case and then to follow the *ratio decidendi*. . . . The decision of this House is authoritative in cases of which the circumstances are not reasonably distinguishable from those which gave rise to the decision.[17]

In this context the 'decision' means the order of the court in the light of all the facts of the case, and the obligation of a court bound by the decision is to follow it unless that court can point to a reasonable, i.e. legally relevant, distinction between the facts of the previous and instant cases. The later court is not bound by any proposition of law stated by the earlier one or by the earlier court's treatment of certain facts as material or immaterial. Each of the last-mentioned considerations is of course crucial so far as a court bound by the *ratio decidendi* of a previous case is concerned.

The view is sometimes expressed that *stare decisis* always means no more than 'keep to decisions' in the narrow sense which has just been examined. Lord Reid is clearly not of that persuasion, and, for England at least,[18] the view is still highly unorthodox as an account of the ordinary meaning of *stare decisis* as distinct from its meaning in exceptional situations.

The object of this chapter is to consider the extent to which the rule of *stare decisis* is followed in the different courts.

No separate paragraph has been devoted to the Privy Council in the following account of the practice of the different courts. This is

---

[14] p. 57 *supra*.   [15] [1962] AC 446.
[16] [1924] AC 522.   [17] [1962] AC at 466.
[18] It may be the orthodox meaning in America; see an important article by Rolf Sartorius in *Archives for Philosophy of Law and Social Philosophy*, 53 (1967), 343.

because the Privy Council is not an English court, and there would, in any event, be little to add to what was said on the subject in Chapter I. The Privy Council is not absolutely bound by its past decisions and its decisions are only of persuasive authority in this country. It is possible to refer to cases in which a decision of the Privy Council has not been followed by an English judge of first instance,[19] but it is also possible to point to cases in which a decision of the Privy Council has been persistently preferred to a decision of the Court of Appeal, although the decision of that Court has never been overruled.[20] This is one of the instances in which a rule of precedent has not been applied with complete consistency, but it is too exceptional to require detailed examination.

2. THE HOUSE OF LORDS

Although the rule was virtually settled in *Beamish* v. *Beamish*,[21] the case which is most often cited as having finally established, for sixty-eight years, that the House of Lords was bound by its past decisions is *London Tramways* v. *London County Council*.[22] The point at issue was the amount of compensation to be paid to the appellant company on its being taken over by the London County Council. The method of calculating this sum had been laid down four years earlier by the House of Lords when hearing a Scots appeal turning on similar legislation,[23] and that method had been applied on an English appeal which had been heard by the House of Lords immediately afterwards.[24] The only question considered in the later case was whether the House of Lords was bound by these earlier decisions and the conclusion reached was that it was

---

[19] *Port Line Ltd.* v. *Ben Line Steamers Ltd.* [1958] 2 QB 146.

[20] See the preference for *Le Mesurier* v. *Le Mesurier* [1895] AC 517 over *Niboyet* v. *Niboyet* (1878) 4 PD 1, before *Indyka* v. *Indyka* [1967] 2 All ER 689. See also the treatment of *re Polemis* [1921] 3 KB 560 as overruled by the *Waggon Mound No. 1* [1961] AC 388 in *Smith* v. *Leech Brain & Co.* [1962] 2 QB 405, and *Doughty* v. *Turner Manufacturing Co. Ltd.* [1964] 2 QB 510.

[21] (1861) 9 HLC 274, p. 27 *supra*.

[22] [1898] AC 375. The name of the appellant is wrongly given as *London Street Tramways* in the title of the case (see the correction in the list of errors in [1898] AC). The mistake is particularly unfortunate because *London Street Tramways*, a different company, was involved in a previous appeal to the House of Lords in 1894.

[23] *Edinburgh Street Tramways* v. *Lord Provost etc. of Edinburgh* [1894] AC 456.

[24] *London Street Tramways* v. *LCC* [1894] AC 489.

bound by them. Lord Halsbury delivered the only speech, and the following is one of the crucial passages:

Of course I do not deny that cases of individual hardship may arise, and there may be a current of opinion in the profession that such and such a judgment was erroneous; but what is that occasional interference with what is perhaps abstract justice, as compared with the inconvenience—the disastrous inconvenience—of having each question subject to being re-argued and the dealings of mankind rendered doubtful by reason of different decisions, so that in truth and in fact there would be no real final court of appeal. My lords, 'interest rei publicae' that there should be 'finis litium' sometime and there could be no 'finis litium' if it were possible to suggest in each case that it might be re-argued because it is 'not an ordinary case' whatever that may mean.[25]

The reference to the maxim 'interest rei publicae ut sit finis litium' suggests a possible confusion between *ratio decidendi* and *res judicata* which has already been mentioned, but the main tenor of the passage is that the House of Lords should follow its past decisions in order to produce finality and certainty in the general law. This argument has two aspects. Were the House of Lords to differ from its past decisions, (i) lower courts would not know which of two cases to follow, the earlier decision of the House of Lords or the later decision in which the House declined to follow that case, and (ii) lawyers would be unable to advise their clients with confidence because of the possibility that a certain decision of the House of Lords would not be followed by a later House of Lords.[26] The first of these dangers would not exist if it came to be the accepted practice that the later decision of the House of Lords should be treated as having overruled the one which was not followed. The second objection would be met if the practice of prospective overruling mentioned in Chapter VIII were ever adopted.

Lord Halsbury's observations also invite a consideration of the problem from the point of view of abstract justice between the individual litigants. Whenever the matter is considered in this way, it should not be forgotten that there is a sense in which a court's failure to follow one of its past decisions inevitably produces a failure of justice. Litigants are entitled to expect that like cases will be decided alike, and they are encouraged to do so by the courts. One litigant must necessarily be disappointed of his just expectations

[25] [1898] AC at 380.   [26] Salmond's *Jurisprudence* (12th edn.), 164.

if the House of Lords holds that, although the facts of his case are as he contended and although, as he likewise contended, there is no reasonable legal distinction between those facts and the facts of a previous case decided by the House, the case is one which ought not to be followed.

Practice Statement of 1966

The manner in which the change of practice was announced was calculated to meet this objection. It was done by a Practice Statement not, as some had thought it might be done, in the course of deciding a case (in which event the point mentioned in the last paragraph might have been highly relevant) nor, as others thought the change would have to be effected, by legislation.

The Statement reads as follows:

Their Lordships regard the use of precedent as an indispensable foundation upon which to decide what is the law and its application to individual cases. It provides at least some degree of certainty upon which individuals can rely in the conduct of their affairs, as well as a basis for orderly development of legal rules.

Their Lordships nevertheless recognize that too rigid adherence to precedent may lead to injustice in a particular case and also unduly restrict the proper development of the law. They propose, therefore, to modify their present practice and, while treating former decisions of this House as normally binding, to depart from a previous decision when it appears right to do so.

In this connection they will bear in mind the danger of disturbing retrospectively the basis on which contracts, settlements of property and fiscal arrangements have been entered into and also the especial need for certainty as to the criminal law. This announcement is not intended to affect the use of precedent elsewhere than in this House.[27]

The logical status and constitutional propriety of this Practice Statement have been the subject of controversy among academic commentators.[28] As to logic, it has been claimed that the Statement, like the ruling in the *London Tramways* case, suffers from the vice of self-reference. Both were 'decisions' of the House of Lords purporting to lay down that decisions of the House are or

---

[27] The statement was read by Lord Gardiner LC, on behalf of himself and the Lords of Appeal in Ordinary, before judgments were delivered on 26 July 1966.

[28] Roy Stone, *Minn. LR* 51 (1967), 655; *CLJ* 26 (1968), 35. Julius Stone, *Col. LR* 69 (1969), 1162. Hicks, *CLJ* 29 (1971), 265. Goldstein, *CLJ* 38 (1979), 373; *CLJ* 43 (1984), 88. Evans, *CLJ* 41 (1982), 162; *CLJ* 43 (1984), 108. Mann, *CJQ* 2 (1983), 320.

are not binding. This allegation was adequately rebutted by Sir Rupert Cross, who pointed out that it was premissed on the false assumption that statements about rules of precedent constitute, as well as referring to, *rationes decidendi*. Once it is recognized that the distinction between *ratio* and *obiter dicta* does not apply to such statements, it can be seen that they themselves do not constitute 'decisions' in the same sense that *rationes decidendi* laying down substantive rules of law are 'decisions'.[29] Precedent rules confer authority on the *rationes decidendi* of various courts; but they derive their authority, not from such *rationes*, but from a more widely diffused judicial practice which transcends the outcome of particular cases. To the extent that this practice is settled, they are conceived of as imposing obligations which are as peremptory as any other legal obligations, and in that sense they constitute rules of law. However, they dwell at a higher level than ordinary rules of substantive case-law whose authenticity they control. There is consequently no problem of self-reference.

The constitutional propriety of the Practice Statement presents more difficulty. Cross asked rhetorically: 'but can there be any doubt that it owes its validity to the inherent power of any court to regulate its own practice?'[30] There are two problems with this suggestion. First it may prove too much. It suggests that rules governing the precedential status of the decisions of a particular court must necessarily include a power in that court to change the rules; whereas there could be a settled practice which excluded such power. As we shall see in the next section, the view that the Court of Appeal has the power to change the rules concerning the bindingness of its own decisions, though asserted by some, has not been generally accepted.

Secondly, Cross's suggestion appears to rely on an inappropriate analogy between precedent rules and ordinary procedural practice rules. There is no doubt that any superior court may from time to time issue practice directions concerning procedural steps to be taken in litigation before that court. It does not follow, merely because precedent rules derive from practice, that they also embody a similar freedom. The word 'practice' can be over-played.

---

[29] R. Cross, 'The House of Lords and the Rules of Precedent', in Hacker and Raz (eds.), *Law, Morality, and Society*, ch. 8.
[30] Ibid. 157.

If there was, in 1966, a settled judicial tradition about precedent which comprised a rule imposing a constitutional obligation on the House of Lords to follow its own *rationes decidendi* on questions of substantive law, how could that rule have been changed by the Practice Statement of that year without constitutional impropriety? There is no doubt that precedent rules, like anything else deriving from a tradition, may evolve. The English rules have changed over the centuries and on many points of detail they are constantly subject to modification, as the discussion of exceptions to *stare decisis* in Chapter IV will reveal. Whenever a judge is faced with some debatable feature of the rules, he may express a view as to what the tradition requires, having regard to past instances reported in the cases and his conception of the underlying purpose of the rule in question. Such a pronouncement, if it subsequently meets with general approval by other judges, may have the effect of crystallizing a particular rule or exception. Such was the case, for example, of Lord Greene's articulation in *Young* v. *Bristol Aeroplane Co. Ltd.* of the circumstances in which the Court of Appeal is or is not bound by its own decisions. It is another thing if judges claim overtly to bring about a change in the rules which have hitherto been settled, as those who participated in the Practice Statement seem to have done. In such a context, power to alter precedent rules, at a stroke, is consciously exercised by participants from within a practice. It is not merely attributed, as an inevitable concomitant of traditionary evolution, by an external commentator on the practice.

Seen in this light, there would appear to be two plausible views of the constitutionality of what was done in 1966. They diverge on a historical understanding of how judges and other lawyers conceived of the tradition at the time. On one view, it was accepted that the House of Lords was bound by its own decisions only until such time as the House should, by some appropriate announcement, change the rule—that is, that the practice then accepted included a power in the House, by a single pronouncement, to bring about the change. The second view is that in 1966 the rule which had emerged in cases such as *Beamish* v. *Beamish* and the *London Tramways* case was so firmly rooted that it could only be changed by legislation—that there was no power in the House itself to alter it. On the former view, the Practice Statement constituted an exercise of an existing constitutional power. On the latter view, it was issued without constitutional authority and so

amounted to a technical 'revolution'.[31] The judges themselves
have, for the most part, tactfully ignored the issue. Support for the
first view may be inferred from Viscount Dilhorne's claim, in
Davis v. *Johnson*, that those who were parties to the 1966
announcement simply concluded, 'as a matter of law' that the
House was not bound to follow its own decisions.[32] This cannot
mean that there never was a rule that it was bound, in view of the
cases asserting that rule and the terms of the Practice Statement
itself which speaks of their Lordships' proposal 'to modify their
present practice'. It must therefore entail that the rule was one
which they were, as a matter of law, free to change. A variant of
the first view is contained in the speech of Viscount Simon in the
Knuller case. He stated that the Practice Statement must 'be
considered to be one of those conventions which are so significant
a feature of the British constitution, as Professor Dicey showed in
his famous work'.[33] That was so, Lord Simon claimed, because
it represented a consensus of the three branches of government:
it was concurred in by all Lords of Appeal in Ordinary, no
objection was raised elsewhere in Parliament, and since the
announcement was made by the Lord Chancellor it must be taken
to have had general Executive approval. In other words, there was
a power to alter the rule exercisable by virtue of such a consensus.
However, as Professor Blackshield has pointed out,[34] the received
notion of constitutional conventions sits ill with what was done in
1966 and in any case does not include the idea of a power to bring
about changes at a stroke.

Either way, the rule has now changed and nobody regrets it.
The previous position led to over-subtle distinguishing of unsatisfactory cases and the Practice Statement has brought England into
line with all other common-law jurisdictions where it is accepted
that final appellate courts are not bound by their own decisions.
The practical significance of the change is considered in Chapter
IV. Given widespread agreement as to its desirability, its initial
constitutionality may not matter very much. The only practical
consequence of acceptance of the first of the two views canvassed
in the last paragraph would be this. By postulating an abiding

[31] See the discussion of Kelsen's theory of revolutions in Ch. VII.

[32] (1979) AC 264, 336, cited *infra* p. 114–15.

[33] *Knuller (Publishing, Printing and Promotions) Ltd.* v. *Director of Public
Prosecutions* (1973) AC 435, 485.

[34] Anthony Blackshield, ' "Practical reason" and "Conventional wisdom"; the
House of Lords and Precedent', in Goldstein (ed.), *Precedent in Law*, ch. 5.

power in the House of Lords to alter rules of precedent as an internal feature of those very rules, it leaves open the possibility that the House could, constitutionally, at any time abrogate or alter the Practice Statement by a new.practice statement announcing new rules governing the binding status of its own and perhaps other courts' decisions.

3. THE COURT OF APPEAL (CIVIL DIVISION)

Young v. *Bristol Aeroplane Co.*,[35] decided before the amalgamation of the Court of Appeal and the Court of Criminal Appeal in 1966, lays down the general rule that the Court of Appeal (Civil Division) is bound by its past decisions and those of older courts of co-ordinate jurisdiction such as the Exchequer Chamber. At different times between the creation of the Court of Appeal in 1875 and the delivery of the judgment in *Young*'s case in 1944, it had been suggested that the Court was not absolutely bound to follow its past decisions and, in *Wynne-Finch* v. *Chaytor*,[36] it declined to follow one such case, but the view which found favour in *Young* v. *Bristol Aeroplane Co.* was undoubtedly borne out by the majority of statements on the subject; and it had found favour with the House of Lords on several occasions.

Another point which emerges from the judgment in *Young*'s case is that decisions of a full Court of Appeal have no greater authority than decisions of any one of its divisions. The Court usually sits in several divisions consisting of three Lords Justices of Appeal, but, when difficult points are raised, the judge presiding over one division occasionally adjourns the case for argument before a full Court consisting of five judges. A similar practice prevailed in the Court of Criminal Appeal, and in *R.* v. *Taylor*,[37] an important decision of that Court considered in the next chapter, it was held, by way of contrast with *Young*'s case, that in certain circumstances a full Court of Criminal Appeal would be justified in refusing to follow the previous decision of an ordinary sitting of the Court.

Young v. *Bristol Aeroplane Co.* eventually reached the House of Lords. Most of the speeches were devoted to the question of substantive law raised by the appeal, but Lord Simon agreed with the conclusion on the question of precedent at which the Master of

[35] [1944] KB 718.   [36] [1903] 2 Ch. 475.   [37] [1950] 2 KB 368.

the Rolls arrived in the Court of Appeal. Lord Simon paraphrased that conclusion in the following words:

If the Court of Appeal, when sitting in one of its divisions, has in a previous case pronounced on a point of law which necessarily covers a later case coming before the Court, the previous decision must be followed (unless, of course, it was given *per incuriam*, or unless the House of Lords has in the meantime decided that the law is otherwise), and . . . the application of the rules governing the use of precedents binds the full Court of Appeal no less than a, division of the Court as usually constituted.[38]

The House of Lords' Statement of 1966 concludes with the words 'This announcement is not intended to affect the use of precedent elsewhere than in this House.' Nevertheless, during the following decade the head of the Court of Appeal, Lord Denning MR, mounted what Lord Diplock was to call a 'one-man crusade'[39] asserting that the Court of Appeal had a freedom to depart from its own past decisions modelled on that assumed for itself by the House of Lords.[40] Despite opposing views expressed both in the Court of Appeal[41] and in the House of Lords,[42] the crusade appeared to have achieved some degree of success by the decision of the Court of Appeal in *Davis* v. *Johnson*.[43] A majority of three out of a court of five took the view that the *stare decisis* rule laid down in Young's case could at least be modified by the recognition of new exceptions. However, when *Davis* v. *Johnson* was taken to the House of Lords, all the members of the House reasserted the doctrine that the Court of Appeal was bound to follow its own decisions save only for the exceptions stated in *Young* v. *Bristol Aeroplane Co.*

---

[38] [1946] AC at 169.   [39] *Davis* v. *Johnson* (1979) AC 264, 325.
[40] *Gallie* v. *Lee* (1969) 2 Ch. 17, 37. *Hanning* v. *Maitland (no. 2)* (1970) 1 QB 580, 587. *Barrington* v. *Lee* (1972) 1 QB 326, 338. *Farrell* v. *Alexander* (1976) QB 345, 359. *Dyson Holdings Ltd.* v. *Fox* (1976) QB 503, 509. Lord Denning expressed a temporary recantation in *Miliangos* v. *George Frank (Textiles) Ltd.* (1975) QB 487, 503, a case in which he was convinced of the merits of the impugned decision of the Court of Appeal.
[41] Russell LJ in *Gallie* v. *Lee* (1969) 2 Ch. 17, 41–2. Stephenson LJ in *Barrington* v. *Lee* (1972) 1 QB 326, 345–6. Scarman LJ in *Tiverton Estates Ltd.* v. *Wearwell Ltd.* (1975) Ch. 146, 172–3; and in *Farrell* v. *Alexander* (1976) QB 345, 371.
[42] Lord Hailsham LC in *Cassell and Co. Ltd.* v. *Broome* (1972) AC 1027, 1055. Lord Simon in *Miliangos* v. *George Frank (Textiles) Ltd.* (1976) AC 443, 470. Lords Dilhorne, Simon, and Russell in *Farrell* v. *Alexander* (1977) AC 59, 81, 92, 104–5.
[43] (1979) AC 264.

Davis v. *Johnson* constitutes a landmark in the modern evolution of *stare decisis* in England. It puts beyond doubt, for the time being, that the House of Lords 1966 Practice Statement is to have no spin-off effects on intermediate courts exercising an appellate jurisdiction. It is necessary, however, to separate two issues which were not kept distinct in the judgments. First, is it desirable in the interests of the administration of justice for the rule in *Young*'s case to be relaxed? Secondly, if it is, where does the authority reside to effect such a change?

As to the first question, the principal factor which swayed the House of Lords and the minority in the Court of Appeal against any change was, of course, certainty. It was said that if the Court of Appeal could depart from a decision of its own which it thought ' mistaken the result would be 'confusion' and 'doubt'. But for whom? To some extent, the argument may have been question-begging. So long as the Court of Appeal is not accorded any such power, a judge at first instance may be in a dilemma if faced with two explicitly conflicting decisions of the Court of Appeal. Should he follow the first, or the second which appears to depart from it? But were the Court of Appeal conceded the same power to depart from its decisions as the Practice Statement confers on the House of Lords, no such dilemma would arise. It has been uniformly assumed that where, in exercise of the Practice-Statement power, the House of Lords departs from one of its decisions, all inferior courts must follow the overruling decision of the House, not the one impugned. Similarly, as Lord Denning argued,[44] courts below the Court of Appeal would be obliged to follow the later of two decisions of the Court, where the second explicitly departed from the first. Pending a further reconsideration by the Court of Appeal, or an appeal to the House of Lords, the law would be settled.

However, the main burden of the uncertainty argument, as it emerged in *Davis* v. *Johnson*, was this. The Court of Appeal consisted of seventeen judges,[45] but sat, usually, in divisions of only three. Differences of opinion as to questions of law among so large a number are inevitable. (In the instant case, there had, in the two cases which the Court of Appeal was purporting not to follow,[46] been six Lords Justices taking one view of a question of statutory construction, whilst four members of the present court

---

[44] (1979) AC 264, 279.   [45] There were 26 in 1989.
[46] *B.* v. *B.* (1978) Fam. 26. *Cantliff* v. *Jenkins* (1978) Fam. 47.

took another.)[47] Hence, if there were power to depart from earlier decisions, there would be 'uncertainty' in the sense of inability to predict whether the Court would change the law it had laid down. More importantly there would be 'uncertainty' in the sense of lack of finality: if one division (in case B) were able to decide that another division (in case A) had been mistaken, who was to say that a third division (in case C), exercising again the power to depart from earlier decisions, might not conclude that the decision in B was erroneous and that in A correct? Such reconsiderations would entail a novel kind of uncertainty.

Comparison with the House of Lords was not spelled out. The clear inference was, however, that, given its smaller size and its invariable practice of sitting in panels of at least five members, rapid voltes-face are much less likely than in the case of the Court of Appeal. They are not unknown. With or without formally exercising its Practice-Statement power, the House of Lords sometimes announces that the law is the contrary of that which it itself has recently declared. In *D. and F. Estates Ltd.* v. *Church Commissioners for England*,[48] the House radically restricted the classes of economic loss recoverable in negligence, and purported to distinguish two of its earlier decisions[49] which had been supposed to establish a wider range of recovery. Such *bouleverse-ments* may result from a change in membership of the five Law Lords allocated to the hearing of the cases, as when a fundamental rule of the law of trusts thought to be established by the decision in *Re Gulbenkian's Settlement Trusts*[50] was abrogated two years later in *McPhail* v. *Doulton*.[51] Or they may be the consequence of a change of mind by one or more of their Lordships. This occurred in the field of immigration law when, in *R.* v. *Secretary of State for the Home Department, ex parte Khawaja*,[52] the House overruled a decision arrived at three years earlier,[53] with Lord Fraser disavowing the opinion with which he had previously concurred. Two recent developments in criminal law provide even more striking examples. The interpretation of the Criminal Attempts

---

[47] Of the members of the Court of Appeal who dissented, Goff LJ would have decided with the majority if the matter had been *res integra*.

[48] (1989) AC 177.

[49] *Anns* v. *Merton London Borough Council* (1978) AC 728. *Junior Books Ltd.* v. *Veitchi Co. Ltd.* (1983) 1 AC 520.

[50] (1970) AC 508.   [51] (1971) AC 424.   [52] (1984) AC 74.

[53] *R.* v. *Secretary of State for the Home Department, ex parte Zamir* (1980) AC 1148.

Act 1981 put forward in *Anderton* v. *Ryan*[54] was, by exercise of the 1966 power, rejected within a year in *R.* v. *Shivpuri*,[55] with Lord Bridge frankly announcing that his views had changed. Guidelines appropriate for directions to juries as to the mental element in murder were laid down by the House of Lords in *R.* v. *Moloney*,[56] and repudiated (again within the year) in *R.* v. *Hancock*,[57] with Lord Keith assenting to both judgments.

There has as yet been no instance of lack of finality, no case in which the House of Lords, having once exercised its power to overrule one of its past decisions, has thereafter exercised it to revive the decision. Whether that special kind of uncertainty-provoking occurrence would follow from the Court of Appeal being granted power to depart from its own decisions can be only a matter of speculative guesswork.

For the majority of the Court of Appeal in *Davis* v. *Johnson*, there were three factors which together outweighed any derogation from certainty. First, if the Court of Appeal deferred to an earlier decision of its own which it was convinced was mistaken, and the losing party did not take the matter on appeal to the House of Lords, there could be no assurance that the House would have another opportunity of considering the point and, in consequence, error in the law would be perpetuated. Secondly, the party adversely affected by the Court following a wrong decision would be faced with the alternative of suffering an injustice, or undertaking the trouble, hazard and (above all) expense of an appeal to the House of Lords. If he was neither rich nor so poor as to qualify for legal aid, he might be forced to suffer injustice through lack of means.

These familiar arguments of detriment to the law and injustice to individuals have convinced most academic commentators that the *Young* v. *Bristol Aeroplane* rule should be abandoned. The third argument was tailored more specifically to the facts of *Davis* v. *Johnson*: even if an appeal was taken to the House of Lords and was successful, the delay itself might cause injustice. The issue in the case was whether section 1 of the Domestic Violence and Matrimonial Proceedings Act 1976 conferred jurisdiction on a county court judge to order a man who was joint tenant of a council flat to vacate the premises on the application of the female co-habitee who had suffered horrifying violence at his hands. If the

[54] (1985) AC 560.   [55] (1987) AC 1.   [56] (1985) AC 905.
[57] (1986) AC 455.

Court of Appeal followed its earlier decisions and held that there was no jurisdiction, the woman and her child would be forced to remain in a battered wives' refuge pending an appeal. Although in most cases ultimate success in the House of Lords would give justice, that was not so in urgent issues of this sort.

These arguments did not persuade the House of Lords or the minority in the Court of Appeal. As to delay, Lord Diplock pointed out that, had the Court of Appeal simply dismissed the appeal on the authority of the cases by which it was bound instead of hearing lengthy argument, the appeal to the House of Lords could have come on much sooner.[58] As to the danger that, in such a case, no appeal might be taken (with consequent injustice and perpetuation of error), that was a risk which was clearly outweighed by the disadvantages, in terms of certainty, should the present *stare decisis* rule be abandoned. Cumming-Bruce LJ and Lord Salmon suggested that it could be reduced were Parliament to empower costs of an appeal to be paid from public funds, in a case where it was certified that an appeal to the House of Lords was necessary because the Court of Appeal was bound by a decision of which it disapproved.[59]

It was suggested above that the question of the desirability of altering the rule laid down in *Young* v. *Bristol Aeroplane Co. Ltd.* should be distinguished from the question of where the authority resides to bring about such a change. It is unlikely that the whole issue will never resurface, so that this question remains of vital concern. In *Davis* v. *Johnson*, Lord Denning MR, Sir George Baker P, and Shaw LJ concluded that the present five-man Court of Appeal could modify the rule.[60] Goff LJ and Lord Salmon took the view that this could be done only by a unanimous decision of all the members of the Court of Appeal.[61] Cumming-Bruce LJ stated: 'I consider that the constitutional functions of their Lordships sitting in their judicial capacity include the function of declaring with authority the extent to which the Court of Appeal is bound by its previous decisions.'[62] Lord Diplock,[63] with whom

---

[58] (1979) AC 264, 326. He also pointed out that the 'delay' argument could be used to justify any high court or county court judge in refusing to follow a decision of the Court of Appeal which he thought was wrong.

[59] (1979) AC 264, 311, 344.

[60] (1979) AC 264, 278–83, 288–90, 307–9.

[61] (1979) AC 264, 295, 344.   [62] (1979) AC 264, 311.

[63] (1979) AC 264, 323–8.

Viscount Dilhorne and Lord Scarman agreed,[64] assumed that the *stare decisis* rule, being a rule of law, could be authoritatively declared only by the House of Lords. Lord Diplock said:

> So far as civil matters are concerned the law on this question is now clear and unassailable. . . . In my opinion, this House should take this occasion to re-affirm expressly, unequivocally and unanimously that the rule laid down in the *Bristol Aeroplane* case as to stare decisis is still binding on the Court of Appeal.[65]

The view that *stare decisis* rules can be laid down as rules of law does, indeed, appear to have been the assumption on which the Court of Appeal acted in *Young* v. *Bristol Aeroplane Co. Ltd.* There is, however, an alternative view, stemming from Lord Brett MR in *The Vera Cruz*, to the effect that where courts follow their own decisions they do so 'on the ground of judicial comity' and are not constrained by any common-law or statutory rule.[66] This 'practice' view of the nature of *stare decisis* rules was revived, following the 1966 Practice Statement. In *Boys* v. *Chaplin* Diplock LJ himself had expressed the opinion that the Court of Appeal's fetters were 'self-imposed';[67] and in *Gallie* v. *Lee* Salmon LJ had suggested that the Court of Appeal could make a pronouncement modelled on the House of Lords Practice Statement, although this would require the concurrence of the whole court.[68]

In *Davis* v. *Johnson*, Lord Denning argued that the 1966 Practice Statement

> shows conclusively that a rule as to precedent (which any court lays down for itself) is not a rule of law at all. It is simply a practice or usage laid down by the court itself for its own guidance: and, as such, the successors of that court can alter that practice or amend it or set up other guide lines, just as the House of Lords did in 1966.[69]

Viscount Dilhorne countered this argument with an assertion of law:

> In 1966 consideration was given to whether as a matter of law this House was bound to follow its earlier decision. After considerable discussion it

---

[64] (1979) AC 264, 336, 349. Lord Kilbrandon agreed with all his colleagues, without distinguishing between the views of Lord Diplock and Lord Salmon (ibid. 340).   [65] (1979) AC 264, 323, 328.
[66] (1880) 9 PD 96, 97, cited p. 87 *supra*.   [67] (1968) 2 QB 1, 35.
[68] (1969) 2 Ch. 17, 49. When, in *Davis* v. *Johnson*, Lord Denning cited the views of Salmon LJ, he omitted the reference to the necessity of the whole court concurring in a changed practice: (1979) AC 264, 280.
[69] (1979) AC 264, 281.

was agreed that it was not, and so the announcement . . . was made. . . . This House is not bound by any previous decision to which it may have come. It can, if it wishes, reach a contrary conclusion. This is so whether or not the House is sitting to discharge its judicial functions. That is the ground on which those who were parties to the announcement made in 1966 felt, I think, that it could be made without impropriety. It is not a ground available to any other court and the fact that this House made that announcement is consequently no argument which can properly be advanced to support the view that the Court of Appeal or any other court has similar liberty of action.[70]

In the House of Lords only Lord Salmon dissented from the view that rules of precedent are straightforwardly rules of law. Reiterating the opinion he had expressed in *Gallie* v. *Lee*, he said, having approved the rule that the Court of Appeal is bound by its own decisions:

In the nature of things, however, the point could never come before your Lordships' House for decision or form part of its *ratio decidendi*. This House decides every case that comes before it according to the law. If, as in the instant case, the Court of Appeal decides an appeal contrary to one of its previous decisions, this House, much as it may deprecate the Court of Appeal's departure from the rule, will nevertheless dismiss the appeal if it comes to the conclusion that the decision appealed against was right in law.[71]

The appeal was accordingly dismissed, since the House unanimously sided with the majority of the Court of Appeal on the merits.

It has already been suggested that the *obiter–ratio* distinction is irrelevant in the context of judicial statements about the rules of precedent.[72] If this is correct, it follows that neither the House of Lords nor any other court can lay down rules of precedent in the way they lay down rules of common law. But it does not follow that precedent rules binding on the Court of Appeal are exclusively within the purview of that court, that they are, so to speak, 'none of the Lord's business'. Lord Salmon asserted that approving comments in the House of Lords on the *Bristol Aeroplane* case had 'greatly strengthened the rule'.[73] Institutional practices, as well as *rationes decidendi*, may give rise to rules; and

[70] (1979) AC 264, 336.
[71] (1979) AC 264, 344. The same point was made in the Court of Appeal both by Lord Denning MR (ibid. 280), and by Cumming-Bruce LJ (ibid. 311), and again by Lord Salmon in *Attorney-General of St Christopher Nevis and Anguilla* v. *Reynolds* (1980) AC 637, 659.
[72] p. 105 *supra*.
[73] (1979) AC 264, 344.

if such rules are perceived as binding by judges it may not be thought inappropriate, although it may add little, to term them 'rules of law'.[74] English judges recognize that views expressed in the House of Lords about precedent rules binding lower courts are, at the very least, an important part of the evidence for the existence of such practices.

The differences of view expressed in *Davis* v. *Johnson* leave one important detail of our practice rules unsettled. Do they empower the Court of Appeal, acting by unanimous pronouncement, to change the rule in *Young* v. *Bristol Aeroplane Co. Ltd.* (as Lord Salmon, Goff LJ, and the majority of the Court of Appeal supposed)? Or do they vest this authority exclusively in the House of Lords (as explicitly stated by Cumming-Bruce LJ, and as assumed by the majority of the House of Lords)? Or was Lord Simon of Glaisdale right when, in *Miliangos* v. *George Frank (Textiles) Ltd.*, he claimed that the rule, although originating in judge-made law, is now so firmly established that only legislation can alter it?[75] Wherever the power to change the rule may reside, it has not yet been exercised. The members of the Court of Appeal have uniformly assumed, since *Davis* v. *Johnson*, that the Court is absolutely bound by its own decisions, subject to the exceptions considered in the next chapter.

4. THE COURT OF APPEAL (CRIMINAL DIVISION)

When considering the extent to which *stare decisis* is or ought to be the rule in criminal cases, it is necessary to remember that there may be good grounds for a less rigid application of that doctrine in appellate courts than in courts which are exclusively or primarily concerned with civil litigation. The Court of Criminal Appeal, since 1907 the successor of the Court for Crown Cases Reserved, was amalgamated with the Court of Appeal in 1966; but the Court of Appeal is now divided into two divisions, Civil and Criminal, whereas it was only concerned with civil cases before 1966. One of the arguments in favour of a strict doctrine of precedent is that it protects vested rights. If, as a result of certain transactions, A, B, and C have been held to have acquired proprietary rights in

---

[74] See Brownsword and Hayes, *NILQ* 29 (1978), 296; Kidd, *ALJ* 52 (1978), 274; Rickett, *MLR* 43 (1980), 136; Carty, *LS* 1 (1981), 68; Aldridge, *MLR* 47 (1984), 187.
[75] (1976) AC 443, 470.

consequence of case 1 decided by the Court of Appeal (Civil Division), however weak the arguments leading to that conclusion may have been, any English court would be most loath to hold that similar transactions did not confer similar rights on D, for many other people may have received legal advice based on case 1 before entering into the transactions in question. The criminal law does not confer rights on the citizen. Very occasionally a man may decide to act in a particular way because he is advised that the conduct is not criminal, but, generally speaking, the argument that a strict doctrine of precedent is necessary in order to protect vested rights has less application to criminal than to civil law. There is, however, another argument which suggests the opposite conclusion. If ever there was a branch of the law in which uniformity was of the utmost importance, it is the criminal law. If A was acquitted by the Court of Criminal Appeal in case 1, most people would consider it a travesty of justice if B's conviction on substantially identical facts were upheld in case 2.

Up to this point the arguments for and against different rules of precedent in civil and criminal law respectively are about evenly balanced, but a variation in the facts of the last example shows why there may be a case for some relaxation in criminal law. Suppose B were acquitted in case 2 on facts similar to those on which A had been convicted in case 1, it is at least doubtful whether the average man's sense of justice would be as gravely offended as it would be in the case of a conviction on facts substantially similar to those on which an acquittal had previously been recorded. Whether this is so or not, we shall see when we consider *R. v. Taylor*[76] in the next chapter that relaxations in the doctrine of *stare decisis* have been allowed in the interest of the liberty of the subject in criminal cases in circumstances in which they have not been countenanced in civil law. *Stare decisis* is, nevertheless, still the general rule in the Court of Appeal (Criminal Division) just as it was in the earlier Court for Crown Cases Reserved.

It is possible to point to statements of judges in the Court for Crown Cases Reserved in which a previous decision of that Court has been treated as binding, although the judges making the statements considered that the earlier cases had been wrongly decided.[77] But it is also possible to point to cases in which a later decision of the Court was said to have overruled an earlier one.[78]

[76] [1950] 2 KB 368.   [77] *R. v. Glyde* (1868) 1 CCR 139 at 144.
[78] *R. v. Ring* (1892) 61 LJMC 116.

In short, the doctrine of *stare decisis* was not rigidly enforced, and it is pertinent to observe that the case in which an earlier decision was said to have been overruled was one in which the accused's conviction was affirmed although an acquittal had previously been held to be the correct verdict on substantially similar facts.

The Court of Criminal Appeal was bound by decisions of the Court for Crown Cases Reserved,[79] but, as that Court did not always follow its own decisions, this does not involve a particularly rigorous approach to *stare decisis*. There are, in fact, several well-known cases in which the Court of Criminal Appeal did not follow one of its own earlier decisions,[80] but there may well be more cases in which the judgment of the Court of Criminal Appeal asserted that the Court was bound to follow one of its previous decisions.

In *R. v. Gould* Diplock LJ expressed the view that, in its criminal jurisdiction, the Court of Appeal was not bound by decisions either of its own or of the Court of Criminal Appeal, even if they fell outside the exceptions laid down in *Young* v. *Bristol Aeroplane Co. Ltd.* His opinion was not limited to cases where a departure from an earlier decision would favour the accused.[81] In practice, the Court of Appeal (Criminal Division) has assumed that it is bound by earlier decisions,[82] and Diplock LJ's statement to the contrary has been disapproved. In *R. v. Spencer*, May LJ, giving the judgment of the Court, said:[83]

> As a matter of principle we respectfully find it difficult to see why there should in general be any difference in the application of the principle of *stare decisis* between the civil and criminal divisions of this Court, save that we must remember that in the latter we may be dealing with the liberty of the subject and if a departure from authority is necessary in the interests of justice to an appellant, then this Court should not shrink from so acting. In our opinion the dictum from *Reg. v. Gould* . . . must be read in this sense and subject to this the principles laid down in *Young* v. *Bristol Aeroplane Co. Ltd.* . . . . should apply.

[79] *R. v. Cade* [1914] 2 KB 209 at 211–12.
[80] *R. v. Power* [1919] 1 KB 572; *R. v. Norman* [1924] 2 KB 315.
[81] (1968) 2 QB 65, 68–9.
[82] See e.g. *R. v. Sheppard* (1980) 70 Cr. App. Rep. 210. *R. v. Pigg* (1982) 74 Cr. App. Rep. 352. *R. v. Terry* (1983) RTR 321. Speaking in the House of Lords, Lord Diplock has himself indicated that the Criminal Division of the Court of Appeal should generally consider itself bound, *Director of Public Prosecutions* v. *Merriman* (1973) AC 584, 605; *R. v. Chard* (1984) AC 279, 290. See Rosemary Pattenden, 'The Power of the Criminal Division of the Court of Appeal to Depart From its Own Precedents', *Cr. LR* (1984), 592.
[83] (1985) QB 771, 779.

There was an unsettled question of the relations between the Court of Appeal and the Court of Criminal Appeal. In *Hardie & Lane* v. *Chilton*[84] the Court of Appeal questioned and declined to give effect to the decision of the Court of Criminal Appeal in *R.* v. *Denyer*.[85] According to Denyer's case, the Secretary of the Motor Trade Association was guilty of blackmail when he wrote to a member demanding a sum of money as an alternative to placing his name on the Association's stop list. The logical consequence of this view of the law is that any sum paid to the Association by a member in consideration of not having his name put on a stop list can be recovered in a civil action, but the Court of Appeal held that such an action failed in *Hardie & Lane* v. *Chilton*. Shortly after that case was decided Lord Hewart stated in the Court of Criminal Appeal that, for the purposes of the administration of the criminal law, unless and until the decision in *R.* v. *Denyer* was reversed by the only competent tribunal, it was binding upon and would be enforced by the Court of Criminal Appeal.[86] *R.* v. *Denyer* was subsequently disapproved by the House of Lords in a civil case, but nothing was said about the relationship of the Court of Appeal and the Court of Criminal Appeal so far as the rule of *stare decisis* is concerned. Although the occasions for it are rare, a similar problem could arise concerning the relationship between the decisions of the two divisions of the Court of Appeal.

5. DIVISIONAL COURTS

Until recently it was thought that divisional courts regarded themselves as bound by previous decisions of divisional courts in the same way that the Court of Appeal is bound by its own decisions. That was regarded as having been established for civil cases by *Huddersfield Police Authority* v. *Watson*[87] and for criminal cases by *Younghusband* v. *Luftig*.[88] However, in *R.* v. *Manchester Coroner, ex parte Tal*,[89] a divisional court of the Queen's Bench Division (Robert Goff LJ, McCullough, and Mann Jj) departed from an earlier divisional court decision on the question of the court's jurisdiction to exercise judicial review over the conduct of an inquest. Goff LJ, delivering the judgment of the Court, equated the position of a divisional court, when exercising

---

[84] [1928] 2 KB 306.
[86] 20 Cr. App. Rep. 186.
[88] (1949) 2 KB 354.
[85] [1926] 2 KB 258.
[87] (1947) KB 842.
[89] (1985) QB 67.

such supervisory jurisdiction, with that of a single judge of the High Court. He pointed out that there is no single court known as 'the Divisional Court' in the way that the Court of Appeal is one court.

> . . . every divisional court is simply a court, constituted of not less than two judges, held for the transaction of business of the High Court, which is (by rules of court or statute) required to be heard by a divisional court. Among the business of the High Court required to be so heard are to be found applications for judicial review in any criminal cause or matter, or in other causes or matters where the Court so directs: . . . when a divisional court is constituted to hear an application for judicial review, it is not sitting in an appellate capacity. It is not hearing an appeal from another court, nor is it considering a question of law on a case stated by another court, as in the case of appeals by way of cases stated by Magistrates' courts. It is exercising what is often called a supervisory jurisdiction. . . .
> If a judge of the High Court sits exercising the supervisory jurisdiction of the High Court then it is, in our judgment, plain that the relevant principle of *stare decisis* is the principle applicable in the case of a judge at first instance exercising the jurisdiction of the High Court, viz., that he will follow a decision of another judge of first instance, unless he is convinced that that judgment is wrong, as a matter of judicial comity; but he is not bound to follow the decision of a judge of equal jurisdiction . . .
> In our judgment, the same principle is applicable when the supervisory jurisdiction of the High Court is exercised, not by a single judge, but by a divisional court, where two or three judges are exercising precisely the same jurisdiction as the single judge. We have no doubt that it will be only in rare cases that a divisional court will think it fit to depart from a decision of another divisional court exercising this jurisdiction. Furthermore, we find it difficult to imagine that a single judge exercising this jurisdiction would ever depart from a decision of a divisional court.[90]

This judgment has been applied in subsequent cases. Divisional courts have held that when exercising supervisory jurisdiction, whether in criminal or civil cases, divisional courts are not bound by prior decisions,[91] whereas when they are hearing appeals by way of case stated they are.[92] In none of these cases was reference

---

[90] (1985) QB 67, 80–1. Similarly, the erstwhile National Industrial Relations Court did not regard itself as bound by decisions either of its own or of divisional courts, *Chapman* v. *Goonvean* (1973) 1 WLR 678.

[91] *Hornigold* v. *Chief Constable of Lancashire* (1985) Cr. LR 792. *R.* v. *Chief Metropolitan Magistrate, ex parte Secretary of State for the Home Department* (1989) 1 All ER 151.

[92] *Rogers* v. *Essex County Council* (1985) 2 All ER 39.

made to the decision in *Davis* v. *Johnson*.[93] It emerged from our discussion of that case earlier in this chapter that, at the very least, something like a unanimous change in practice by the members of the Court of Appeal was required before the rule in *Young* v. *Bristol Aeroplane Co. Ltd.* could be altered. Nothing of the sort has occurred in regard to the judges of the High Court who sit in divisional courts concerning the principle of *stare decisis* to be applied in the case of divisional courts. In *Tal*'s case, Robert Goff LJ suggested that the basis of the judgment in *Huddersfield Police Authority* v. *Watson*, which had been modelled on *Young*'s case, had been undermined by the House of Lords 1966 Practice Statement.[94] Yet that Statement insisted in terms that it was not to affect the doctrine of precedent otherwise than in the House of Lords.

Nevertheless, the rather technical distinction between supervisory and strictly appellate jurisdiction established in *Tal* has gained general acceptance. It evinces an approach similar to that underlying the construction of the *per incuriam* exception in the Court of Appeal, namely, that the obligation to follow precedents is not felt to be so strong in the context of procedural and jurisdictional law as it is in matters of substantive law.[95]

A divisional court exercising criminal jurisdiction was bound by decisions of the Court of Criminal Appeal[96] although no appeal lay to that Court from its decisions. A divisional court exercising criminal jurisdiction was also and presumably still is bound by decisions of the Court of Appeal[97] on the comparatively rare occasions when similar issues come before the two courts as may be the case, for instance, when a claim for compensation in tort for breach of statutory duty under the Factory Acts comes before the Court of Appeal, and the prosecution for the infringement of the same provision reaches the divisional court by way of case stated from magistrates. A divisional court exercising civil jurisdiction is bound by decisions of the Court of Appeal.[98]

---

[93] (1979) AC 264.   [94] (1985) QB 67, 79.   [95] p. 150 *infra*.
[96] *Ruse* v. *Read* [1949] 1 KB 370 at 384.
[97] *Carr* v. *Mercantile Products Ltd.* [1949] 2 KB 601.
[98] *Read* v. *Joannon* (1890) 25 QBD 300 at 302–3.

6. THE HIGH COURT

The position of a judge of the High Court with regard to *stare decisis* was summed up in the following passage in Lord Goddard's judgment in *Huddersfield Police Authority* v. *Watson*.[99]

I think the modern practice and the modern view of the subject is that a judge of first instance, unless he is convinced that the judgment is wrong, would follow it as a matter of judicial comity. He certainly is not bound to follow the decision of a judge of equal jurisdiction. He is only bound to follow the decisions of the Court of Appeal, the House of Lords and divisional courts.

The obligation of a first instance judge to apply the law as laid down by the Court of Appeal has been held to extend to Court of Appeal decisions given *ex parte*, even though, argument having been heard on one side only, the decision would not bind a lower court determining the same issue *inter partes*.[100] There is, however, an exception in the rare case where the judge is exercising his discretion to strike out a claim as disclosing no cause of action and he is faced with a ruling by the Court of Appeal which is presently the subject of an appeal to the House of Lords. In such a case he is not bound to apply the law as stated by the Court of Appeal if he considers there are good grounds for supposing that its decision will be reversed by the House.[101] So far as decisions of divisional courts are concerned, we saw in the last section that Robert Goff LJ in *Tal*'s case equated the position of a divisional court exercising supervisory jurisdiction with that of a single judge of the High Court. He nevertheless stated that: 'We find it difficult to imagine that a single judge exercising this jurisdiction would ever depart from a decision of a divisional court.'

In *Colchester Estates (Cardiff)* v. *Carlton Industries plc*,[102] Nourse J indicated that, where one judge had expressly declined to follow the decision of another, a judge in a third case is bound by something stronger than comity to abide by the second decision:

. . . It is desirable that the law, at whatever level it is declared, should generally be certain. If a decision of this court, reached after full consideration of an earlier one which went the other way, is normally to

---

[99] [1947] KB 842 at 848.   [100] *The Alexandros P* (1986) 1 All ER 278.
[101] *Derby and Co. Ltd.* v. *Weldon (no. 3)* (1989) 3 All ER 118.
[102] (1986) Ch. 80, 85.

be open to review on a third occasion when the same point arises for decision at the same level, there will be no end of it. Why not in a fourth, fifth or sixth case as well? . . . There must come a time when a point is normally to be treated as having been settled at first instance. I think that that should be when the earlier decision has been fully considered, but not followed, in a later one. . . . I would make an exception only in the case, which must be rare, where the third judge is convinced that the second was wrong in not following the first. An obvious example is where some binding or persuasive authority has not been cited in either of the first two cases. If that is the rule then, unless the party interested seriously intends to submit that it falls within the exception, the hearing at first instance in the third case will, so far as the point in question is concerned, be a formality, with any argument upon it reserved to the Court of Appeal.

7. THE CROWN COURT

The Crown Court was instituted by the Courts Act 1971 as a superior court of record, as the successor to assizes and quarter sessions. The judges who sit in it include High Court judges, circuit judges, recorders, and part-time deputies. It has been convincingly argued by Professor Ashworth that the precedential effect of Crown Court decisions does not vary with the status of the presiding judge and that, in view of the absence of any systematic reporting of such decisions, a Crown Court ruling does not bind another Crown Court or a magistrates' court. For both, it is merely of persuasive authority.[103]

8. INFERIOR COURTS

It is almost invariably assumed that Magistrates and County Court judges are bound by the decisions of the High Court and all appellate tribunals. The only challenge to this assumption comes from a suggestion that it is just arguable that a County Court judge is not bound by the decision of a judge of the High Court because appeals from the County Court go to the Court of Appeal.[104] The argument assumes that, strictly speaking, a lower court is only obliged to follow the decisions of a court above it when its own decisions can be taken to that court. But the argument has only been advanced most tentatively.

---

[103] Andrew Ashworth, 'The Binding Effect of Crown Court Decisions', *Cr. LR* (1980) 502.
[104] Salmond's *Jurisprudence* (12th edn.), 163 n. (w).

Statutory tribunals are bound by decisions on points of law rendered by the High Court in the exercise of its general supervisory jurisdiction. Where, however, statute confers a limited appellate jurisdiction over administrative decisions on judges of the High Court, and a subsequent statute removes that jurisdiction and confers it instead upon a tribunal, the tribunal is not bound by High Court decisions arising from the exercise of that limited jurisdiction.[105] Where an appeal tribunal lays down guidelines for the exercise of statutory discretion, they are not binding legal rules, failure to follow which would amount to an error of law.[106] Decisions of social security tribunals and commissioners are reported when they involve questions of legal principle; but the strict doctrine of *stare decisis* has not been adopted, so that a tribunal is not absolutely bound to follow the decision of a previous tribunal.[107]

---

[105] *Chief Supplementary Benefit Officer* v. *Leary* (1985) 1 All ER 1061.
[106] *Wells* v. *Derwent Plastics Ltd.* (1978) ICR 424. *Anandarajah* v. *Lord Chancellor's Department* (1984) IRLR 131.
[107] Ogus and Barendt, *Social Security Law* (3rd edn.), 583.

IV

EXCEPTIONS TO *STARE DECISIS*

1. INTRODUCTORY

One of the defects of the preliminary statement of the English rules of precedent in Chapter I is that, the House of Lords apart, it does not refer to the existence of important exceptions to the rule of *stare decisis*. The purpose of the present chapter is to analyse those exceptions. They have varied from period to period for *stare decisis* has been the general rule in England for a considerable time. It will be convenient to begin by saying something of Sir William Holdsworth's views on this subject before discussing the notion of overruling a case which is essential to a proper understanding of the rest of the chapter.

Holdsworth's views

Holdsworth's general thesis was that the English doctrine of precedent

hits the golden mean between too much flexibility and too much rigidity; for it gives to the legal system the rigidity which it must have if it is to possess a definite body of principles, and the flexibility which it must have if it is to adapt itself to the needs of a changing society.[1]

This cheerful and prima facie surprising conclusion was reached after a consideration of four reservations to which the English doctrine has been subject. The first of these reservations is that cases do not make the law, for they are only evidence of what the law is. We have already seen that this was a most important reservation in the days when the declaratory theory held sway,[2] but it has lost most of its significance since the middle of the nineteenth century.

---

[1] *History of English Law*, xii. 160. The views discussed in the text were originally stated in *LQR*, 50 (1934), 180 ff. The article is reproduced in *History of English Law*, xii. 146–62.

[2] p. 27 supra.

The second reservation is that before and during the eighteenth century a judge could always say that a case of which he disapproved had been badly reported. No doubt this is true, but it is a luxury which can seldom be available to a judge of the twentieth century. Some of the old private law reporting left a great deal to be desired, but, since the foundation of the Incorporated Society of Law Reporting in 1866 the standard of law reporting in England has been very high indeed.

The third reservation is that it used to be a recognized fact that some of the decisions of different courts of co-ordinate jurisdiction conflicted, as was pointed out by Pollock CB in *Taylor* v. *Burgess.*[3] But, under the modern organization of the courts, the opportunities for what may be termed deliberate conflicts of the kind contemplated by Holdsworth and Pollock CB are greatly reduced. The type of conflict which they contemplated is that which would have occurred when the Court of Common Pleas, having considered the *ratio decidendi* of a case decided by the Queen's Bench, declined to follow it. Conflicts of this nature are only possible under the modern system so far as High Court judges are concerned, and as between the two divisions of the Court of Appeal. There may, of course, be any number of conflicts of a different nature, the inadvertent conflicts that arise either from the fact that a previous case was not cited to the court deciding a further one, or else from the failure of the later court to indicate a sound distinction between the case before it and a previous case which the later decision appears to contradict. Infringements of the rule of *stare decisis* only rank as exceptions to it when they are the result of deliberate action on the part of the courts.

The last reservation mentioned by Holdsworth is that a precedent conflicting with 'general rules and principles' is not binding. Some judges of the eighteenth century undoubtedly attached more importance to principles than to precedents, although it is to be observed that they laid most stress on principle when there was no precedent.[4] Even today it is by no means infrequent for a judge to cite broad general principles without relying on authority, or to refer to principles which cannot be

---

[3] (1859) 5 H. and N. 1, 5.
[4] Lord Mansfield's famous statement that 'The law would be a strange science if it rested solely upon cases' was made to counter the argument that there was no precedent covering the point before him (*Jones* v. *Randall* (1774) Loft. at 385).

upset by judicial decision. In *Johnston* v. *O'Neill*,[5] for example, Lord Dunedin said:

> To hold that one of the fundamental doctrines of real property can be called in question because it has not been in terms laid down by judgment of the House of Lords is, in my opinion, to invest the judicial proceedings of this House with an authority to which they are not entitled. The A B C of the law is generally not questioned before your Lordships, just because it is the A B C.

These principles spring from most heterogeneous sources. They may, as the foregoing remarks suggest, be the outcome of *rationes decidendi* which are not binding on the court considering a case. They may be the result of judicial *dicta*, statements in textbooks, maxims of Roman and Canon law, or the commonly accepted principles of morality. Whatever their origin, the fact that they are constantly recognized by the courts has an important bearing on the problem of the definition of law briefly discussed in Chapter VII. The concentration on precedent which is inevitable in a book on the subject must not be thought to indicate any insensibility to the importance of these principles on the part of the author, but as has already been said, it is scarcely conceivable that a contemporary English judge would refuse to follow an authority which was binding on him according to the accepted rules of precedent because it was contrary to principle.

Holdsworth's view was that the reservations mentioned in the last two paragraphs enabled the judges, within fairly wide limits, to apply to old precedents a process of selection and rejection which brings the law into conformity with modern conditions. For the reasons stated in connection with each of them, it seems that none of the reservations are recognized at the present time.

Overruling from above

One respect in which there has been a marked change in the practice of the courts of recent years relates to the question of overruling a previous case. This is primarily the prerogative of the court above that which decided the previous case. Overruling may be express or implied. There is nothing particularly novel about the conception of an express overruling. If in case B a court with power to overrule case A says that case A is overruled, the *ratio decidendi* of case A ceases altogether to have any authority so far

[5] [1911] AC 552 at 592.

as the doctrine of precedent is concerned. It is completely 'wiped off the slate', to borrow Lord Dunedin's metaphor. The judgment may be of considerable historical value, and it may even contain *dicta* which can be cited in the course of the argument in subsequent cases, but a case which has been overruled cannot be cited as authority for the proposition of law which constituted its *ratio decidendi*.

The notion of an implied overruling seems to be mainly dependent on recent practice. In 1922 the Court of Appeal followed a previous decision of its own which was admittedly inconsistent with the reasoning of a later decision of the House of Lords because the decision of the Court of Appeal had not been expressly overruled;[6] but the possibility of an implied overruling was a pivotal point in the judgment of the Court of Appeal in *Young* v. *Bristol Aeroplane Co.* in 1944, and, in holding in 1949 that a decision of the Court for Crown Cases Reserved had been impliedly overruled by the House of Lords, Lord Goddard CJ said:

When you find that a case, whether it has been expressly overruled or not by the final court of appeal, has been dealt with, or the facts, which were the governing facts in a particular case, have been regarded in a totally different manner by the final court of appeal, so that it is obvious in the opinion of a final court of appeal that the cause was wrongly decided, then whether they have in terms said they overrule the case or not, I think this court ought to treat the case as overruled.[7]

Intricate problems may arise when the House of Lords, although it is not necessary to its decision, indicates that a case has been wrongly decided by the Court of Appeal. In *Cedar Holdings Ltd.* v. *Green*,[8] a husband who was joint owner with his wife of the matrimonial home purported to charge it to the plaintiffs, the wife's signature being forged by another lady. The question was whether this created a charge over the husband's beneficial interest. It required rulings on two points. First, did section 63 (1) of the Law of Property Act 1925, which provides that a conveyance is effectual to pass any interest which the conveying party has in the property, entail that the husband had charged his beneficial interest? Secondly, was an agreement to create a charge necessarily itself sufficient to give rise to a charge, on the basis that

---

[6] *Consett Industrial & Provident Society* v. *Consett Iron Co. Ltd.* [1922] 2 Ch. 135.
[7] *R.* v. *Porter* [1949] 2 KB 128 at 132.   [8] (1981) Ch. 129.

it was specifically enforceable? The Court of Appeal, in holding that the plaintiffs had no charge, answered 'no' to both questions. In *Williams and Glyn's Bank Ltd.* v. *Boland*,[9] one of the issues before the House of Lords was whether a beneficial co-owner of land had an interest subsisting in reference to the land so as to constitute an overriding interest within section 70 of the Land Registration Act 1925. It was held that she did, and that *Cedar Holdings* had been 'wrongly decided'.

The issues in the cases concerned the construction of different statutory provisions. The rulings in them could stand together without logical contradiction and might both be sustainable in terms of policy. However, a step in the reasoning to the first ruling in *Cedar Holdings* was that the beneficial interest of the husband, since it subsisted behind a trust for sale, was not an interest in the land. That doctrinal step was negated in *Boland*. In the result, it has been held that the contrary of the first ruling in *Cedar Holdings* now represents the law,[10] but that the binding force of the second ruling has not been affected by *Boland*.[11]

Undermining

The usual effect of overruling a case is to make the law in some sense the contrary of the proposition for which the *ratio decidendi* was formerly authoritative. This is because the judgment of the court which decides the later case by which an earlier decision is overruled will indicate, expressly or by implication, that the court order in the earlier case was made in favour of the wrong party. The consequence of the *ratio decidendi* of the later case will be that, on facts similar to those of the earlier one, judgment should in future be entered for the party who was unsuccessful in the earlier case. In certain circumstances, however, though an earlier decision may cease to be authoritative in consequence of a later one, it does not follow that a court bound by the later case will be bound to give judgment for the plaintiff because the defendant succeeded in the earlier case, or for the defendant because the plaintiff was previously successful. A High Court judge of first instance confronted with a decision of the Court of Appeal which has not been expressly overruled by a later House of Lords' case may cease to be bound by it because the House of Lords

---

[9] (1981) AC 487.
[10] *First National Securities Ltd.* v. *Hegerty* (1985) QB 850.
[11] *Thames Guaranty Ltd.* v. *Campbell* (1985) QB 210.

considered that the Court of Appeal misinterpreted the authorities on which the impugned decision was based. The judge is then not obliged to follow the Court of Appeal, but he is not bound to dissent from their conclusion. The previous decision is undermined rather than directly overruled.

Whatever the right description of the process may be, it is strikingly exemplified by *Cackett* v. *Cackett*.[12] This case came before Hodson J as a judge of first instance. The impugned decision of the Court of Appeal was *Cowen* v. *Cowen*,[13] in which it had been held that both the use of a sheath by the husband and his practice of *coitus interruptus* amounted to wilful refusal to consummate a marriage. The Court of Appeal reached these conclusions on the strength of a passage from the judgment of Dr Lushington in *D.* v. *A.*[14] In *Baxter* v. *Baxter*[15] the House of Lords held that the use of a sheath did not prevent a marriage from being consummated. The only speech was delivered by Lord Jowitt. Although he left open the question whether the practice of *coitus interruptus* amounted to wilful refusal to consummate, he demonstrated that the Court of Appeal had misunderstood the passage in Dr Lushington's judgment on which they relied in *Cowen* v. *Cowen* because that passage was concerned with non-consummation due to malformation. Accordingly, in *Cackett* v. *Cackett* Hodson J, as he then was, felt that he was entitled to disregard *Cowen* v. *Cowen*. He said:

> The whole foundation of the conclusion arrived at by the Court of Appeal having been destroyed, in my judgment the conclusion is also destroyed and for that reason in the full sense of the word left open.[16]

A line similar to that taken by Hodson J has been taken in subsequent cases.[17] It does not, as is sometimes suggested, involve the logical fallacy of asserting that the falsification of the premises necessarily falsifies the conclusion. Hodson J was not saying that, because the premiss was false, the conclusion must also be false. He was simply saying that the conclusion did not follow from the statement of Dr Lushington and, furthermore, that this view had the approval of the House of Lords. Hodson J in fact held that the practice of *coitus interruptus* does not prevent a marriage from being consummated, but he could have held otherwise if he had

---

[12] [1950] P. 253. [13] [1946] P. 36. [14] (1884) 1 Rob. Ecc. 279.
[15] [1948] AC 274. [16] [1950] P. at 258.
[17] See note by Professor J. L. Montrose in 17 *MLR* 462.

been able to point to a reasonable distinction between the case before him and *Baxter* v. *Baxter*. When he said that the question was open in the full sense of the word, he meant that Lord Jowitt had not merely intended to say that the question was open at the level of the House of Lords.

Can a court 'overrule' its own decision?

We have said that the prerogative of overruling a case is primarily that of a court above the court by which the case was decided. Plainly a court bound by its own decisions cannot impliedly overrule one of its own previous decisions. If a divisional court or the Court of Appeal were first to decide case A, and then to decide case B in a manner inconsistent with it, a conflict of authorities would have been produced and a later court would have to choose whether to follow case A or case B.

The question remains whether a court can be said to 'overrule' one of its previous decisions when it acts on a recognized exception to *stare decisis*. So far as the Court of Appeal is concerned, Lord Denning has indicated that acting on one of the exceptions stated in *Young* v. *Bristol Aeroplane Co. Ltd.* (considered below) entails 'overruling'.[18] Other judges have spoken more obscurely of the disapproved and disapproving decisions being 'in conflict'.[19] The House of Lords' Practice Statement of 1966 speaks of an intention to 'depart' from a previous decision when it seems right to do so. The term 'overrule' has, however, been used in this context in the House of Lords sufficiently frequently since 1966 to justify the assertion that the distinction between overruling and departing from what would normally be a binding decision is a distinction without a difference.

Overruling a ratio *and overruling a decision*

When we speak of a court 'overruling' a case, we are usually referring to the overruling of the *ratio decidendi*. This generally means that the decision is also overruled so that, were substantially the same facts to recur, the result would be different; but it is

---

[18] *Tiverton Estates Ltd.* v. *Wearwell Ltd.* (1975) Ch. 146, 161. *Industrial Properties (Barton Hill) Ltd.* v. *Associated Electrical Industries Ltd.* (1977) QB 580, 599.

[19] *Daulia Ltd.* v. *Millbank Nominees Ltd.* (1978) Ch. 231, 249–50 Buckley LJ, 251 Orr LJ.

sometimes necessary to recognize that the decision has survived the *ratio decidendi*. Thus Lord Reid once said:

> Before holding that the decision should be overruled I must be convinced not only that the *ratio decidendi* is wrong, but that there is no other possible ground on which the decision can be supported.[20]

The distinction may be illustrated by two post-1966 decisions of the House of Lords, *Conway* v. *Rimmer*[21] and *British Railways Board* v. *Herrington*.[22]

In *Conway* v. *Rimmer*, the House of Lords can be said to have overruled the *ratio decidendi* of *Duncan* v. *Cammell Laird Ltd.*[23] according to which the court could not go behind a properly formulated ministerial claim that evidence should be excluded as a matter of state interest. Yet the decision in *Duncan's* case that a claim to exclude evidence in wartime concerning the structure of our submarines should be upheld was recognized as correct by all the Law Lords who heard the appeal in *Conway* v. *Rimmer*. The reports reflect the semantic difficulties by saying, in the case of the Law Reports, that *dicta* in *Duncan* v. *Cammell Laird Ltd.* were overruled, and, in the case of the All England Reports, that *Duncan* v. *Cammell Laird Ltd.* was not followed.

In *British Railways Board* v. *Herrington*, the House of Lords laid down new law concerning the liability of the occupiers of land for injuries suffered by child trespassers thereon, a subject which had previously been complicated by the issue whether the children might not be treated as licencees. In *Robert Addie and Sons (Colleries) Ltd.* v. *Dumbreck*,[24] the House of Lords had held that no licence could be implied, and there is little doubt that if the facts were to recur after *Herrington's* case the decision would be different. In these circumstances it is difficult to disagree with the following remarks of Lord Reid:

> I dislike usurping the functions of Parliament, but it appears to me that we are confronted with a choice of following *Addie's* case or putting the clock back and drastically modifying the *Addie* rules. It is suggested that such a modification can be achieved by developing the law as laid down in *Addie's* case without actually overruling any part of the decision. I do not

---

[20] *Ross-Smith* v. *Ross-Smith* [1963] AC at 294, p. 10 *supra*.
[21] [1968] AC 910.   [22] [1972] AC 879.
[23] [1942] AC 624. There is room for argument which would be out of place here about which parts of Lord Simon's speech constituted the *ratio decidendi*.
[24] [1929] AC 358.

think that that is possible. It can properly be said that one is developing the law laid down in a leading case so long, but only so long, as the development does not require us to say that the original case is wrongly decided; but it appears to me that any acceptable development of *Addie's* case must mean that *Addie's* case, if it arose today, would be decided the other way.[25]

The point is, however, a purely semantic one at the level of the House of Lords. To quote from Lord Diplock's speech:

My Lords, this House has since 1966 abandoned its former practice of adhering rigidly to the *ratio decidendi* of its previous decisions. There is no longer any need to discuss whether to discard the fiction of a so-called licence to enter granted by the occupier of land to the person who suffers personal injury on it should be characterised as overruling *Addie's* case or as doing no more than explaining its reasoning in terms which are in harmony with the general development of legal concepts since 1929 as to the source of one man's duty to take steps for the safety of another.[26]

Conflicting decisions

Another marked tendency of recent years, so far as the rules of precedent are concerned, is an increasing willingness on the part of the courts to recognize that past decisions of the same court may conflict with each other. The orthodox judicial approach was stated as follows by Lord Selborne when speaking at the hearing of an appeal in the House of Lords in 1882:

It is your Lordships' duty to maintain as far as you possibly can the authority of all former decisions of this House, and although later decisions may have interpreted and limited the application of earlier, they ought not (without some unavoidable necessity) to be treated as conflicting.[27]

The operative words are of course those in brackets. No doubt Lord Selborne's approach to the problem of conflicting decisions is as representative of current practice today as it was when he spoke, but it is probably true to say that the existence of some unavoidable necessity is more readily recognized nowadays than was formerly the case, although Lord Selborne may well have recognized that it would prove impossible to reconcile all the old

---

[25] [1972] AC at 897–8.   [26] At 934.
[27] *Caledonian Railway* v. *Walker's Trustee* (1882) 7 App. Cas. 259 at 275.

decisions of the House of Lords. Many of these were the result of voting by lay peers, many of them are not properly reported, and, in some cases, no reasons were given for the conclusion.

The problem of what constitutes a conflict of decisions is not altogether free from difficulty. To take an example from cases which are frequently cited in discussions of *Young* v. *Bristol Aeroplane Co.*,[28] in *Morrison* v. *Sheffield Corporation*[29] the Corporation had statutory authority to plant trees in the highway. It did so and protected the trees with dangerous spikes pointing outwards. During the First World War the plaintiff sustained injuries through walking into the spikes in the blackout, and the Court of Appeal held that he was entitled to judgment. The *ratio decidendi* was stated in wide terms, but *Morrison*'s case was not cited in *Woodhouse* v. *Levy*[30] where, during the Second World War, a passenger in a taxi was injured when it ran into an unlighted bollard and the Court of Appeal held that he was not entitled to recover against the local authority. *Morrison*'s case was cited in *Lyus* v. *Stepney Borough Council*[31] where a pedestrian who collided with an unlighted and unwhitened dustbin also failed to recover damages in the Court of Appeal. That Court then held that there was no conflict between *Woodhouse* v. *Levy* and *Morrison* v. *Sheffield Corporation* because the latter case depended on its special facts. In the later case of *Fisher* v. *Ruislip-Northwood Urban District Council*[32] the Court of Appeal decided that *Lyus* v. *Stepney Borough Council* and *Woodhouse* v. *Levy* conflicted with *Morrison*'s case and chose to follow this latter decision. The principle underlying *Morrison*'s case was that a local authority owes a duty to users of the highway to light or, in the case of a blackout, adopt other means of warning against obstruction. This covered *Woodhouse* v. *Levy* and *Lyus* v. *Stepney Borough Council*, although there were facts such as the possibility of rendering the spikes with which *Morrison*'s case was concerned harmless, by means of which that decision could have been distinguished.

If there is an increasing tendency to recognize the possibility that previous decisions of the same court may conflict, it is a tendency which is to be applauded. The court's attention is frequently not drawn to all the relevant authorities, some cases are

---

[28] [1944] KB 718.   [29] [1917] 2 KB 866.   [30] [1940] 2 KB 561.
[31] [1941] KB 134.   [32] [1945] KB 584.

not particularly well argued, and unreserved judgments are often delivered. It is useless to deplore these occurrences because they will continue as long as barristers, judges, and litigants remain human, but there is something to be said for an occasional stocktaking, and especially if it enables a court to overrule one or more of its past decisions which conflict with others.

It is now proposed to consider the exceptions to *stare decisis* which have been recognized in the different courts. The present situation is far from certain, and this renders it necessary to conclude the chapter with another general paragraph.

2. THE HOUSE OF LORDS[33]

Since the announcement of the 1966 Practice Statement (set out on p. 104), the House of Lords has unequivocally exercised its new power to overrule its past decisions on eight occasions. In *The Johanna Oldendorff*,[34] it overruled its decision in *The Aello*,[35] on the question of when a vessel sailing under a port charter-party could be said to have 'arrived' so as to make the charterers liable for lay-time. In *Miliangos* v. *George Frank (Textiles) Ltd.*,[36] it overruled its decision in the *Havana Railways* case,[37] and laid down that judgments could be obtained in English courts in currencies other than sterling. In *Dick* v. *Burgh of Falkirk*,[38] it overruled its decision in *Darling* v. *Gray and Sons*,[39] on the question whether, according to the common law of Scotland, a dependant may bring an action where the victim of an accident had instituted proceedings before his death. In *Vestey* v. *Inland Revenue Commissioners*,[40] it overruled its decision in *Congreve* v. *Inland Revenue Commissioners*[41] on the interpretation of a section of the Income Tax Act 1952 governing the payment of tax by

---

[33] For further discussion, see J. W. Harris, 'Towards Principles of Overruling— When Should a Final Court of Appeal Second Guess?', *OJLS* 10 (1990), 135.

[34] E. L. *Oldendorff and Co. GmbH* v. *Tradax Export SA, The Johanna Oldendorff* (1974) AC 479.

[35] *Societad Financiera de Bienes Raices SA* v. *Agrimpex Hungarian Trading Co. for Agricultural Products, The Aello* (1961) AC 135.

[36] (1976) AC 443.

[37] *Re United Railways of Havana and Regla Warehouses Ltd.* (1961) AC 1007.

[38] (1976) SLTR 21.

[39] (1892) RHL 31 (reported more fully s.n. *Wood* v. *Gray and Sons* (1892) AC 576).

[40] (1980) AC 1148.   [41] (1948) 1 All ER 948.

beneficiaries under discretionary trusts. In *Khawaja*,[42] it overruled its decision in *Zamir*[43] on the interpretation of a section of the Immigration Act 1971. In *R.* v. *Shivpuri*,[44] it overruled its decision in *Anderton* v. *Ryan*[45] on the interpretation of the Criminal Attempts Act 1981. In *R.* v. *Howe*,[46] it overruled its decision in *Lynch* v. *Director of Public Prosecutions for Northern Ireland*,[47] on the highly contentious question of whether duress can be pleaded as a defence to murder. Finally, in *Murphy* v. *Brentwood District Council*,[48] it overruled its decision in *Anns* v. *Merton London Borough Council*,[49] and laid down that liability in the tort of negligence does not extend to diminution in the value of premises caused by a local authority's failure to ensure compliance with building by-laws.

In many other cases it has declined to exercise the Practice-Statement power.[50] It has been frequently asserted that the mere conclusion that, in the view of the present panel, an earlier decision was 'wrong' is not of itself sufficient warrant for departing from it.[51] The Practice Statement indicates that the House will treat its former decisions as 'normally binding'. It speaks of

[42] *R.* v. *Secretary of State for the Home Department, ex parte Khawaja* (1984) AC 74.
[43] *R.* v. *Secretary of State for the Home Department, ex parte Zamir* (1980) AC 930.
[44] (1987) AC 1.   [45] (1985) AC 560.   [46] (1987) AC 417.
[47] (1975) AC 653.   [48] (1990) 2 All ER 908.   [49] (1978) AC 728.
[50] See e.g. *Conway* v. *Rimmer* (1968) AC 910. *F.A. and A.B. Ltd.* v. *Lupton* (1972) AC 634. *British Railways Board* v. *Herrington* (1972) AC 877. *R.* v. *National Insurance Commissioner, ex parte Hudson* (1972) AC 944. *Cassell and Co. Ltd.* v. *Broome* (1972) AC 1027. *R.* v. *Sakhuja* (1973) AC 152. *Knuller (Publishing, Printing and Promotions) Ltd.* v. *Director of Public Prosecutions* (1973) AC 435. *O'Brien* v. *Robinson* (1973) AC 912. *Hyam* v. *Director of Public Prosecutions* (1975) AC 55. *Taylor* v. *Provan* (1975) AC 194. *Fitzleet Estates Ltd.* v. *Cherry* (1977) 3 All ER 996. *R.* v. *Nock* (1978) AC 979. *Hesperides Hotels Ltd.* v. *Muftizade* (1979) AC 508. *Lim Poh Choo* v. *Camden and Islington Health Authority* (1980) AC 174. *Saif Ali* v. *Sydney Mitchell and Co.* (1980) AC 198. *R.* v. *Cunningham* (1982) AC 566. *Pall Wilson and Co. AS* v. *Partenreederei Hannah Blumenthal, The Hannah Blumenthal* (1983) 1 AC 854. *Pirelli General Cable Works Ltd.* v. *Oscar Faber and Partners* (1983) 2 AC 1. *President of India* v. *La Pintada Compania Navigacion SA* (1985) AC 104. *Food Corporation of India* v. *Antclizo Shipping Corporation, The Antclizo* (1988) 2 All ER 513. *Bird* v. *Inland Revenue Commissioners* (1989) AC 300. Commentators are divided as to whether some of these cases, particularly *Herrington*, should be viewed as instances in which, in substance, the power was exercised; see Alan Paterson, *The Law Lords*, ch. 7.
[51] See esp. Lord Reid in *Hudson* (1972) AC at 996, and in *Knuller* (1973) AC at 445; Lord Wilberforce in *Fitzleet* (1977) 3 All ER at 999; Lord Edmund-Davies, ibid. at 1001–3; Lord Brandon in *Blumenthal* (1983) 1 AC at 911–13.

adherence to precedent being too rigid when it 'may lead to injustice in a particular case and also unduly restrict the proper development of the law'. Even when these conditions are met, however, it has been said that the House should not necessarily depart from an earlier decision; it should bear in mind 'the possibility that legislation may be the better course'.[52] There have been comparatively few attempts in the speeches of their Lordships to explain why it is sometimes appropriate to use the power and sometimes not. Most of the reasoning in the cases is directed towards the substantive question of law under review. It was at one time thought that issues of statutory construction, as such, are peculiarly exempt from the Practice-Statement power. This view was rejected in *Vestey*.[53] In *Vestey*, *Khawaja*, and *Shivpuri* cases turning on statutory interpretation were overruled. The Practice Statement suggests caution where contracts, settlements, and fiscal arrangements are concerned and emphasizes the 'especial need for certainty as to the criminal law'. Nevertheless, both *The Johanna Oldendorff* and the *Miliangos* case involved overrulings which might have affected the basis upon which commercial contracts had been entered into, Vestey overruled a tax case and in *Shivpuri* and *Howe* decisions on issues of criminal law were overturned with the effect, in both cases, that the scope of the criminal law was extended. The power has been applied to decisions whose antiquity varied from eighty years (*Dick*) to one year (*Shivpuri*). Indeed, the age of the decision from which the House is asked to depart has been described as a 'neutral factor'.[54]

In one case Lord Roskill expressed the view that no useful purpose would be served by reviewing other decisions where the House had or had not departed from earlier decisions, since cases where the 1966 practice direction should or should not apply 'cannot be categorised'.[55] If it is to be inferred from this that there are not and cannot be any principles governing the exercise of the power, it follows that the many occasions on which counsel have been invited to address their Lordships specifically on this question have been a waste of time. One can say no more than that 'wrongness' is sometimes enough and sometimes not, everything

---

[52] *Khawaja* (1984) AC 74, 106 Lord Scarman.
[53] (1980) AC 1148, 1186 Viscount Dilhorne, 1196 Lord Edmund-Davies.
[54] *Khawaja* (1984) AC 74, 125 Lord Bridge.
[55] *The Hannah Blumenthal* (1983) 1 AC 854, 922.

turning on an *ad hoc* subjective assessment as to just how wrong
the impugned decision is felt to be.

It is suggested, nevertheless, that the cases do reveal certain
underlying considerations as of the highest importance in determining whether the Practice-Statement power should or should
not be exercised.

In the first place, the House must be convinced that it is in a
position to substitute for the former decision some ruling which
will bring about a net improvement in the law. Much may turn on
whether the impugned ruling can be dealt with in isolation, as was
held to be true of the prohibition on dependants' actions in *Dick*'s
case, or on whether a reversal might produce a proposition which
does not cohere with the rest of the law. In *President of India* v. *La
Pintada*,[56] for example, the House of Lords refused an overruling
which would have abrogated the common-law rule that denies to
creditors who receive late payment interest on their debts by
way of general damages. They considered the rule unjust but
concluded that its reversal would not fit with the legislative code
on the subject which was already in place. It should be noted that,
although wrongness is not enough, neither is it necessary for the
power to be exercised. If the House is satisfied that the present law
would be improved were it to substitute some new ruling for the
impugned decision, it may exercise the power without necessarily
concluding that the earlier decision was wrong at the time when it
was given. That was the view expressed in the *Miliangos* case by
most members of the House as regards *Havana Railways*.[57] It was
sufficient to determine that present-day fluctuations in exchange
rates rendered it unjust to force creditors to accept the sterling
equivalent of the contract debt.

Secondly, the House will usually decline to overrule a decision
where the contentions now put forward for or against the issue of
law in question are the same as those advanced in the earlier
case—that is, where nothing of significance was overlooked in the
earlier case and there has been no material change in circumstances
since it was decided. In *Vestey*, the House concluded that the
Congreve reasoning had overlooked the constitutional impropriety
of the revenue being able to pick which trust beneficiaries should
pay tax; and in *Shivpuri*, it was found that *Anderton* v. *Ryan* had

[56] (1985) AC 104.
[57] (1976) AC 443, 460 Lord Wilberforce; 498 Lord Edmund-Davies, 501 Lord
Fraser.

not taken account of a Law Commission report as evidence of the mischief at which the Criminal Attempts Act was directed. In *Murphy*, it was said that their Lordships in *Anns* had failed to explore the logical and practical implication of their ruling. *Miliangos* emphasized the inflation which those who decided *Havana Railways* could not have foreseen. Where there are no new reasons of this sort, an overruling affronts finality. Even if the present panel thinks the earlier decision may have been mistaken, there are said to be two 'tenable' views, and therefore, should the House in case B depart from case A, there is nothing to prevent a third panel, in case C, restoring case A.[58] This constraint is most obviously present where everything turns on an impression as to the meaning of statutory words, but it can apply also to questions of common law. The following passage from Lord Wilberforce's speech in *Fitzleet Estates Ltd.* v. *Cherry*[59] (a case turning on the interpretation of a taxing statute) was cited and applied in *The Hannah Blumenthal*[60] (a case involving a question of commercial common law). Lord Wilberforce was explaining why it would not be right to reverse an earlier decision reached in 1966:[61]

My Lords, two points are clear. (1) Although counsel for the tax payer developed his argument with freshness and vigour, it became clear that there was no contention advanced or which could be advanced by him which was not before this House in 1966 . . . (2) There has been no change of circumstances such as some of their Lordships found to exist in *Miliangos* v. *George Frank (Textiles) Ltd.*, such as would call for or justify a review of the 1966 decision . . .

There is therefore nothing left to the taxpayer but to contend, as it frankly does, that the 1966 decision is wrong. This contention means, when interpreted, that three or more of your Lordships ought to take the view which appealed then to the minority.

My Lords, in my firm opinion, the 1966 Practice Statement was never intended to allow and should not be considered to allow such a course. Nothing could be more undesirable, in fact, than to permit litigants, after a decision has been given by this House with all appearance of finality, to return to this House in the hope that a differently constituted committee might be persuaded to take the view which its predecessors rejected. True that the earlier decision was by a majority: I say nothing as to its

[58] *R.* v. *National Insurance Commissioner, ex parte Hudson* (1972) AC 944, 996–7 Lord Pearson; *The Hannah Blumenthal* (1983) 1 AC 854, 922–3 Lord Roskill.
[59] (1977) 3 All ER 996, 999.
[60] (1983) 1 AC 854, 911–12 Lord Brandon.
[61] *Chancery Lane Safe Deposit and Offices Co. Ltd* v. *Inland Revenue Commissioners* (1966) AC 85.

correctness or as to the validity of the reasoning by which it was supported. That there were two eminently possible views is shown by the support for each by at any rate two members of the House. But doubtful issues have to be resolved and the law knows no better way of resolving them than by the considered majority opinion of the ultimate tribunal. It requires much more than doubts as to the correctness of such opinion to justify departing from it.

This constraint is not, however, absolute. The House may entertain more than mere 'doubts as to the correctness' of its earlier ruling. It may conclude that the earlier case erred as to some matter of fundamental principle. In *Howe*, nothing was contended in argument which had not been urged in *Lynch* and there had been no significant change in circumstances in the intervening twelve years. Their Lordships found, however, that, in admitting duress as a defence to murder, the *Lynch* majority had improperly sought to alter a fundamental principle of the historic common law, something which only the legislature should do. What divided the House in *Knuller (Publishing, Printing and Promotions) Ltd.* v. *Director of Public Prosecutions*[62] was, at bottom, the question whether the decision in *Shaw* v. *Director of Public Prosecutions*,[63] which they were invited to overrule, had or had not involved such a fundamental principle. Lord Diplock, who favoured overruling, opined that it was part of the *ratio decidendi* of *Shaw* that there was a residual power in the judiciary to create new offences so that a basic issue of constitutional liberty was at stake.[64] All the other members of the House decisively rejected this view. They held that *Shaw* was authority merely for the proposition that the common law recognized the existence of one particular offence, a conspiracy to corrupt public morals.[65] That conclusion might have been mistaken—Lord Reid was quite sure that it was—but all the arguments for or against it advanced in *Knuller* had been considered in *Shaw*, and the evidence from convictions subsequently made for the offence showed that the rule had not produced consequences not foreseen in *Shaw*. The majority concluded, therefore, that the issue was not one of such fundamental importance as to escape the finality constraint.

[62] (1973) AC 435.   [63] (1962) AC 229.
[64] (1973) AC 435, 469, 479.
[65] (1973) AC 435, 457–8 Lord Reid, 464–5 Lord Morris, 490 Lord Simon, 496 Lord Kilbrandon.

A third consideration mentioned in the cases concerns justified reliance. If it can be plausibly surmised that citizens may have arranged their affairs on the basis of some impugned ruling, that would be a reason for not departing from it.[66] In practice, the significance of this constraint has been small. In *Dick* v. *Burgh of Falkirk*, it was said that 'no prospective liability could possibly have been calculated, either by an employer or his underwriters, according to the contingency of whether a hypothetical injured man would or would not have instituted proceedings before his death'.[67] In *Murphy*, it was said that, although the *Anns* decision had stood for some thirteen years, it was not of a type that was to a significant extent taken into account by citizens or local authorities in ordering their affairs.[68] Similarly, in *Shivpuri* it was stressed that no one could have acted on the faith of *Anderton* v. *Ryan*[69]—no one would do what he thought was criminal, relying on the rule that, should he be mistaken, he would not be convicted of an attempt.

Fourthly, importance has been attached in some cases to the fact that legislation appears to have been enacted on the assumption that the impugned decision represents the law. The assumption seems to be that if Parliament has deliberately chosen to leave the law as it stands, it would breach comity between the judiciary and the legislature were the House of Lords to alter it. This was accepted as a further reason for not exercising the Practice-Statement power in the *La Pintada* case,[70] and it constituted a subsidiary consideration in the reasoning of some of their Lordships in *Knuller*.[71] In *British Railways Board* v. *Herrington*,[72] the principal reason for the House equivocating on the question of whether it should depart from its decision in *Addie*'s case[73] was the consideration that the rule that occupiers owe no duty of care to trespassers appeared to have been accepted by Parliament when it

---

[66] See e.g. *O'Brien* v. *Robinson* (1973) AC 912, 925 Lord Morris, 930 Lord Diplock.

[67] (1976) SLTR 21, 28–9 Lord Kilbrandon.

[68] (1990) 2 All ER 908, 923, Lord Keith.

[69] (1987) AC 1, 23 Lord Bridge.   [70] (1985) AC 104, 130.

[71] (1973) AC 435, 465, 466 Lord Morris; 489 Lord Simon; 496 Lord Kilbandon. The argument was rejected by Lord Reid (ibid. 455–6), and by Lord Diplock (ibid. 480–1). Some reliance was placed upon it in *O'Brien* v. *Robinson* (1973) AC 912, 930 Lord Diplock; *Taylor* v. *Provan* (1975) AC 194, 220–1 Lord Simon; *Hesperides Hotels Ltd.* v. *Muftizade* (1979) AC 508, 545 Lord Fraser.

[72] (1972) AC 877, 897 Lord Reid, 904 Lord Morris, 921 Lord Wilberforce.

[73] *Addie (Robert) and Sons (Collieries) Ltd.* v. *Dumbreck* (1929) AC 358.

enacted the Occupiers Liability Act 1957. This comity argument is inherently problematic. By hypothesis, Parliament has not expressly re-enacted the rule in question, so that everything turns on inferences about what it must have silently assumed. The inference will be most plausible where, as in *La Pintada*, Parliament has enacted legislation giving effect to some proposals of a law reform body but has omitted to enact a proposal which would have reversed the earlier decision of the House. It is noteworthy than in *Vestey* it was never even suggested that the passing of finance acts subsequent to *Congreve* constituted any ground for declining to overrule that decision.

Finally, there is some support for the view that the House should not overrule an earlier decision, even if thought to be mistaken, where the issue is moot—that is where, on the facts of the instant case, it would make no difference to the outcome whether the impugned ruling were part of the law or not. In *The Antclizo*, this was the sole ground for declining to exercise the Practice-Statement power. Lord Goff said:

> Your Lordships' House has repeatedly stressed that they will not embark on an inquiry into an issue which is only of academic interest: . . . A fortiori they should not do so where the inquiry involves a review of a previous decision of your Lordships' House, because it cannot be right to hold, *obiter*, that such a previous decision was wrong.[74]

Antclizo was a civil case. This putative constraint was ignored in the context of the criminal law in *Shivpuri* and *Howe*. In *Howe*, overruling *Lynch* was not strictly required in order to dismiss the appeals since *Lynch* had ruled that duress could be pleaded by those charged as accessories to murder and in *Howe* the defence had been allowed at trial to those defendants charged with such secondary participation. In *Shivpuri*, all the members of the House concurred in overruling *Anderton* v. *Ryan*, yet at least two of their Lordships took the view that Ryan was distinguishable and that *Shivpuri*'s appeal would have been dismissed even if *Ryan* had not been overruled.[75] It may be that what is referred to in the Practice Statement as 'the especial need for certainty as to the criminal law', which is generally understood as a caution against overruling,

[74] (1988) 2 All ER 513, 516.
[75] (1987) AC 1, 12 Lord Hailsham LC, 23–4 Lord Mackay. The report of *Shivpuri* appearing in the All England Law Reports contains a sentence in which Lord Elwyn-Jones agreed with this view (1986) 2 All ER at 337. This sentence is omitted from the report in Law Reports Appeal Cases (1987) AC at 13.

operates, in this context, the other way. In *Shivpuri* and *Howe*, rather than perpetuate subtle distinctions, the House exercised its overruling power even though, strictly speaking, it did not have to do so in order to dispose of the appeals.

3. THE COURT OF APPEAL (CIVIL DIVISION)

Three exceptions to the rule of *stare decisis* were mentioned by the Court of Appeal in *Young* v. *Bristol Aeroplane Co.*[76] Although they were pronounced in a civil case, they have also been applied in the Criminal Division of the Court of Appeal and in divisional courts.

Writing in 1947 (three years after the decision in *Young*'s case), Dr Goodhart condemned them because they promote uncertainty concerning the exact state of the law at any given moment. His comment was that

an absolute rule concerning precedent authority has at least the virtue of certainty. A semi-absolute precedent has no more virtue than a semi-fresh egg.[77]

It does seem, however, that, if they are properly limited, the beneficent effect of the exceptions in enabling the court to correct its past errors is likely to outweigh the harmful effects of any uncertainty which they may induce.

The exceptions as summarized by Lord Greene MR in the course of his judgment in *Young*'s case are, first, 'The court is entitled and bound to decide which of two conflicting decisions of its own it will follow'; secondly, 'The court is bound to refuse to follow a decision of its own which, though not expressly overruled, cannot, in its opinion, stand with a decision of the House of Lords'; thirdly, 'The court is not bound to follow a decision of its own if it is satisfied that the decision was given *per incuriam*, for example, where a statute or rule having statutory effect which would have affected the decision was not brought to the attention of the earlier court'. Something must now be said about each of these exceptions to *stare decisis*.

---

[76] [1944] KB 718. This paragraph is largely based on 3 articles, 'Precedents in the Court of Appeal', by A. L. Goodhart, 9 *CLJ* 339; '*Young* v. *Bristol Aeroplane Co.*', by R. M. Gooderson, 10 *CLJ* 432; and '*Stare Decisis* in the Court of Appeal', by G. F. Peter Mason, 20 *MLR* 136.

[77] 9 *CLJ* 357.

Conflicting decisions

Dr Goodhart criticizes the first exception on the ground that it makes no provision for finality. He suggests that there should be a fixed rule that, where two decisions of the Court of Appeal conflict, the later should prevail. To this Mr R. M. Gooderson retorts that logically the earlier case should be binding authority because in theory the court in the later case had no jurisdiction to come to a conflicting conclusion. Either rule would be an arbitrary one and in practice the Court has regarded itself as completely free to choose.[78] But the principal answer made by Mr Gooderson to Dr Goodhart's criticism is that finality is achieved as soon as the conflict is resolved. When, in case C, the court finds that the *rationes* propounded by it in cases A and B conflict, the choice of one of these last-mentioned cases involves the overruling of the other. It is submitted that the answer is correct and that the first exception to *stare decisis* mentioned in *Young*'s case is best expressed by saying that if, in any case, the Court of Appeal finds two of its past decisions to be in conflict, it must choose which to follow, and, when it has done so, the decision not followed is overruled.[79]

On occasions a liberal answer has been given to the question what constitutes a conflict. In *Casey* v. *Casey*[80] the Court of Appeal held that the English courts had no jurisdiction to hear a petition for nullity when the marriage was alleged to be voidable, and the only connecting links with England were the facts that the marriage was celebrated in England and the petitioner resided in England. This case was distinguished by the Court of Appeal in *Ramsay Fairfax* v. *Ramsay Fairfax*[81] where it was held that the English courts had jurisdiction to annul a marriage, wherever it was celebrated, and whether it is alleged to be void or voidable, provided both parties were resident in England. In *Ross-Smith* v. *Ross-Smith*,[82] the Court of Appeal treated the two cases as irreconcilable and chose to follow *Ramsay Fairfax* v. *Ramsay Fairfax*. Whatever definition of *ratio decidendi* is adopted, the *rationes decidendi* of *Casey* v. *Casey* and *Ramsay Fairfax* v. *Ramsay Fairfax* can hardly be said to conflict; but there is a conflict

---

[78] See e.g. *R.* v. *Martindale* [1986] 3 All ER 25; *National Westminster Bank plc* v. *Powney* [1990] 2 All ER 416.
[79] This would accord with the view of Lord Denning mentioned at p. 131 *supra*.
[80] [1940] P. 420.   [81] [1956] P. 115.   [82] [1961] P. 39.

of assumptions underlying the decisions. One assumes that there is, and the other that there is not, a distinction, so far as jurisdiction in nullity is concerned, between void and voidable marriages.[83]

If the resolution in case C of a conflict between cases A and B in favour of case B means that case A is overruled, with the result that in case D the Court of Appeal cannot revert to its decision in case A, does the decision in case C that there is no conflict between cases A and B preclude the Court of Appeal from reopening that question in case D? Lord Greene himself gave an affirmative answer to this question in *Hogan* v. *Bentick Collieries*.[84] It could have the consequence, however, that subtle distinctions become encrusted. In practice the Court of Appeal has considered itself free to reopen questions of conflict where in previous decisions it has held cases to be reconcilable.[85]

Inconsistency with a subsequent decision of the House of Lords

When Lord Greene MR delivered the judgment of the Court of Appeal in *Young* v. *Bristol Aeroplane Co.* he probably intended to confine the second exception to cases in which a decision of the Court of Appeal is thought to have been impliedly overruled by a later decision of the House of Lords. This conclusion is supported by *Young*'s case itself, and by *Williams* v. *Glasbrook Bros*.[86] In *Young*'s case the court was invited to refuse to follow its decision in *Perkins* v. *Stevenson & Sons Ltd*.[87] because it was inconsistent with the earlier decision of the House of Lords in *Kinneil Cannel & Coking Coal Co.* v. *Waddell*.[88] Lord Greene replied that

It is a conclusive answer to this submission that *Kinneil*'s case was cited to this court in *Perkin*'s case.[89]

Elsewhere in the judgment Lord Greene speaks of the exception under discussion as

comprising the class of case where this court comes to the conclusion that a previous decision, although not expressly overruled, cannot stand with a *subsequent* decision of the House of Lords.[90]

[83] For a similar liberal approach to 'conflict', see *Tiverton Estates Ltd.* v. *Wearwell Ltd.* [1975] Ch. 146.
[84] 40 BWCC 268, 276.
[85] *Fisher* v. *Ruislip-Northwood UDC* (p. 134 *supra*). *R.* v. *Ghosh* (1982) QB 1053. *Turton* v. *Turton* (1988) Ch. 542.
[86] [1947] 2 All ER 884.   [87] [1940] 1 KB 56.
[88] [1931] AC 575.   [89] [1944] KB at 722.   [90] At 725, italics added.

The word 'subsequent' was omitted in Lord Greene's summary of his conclusions and in the headnote in most of the reports.[91] In *Williams. v. Glasbrook Bros.* it was conceded that the facts of *Wilds* v. *Amalgamated Anthracite Collieries Ltd.*[92] were similar in all material respects to those of the case before the court, but it was argued that *Wilds*'s case, a decision of the Court of Appeal in 1944, was inconsistent with *Jones* v. *Amalgamated Anthracite Collieries Ltd.*,[93] decided by the House of Lords three years earlier. To this Lord Greene retorted in the course of his judgment:

> In my opinion, even assuming it were the fact that this court did misunderstand the decision of the House of Lords in *Jones*'s case, that does not justify us in refusing to follow *Wilds*'s case today. If in *Wilds*'s case this court thought that the House of Lords in *Jones*'s case decided something that it did not, nobody but the House of Lords can put that mistake right. There is all the difference in the world between such a case as that and the matters to which we referred in our judgment in *Young* v. *Bristol Aeroplane Co. Ltd.*, as, for instance, where a subsequent case in the House of Lords is found either expressly or by implication in effect to overrule an earlier decision of the Court of Appeal. No doubt if *Jones*'s case had been subsequent to *Wilds*'s case, it would have been open to counsel for the employers (Glasbrook Bros.) to argue that *Jones*'s case impliedly overruled *Wilds*'s case and we should have had to decide whether he was right or wrong.

On occasions, an even more liberal interpretation has been placed on the notion of implied overruling than on that of conflicting decisions. In *Browning* v. *The War Office*,[94] the question was whether sums payable as of right by way of disability pension should be deducted from the damages due to the plaintiff in respect of negligence for which the defendants were responsible. The Court of Appeal held by a majority that the deductions should be made. It was necessary for the majority to deal with *Payne* v. *The Railway Executive*[95] in which the Court of Appeal had unanimously held that deductions ought not to be made in respect of a pension which was not payable as of right. This latter fact had formed the basis of a *ratio decidendi* concurred in by two members of the court, but there was a second *ratio* in *Payne*'s case, also concurred in by two members of the Court, which was wide

---

[91] It was not omitted from the *Law Journal* report.
[92] [1947] 1 All ER 551.
[93] [1944] 1 All ER 1.   [94] [1963] 1 QB 750.   [95] [1952] 1 KB 56.

enough to cover *Browning*'s case. This was that the injuries inflicted by the defendant were only the *causa sine qua non* of the payment of the pension to Payne and something from which a wrongdoer ought not to benefit, the real cause of the payment being the antecedent fact of Payne's membership of the navy. Diplock LJ disposed of this second *ratio* by holding that it had been overruled by the decision of the House of Lords in *Gourley* v. *British Transport*,[96] the case in which it was held that the defendants were entitled to deduct from the plaintiff's damages for loss of earnings the amount in respect of which he would have been liable for tax had he earned the sum in question. At first sight, the conclusion of Diplock LJ is a surprising one, for *Payne*'s case was not mentioned in *Gourley* v. *British Transport* and *Gourley*'s case was concerned with deductions due from the plaintiff to third parties, not with payments due from third parties to the plaintiff. Nevertheless, Diplock LJ stressed the fact that *Gourley*'s case had proceeded on the assumption that the basis of the law of tort is compensatory and not punitive.[97]

Inconsistency with a prior decision of the House of Lords

As we have seen, Lord Greene himself regarded the second exception to *stare decisis* set out in *Young*'s case as confined to situations in which an earlier decision of the Court of Appeal conflicts with a subsequent decision of the House of Lords.[98] *Dicta* of Lord Buckmaster,[99] Lord Denning,[100] and Lord Simon of Glaisdale[101] support this view. Support for the contrary view, that the exception applies where the Court of Appeal has misinterpreted a previous decision of the House of Lords, is to be found in *dicta* of Lord Wright[102] and Lord Cross.[103] This latter understanding of the exception has been occasionally acted upon by the Court of

[96] [1956] AC 184.
[97] Similarly in *Family Housing Association* v. *Jones* [1990] 1 All ER 385, the Court of Appeal regarded itself as bound, under the second exception in *Young*'s case, to refuse to follow 3 earlier decisions of its own on the ground that they proceeded on a basis which was inconsistent with general statements of principle, made in subsequent House of Lords decisions, about the distinction between tenancies and licences.
[98] pp. 145–6 *supra*.
[99] *English Scottish and Australian Bank* v. *Commissioners of Inland Revenue* (1932) AC 232, 242.
[100] *Miliangos* v. *George Frank (Textiles) Ltd.* (1975) QB 487, 572.
[101] *Miliangos* v. *George Frank (Textiles) Ltd.* (1976) AC 443, 479.
[102] *Noble* v. *Southern Railway Co.* (1940) AC 583, 598.
[103] *Miliangos* v. *George Frank (Textiles) Ltd.* (1976) AC 443, 496.

Appeal,[104] most recently in *Holden and Co.* v. *Crown Prosecution Service*.[105] In that case, it was held that the court's jurisdiction to order a solicitor to pay costs was limited to instances of conduct which involved a serious dereliction on the part of the solicitor of his duty to the court. The Court refused to follow its decision in *Sinclair-Jones* v. *Kay*[106] where it had been ruled that the jurisdiction extended to mere improper acts or omissions. In *Holden* the Court of Appeal concluded that the Court of Appeal in *Sinclair-Jones* had wrongfully distinguished the decision of the House of Lords in *Myers* v. *Elman*[107] when it interpreted that decision as laying down principles applicable only to the court's inherent jurisdiction, whereas the right view was that the House of Lords' decision covered both the court's common-law jurisdiction and its jurisdiction under the Rules of the Supreme Court. It was said that, although ordinarily the second exception in *Young* v. *Bristol Aeroplane Co. Ltd.* applied only to subsequent decisions of the House of Lords, it was the Court's duty to apply the law as it believed it had been laid down by a decision of the House which had been wrongly distinguished in an earlier decision of the Court of Appeal.

As we shall see, the fact that, in the view of the present Court, an earlier Court of Appeal decision has misunderstood a decision of the House of Lords, has been classified in another recent case (*Rickards* v. *Rickards*) as an instance of a decision made *per incuriam*. It thus appears that the tendency to extend the scope of the exceptions laid down in *Young*'s case entails a degree of overlap between them.

Decisions reached per incuriam

We have seen that the example of a decision given *per incuriam* by Lord Greene MR was a case in which a statute or rule having statutory effect is not brought to the attention of the court. Lord Greene had already given judgment in the Court of Appeal in *Lancaster Motor Co. (London) Ltd.* v. *Bremith*[108] in which a previous judgment of the court was ignored because it contravened the terms of a rule of the Supreme Court. Lord Greene characterized that judgment as one 'delivered without argument and delivered without reference to the crucial words of the rule

---

[104] *Lyus* v. *Stepney Borough Council* (1941) KB 134.
[105] (1990) 2 QB 261.   [106] (1988) 2 All ER 611.
[107] (1940) AC 282.   [108] [1941] 2 All ER 11.

and without any citation of authority'. It has since been doubted whether a decision on the interpretation of a statute given without reference to a well-recognized general rule of statutory construction can be said to have been given *per incuriam*.[109] But the most important development under this head has been the clear recognition of the fact that a decision given in ignorance of a case which would have been binding on the court is given *per incuriam*. The following is what must probably be treated as the leading statement of the principle:

> As a general rule the only cases in which decisions should be held to have been given *per incuriam* are those of decisions given in ignorance or forgetfulness of some inconsistent statutory provision or of some authority binding on the court concerned, so that in such cases some feature of the decision or some step in the reasoning on which it is based is found on that account to be demonstrably wrong. This definition is not necessarily exhaustive, but cases not strictly within it which can properly be held to have been decided *per incuriam*, must in our judgment, consistently with the *stare decisis* rule which is an essential part of our law, be of the rarest occurrence.[110]

This formulation has been held to encompass a decision of the Court of Appeal which was based on an inadequate report of a case, a fuller report not having been cited.[111] Furthermore, three recent decisions of the Court of Appeal have exploited the 'rare instance' allowed for by the formulation in such a way as to suggest that some of its members are prepared to find ways round the affirmation of the *Young* v. *Bristol Aeroplane* rule which, as we saw in the last chapter, occurred in *Davis* v. *Johnson*.

Williams v. *Fawcett*[112] concerned a notice requiring a respondent to show cause why he should not be committed to prison for contempt for breach of an undertaking. Previous decisions of the Court of Appeal had laid down that such a notice must be signed by a proper officer of the court. They were held to be *per incuriam* for three reasons. First, the growth of the error could be clearly detected. Second, the cases were all concerned with the liberty of the subject—it was recognized that they were in fact favourable rather than adverse to such liberty, but 'the other side of the coin is

---

[109] *Royal Court Derby Porcelain Co.* v. *Raymond Russell* [1949] 2 KB 417.

[110] *Per* Lord Evershed MR in *Morrelle Ltd.* v. *Wakeling* [1955] 2 QB 389 at 406.

[111] *Industrial Properties (Barton Hill) Ltd.* v. *Associated Electrical Industries Ltd.* (1977) QB 614.

[112] (1986) QB 604.

that these cases are also concerned with the maintenance of the authority of the courts to insist upon obedience to their orders'.[113] Third, if the cases were not declared *per incuriam*, it was most likely that the point would be taken to the House of Lords for the error to be corrected.

In *Rickards* v. *Rickards*,[114] the issue was whether the Court of Appeal had jurisdiction to entertain an appeal from the refusal of an inferior court to grant an extension of time for appealing against an order. A previous decision of the Court of Appeal had ruled that it did not. The Court was satisfied that this decision was *per incuriam*, since it had misunderstood a decision of the House of Lords. It concluded that the cases from *Young* v. *Bristol Aeroplane Co. Ltd.* to *Williams* v. *Fawcett* showed that the Court of Appeal was justified in refusing to follow one of its own decisions, not only where that decision had been given in ignorance or forgetfulness of some inconsistent statutory provision or binding authority, but also (in the words of Lord Donaldson MR):

in rare and exceptional cases, if it is satisfied that the decision involved a manifest slip or error. In previous cases the judges of this court have always refrained from defining this exceptional category and I have no intention of departing from that approach save to echo the words of Lord Greene M.R. (in Young's case), and Sir Raymond Evershed M.R. (in Morelle's case), and to say that they will be of the rarest occurrence.[115]

However, he indicated that invocation of the category was peculiarly appropriate in the context of procedural questions involving jurisdiction, and where it was most unlikely that any appeal would be taken to the House of Lords. It is to be noted that this last consideration (unlikelihood of appeal to the House), which was prominent in both these cases, was one of the arguments advanced and rejected in *Davis* v. *Johnson* for a general relaxation in the rule that the Court of Appeal is bound by its own decisions.

In *Rakhit* v. *Carty*,[116] the Court of Appeal departed from two decisions of its own in which it had been held that a fair rent registered in respect of unfurnished premises which were the subject of a regulated tenancy within the Rent Act 1977 did not

---

[113] (1986) QB 604, 616 Sir John Donaldson MR.
[114] (1990) Fam. 194   [115] (1990) Fam. 194, 203.
[116] (1990) 2 QB 315.

apply to a subsequent furnished letting. The Court found that the first decision was *per incuriam*, because the Court of Appeal had not been referred to a particular subsection of the Act in the light of which its decision was clearly erroneous. The second decision was classified as falling within the 'rare and exceptional' category mentioned by Lord Donaldson in *Rickards* v. *Rickards*, because the Court of Appeal in the second case had mistakenly considered itself bound by the first decision (the *per incuriam* argument not having been addressed to it).

In other cases, the Court of Appeal has affirmed the rule to be that a decision is not *per incuriam* unless some pertinent authority was overlooked, and even then the present Court must be satisfied that the omission produced an essential flaw in the reasoning in the earlier case. In *Johnson* v. *Agnew*,[117] the Court held that its prior decision could not be regarded as *per incuriam* merely because a decision of the House of Lords had not been cited, where the House of Lords case was one which did not clearly cover the point in issue and could, at best, have been persuasive authority for a contrary ruling. In *Duke* v. *Reliance Systems Ltd.*,[118] the Court of Appeal refused to regard a decision of the Court as *per incuriam* merely because an EEC directive, which might have influenced its construction of a statute, had not been cited to it.[119] Sir John Donaldson MR, who also presided over the court in *Williams* v. *Fawcett*, *Rickards* v. *Rickards*, and *Rakhit* v. *Carty*, stated:

I have always understood that the doctrine of *per incuriam* only applies where another division of this Court has reached a decision in the absence of knowledge of a decision binding upon it or a statute, and that in either case it has to be shown that, had the court had this material, it *must* have reached a contrary decision. That is *per incuriam*. I do not understand the doctrine to extend to a case where, if different arguments had been placed before it, it *might* have reached a different conclusion. That appears to me to be the position at which we have arrived to-day.[120]

'*Must*' may be overstating the matter. In *Ashburn Anstalt* v. *Arnold*,[121] the Court of Appeal departed from its famous decision in *Errington* v. *Errington*[122] in which it had been held that a

---

[117] (1978) Ch. 176.   [118] (1988) QB 108.

[119] The House of Lords dismissed an appeal from the Court of Appeal on the ground that, since the directive came into effect after the enactment of the statute, it could not be inferred that the purpose of the statute was to implement the directive, *Duke* v. *GEC Reliance Ltd.* (1988) AC 618.

[120] (1988) QB 108, 113 (emphasis in original).   [121] (1989) Ch. 1.

[122] (1952) 1 KB 290.

contractual licence to occupy constituted an equitable interest in land. That decision, it was said, was '*per incuriam* in the sense that it was made without reference to authorities which, if they would not have compelled, would surely have persuaded the court to adopt a different *ratio*'.[123]

Further exceptions to stare decisis *in the Court of Appeal*

In *Davis* v. *Johnson*,[124] the House of Lords asserted, not merely that the Court of Appeal was bound by its own decisions, but also that the Court of Appeal had no power to lay down any exceptions going beyond those set out in *Young* v. *Bristol Aeroplane Co. Ltd.* The issue in *Davis* v. *Johnson* related to the interpretation of section 1 of the Domestic Violence and Matrimonial Proceedings Act 1976, which confers jurisdiction on a county court to grant an injunction excluding one party from a joint home. The Court of Appeal in two previous cases[125] had held that Parliament could not have intended this provision to be read literally, and that it could not be invoked against someone with a proprietary right in the premises. In consequence, a county court judge had refused to make an order excluding Mr Johnson from the council flat of which he was a joint tenant, even though he had subjected Miss Davis to violence of a horrifying nature. The majority of the Court of Appeal upheld Miss Davis's appeal and refused to follow the two previous decisions of the Court of Appeal. As we saw in the last chapter, Lord Denning MR was prepared to abandon the rule in *Young*'s case altogether. His colleagues, finding that the instant case did not come within any of the three exceptions to the rule, announced new exceptions.

Sir George Baker P suggested that the Court should not be bound by a decision which led to injustice and restricted proper development of the law and 'cannot stand in the face of the will and intention of Parliament expressed in simple language in a recent statute passed to remedy a serious mischief or abuse'.[126] Shaw LJ held that the rule should be relaxed when its application 'would have the effect of depriving actual and potential victims of violence of a vital protection which an act of Parliament was plainly designed to afford to them'.[127]

[123] (1989) Ch. 1, 22.   [124] (1979) AC 264.
[125] *B.* v. *B.* (1978) Fam. 26. *Cantliff* v. *Jenkins* (1978) Fam. 47.
[126] (1979) AC 264, 290.   [127] (1979) AC 264, 308.

These putative general exceptions were rejected by the House of Lords,[128] Sir George Baker's on the ground that it was too wide and might cover any decision on the construction of a statute, Shaw LJ's on the opposite ground that it was so narrow as to amount to a 'one-off' exception. No reference, however, was made by their Lordships to certain other exceptions to, or qualifications of, the rule in *Young* v. *Bristol Aeroplane Co. Ltd.* for which some authority exists. These further exceptions have been little discussed and the status of all of them is unclear. They may be listed as follows:

(1) The Court of Appeal is not bound by a prior decision of the Court of Appeal which was given in interlocutory proceedings. In *Boys* v. *Chaplin*,[129] the Court held that the rule in *Young*'s case applied only to final decisions. The prior decision there in question was an interlocutory order of a court composed of only two Lords Justices, but the grounds for holding that interlocutory decisions are not within the rule—because they are often *ex tempore* and may not have followed on full argument—would, if sound, seem to hold for interlocutory decisions in general.

(2) The Court of Appeal is not bound by a decision of a two-judge court. This proposition is sometimes assumed to be true[130] and sometimes denied.[131] It is surprising that this issue remains unsettled since hearing of appeals by two-judge courts has become increasingly common. New guidelines were issued in 1982, with a view to reducing the enormous backlog of appeals. These provided that, save in exceptional circumstances, all appeals from interlocutory decisions and all appeals from county courts should be heard in the Court of Appeal only by two judges.[132]

(3) The rule in *Young*'s case does not apply where, exceptionally, the Court of Appeal is the final appellate court.[133]

(4) The Court of Appeal is at liberty to depart from an earlier decision of its own which has been disapproved by the Privy

---

[128] (1979) AC 264, 327–8 Lord Diplock, 344–5 Lord Salmon.

[129] (1968) 2 QB 1.

[130] *Ronex Properties Ltd.* v. *John Laing Construction Ltd.* (1982) 3 All ER 961, 966 Donaldson LJ.

[131] *Verrall* v. *Great Yarmouth Borough Council* (1981) QB 202, 219 Roskill LJ.

[132] Practice Note (1982) 3 All ER 376, 383–4.

[133] *Davis* v. *Johnson* (1979) AC 264, 282 Lord Denning MR, 292 Goff LJ. The view that there might be a difference, so far as the doctrine of precedent is concerned, between cases in which there is or is not a right of appeal may be traced back to Pollock CB in *Taylor* v. *Burgess* (1859) 5 H. and N. 1, 5.

Council. This proposition has been asserted in cases in which the rule in *Young* v. *Bristol Aeroplane Co.* has not been discussed.[134]

(5) The Court of Appeal is not bound by the ordinary rules of precedent where the validity of an otherwise binding decision has been affected by changes in public international law. This proposition was asserted by the former Master of the Rolls, Lord Denning, in *Trendtex Trading Corporation* v. *Central Bank of Nigeria*,[135] and two years later it was denied by the present Master of the Rolls, Lord Donaldson of Lymington (then Donaldson J), in *Uganda Co. (Holdings) Ltd.* v. *Government of Uganda*.[136]

(6) The Court of Appeal is not bound by a decision of its own where the earlier decision was taken on appeal to the House of Lords and the House decided that the point on which the Court of Appeal had given a ruling did not arise for decision. In *Balabel* v. *Air India*, Taylor LJ assumed this proposition to be true on the ground that, given the final outcome in the House of Lords, the ruling of the Court of Appeal constituted mere *dicta*.[137] In *R.* v. *Secretary of State, ex parte Al-Mehdawi*,[138] the same judge seems to have treated it as an exception to the *stare decisis* rule. The Court accepted the submission that the statement of exceptions contained in *Young* v. *Bristol Aeroplane Co. Ltd.* was not exhaustive. No mention was made in the judgments of *Davis* v. *Johnson*, although that case was apparently cited in argument. Taylor LJ suggested that, should the present case be taken on appeal, it might be appropriate for their Lordships to consider *stare decisis* in such a context.[139] This suggestion was not taken up when *Al-Mehdawi* reached the House of Lords.[140] Resolution of the matter would indeed seem desirable. Commentators frequently assume that the *ratio decidendi* of a Court of Appeal decision has settled the law (at the level of that Court) even when the case went to the House of Lords on an entirely different point.

4. THE COURT OF APPEAL (CRIMINAL DIVISION)

The exceptions stated in *Young* v. *Bristol Aeroplane Co. Ltd.* apply equally to the Criminal Division of the Court of Appeal.[141]

---

[134] *Doughty* v. *Turner Manufacturing Co. Ltd.* (1964) 1 QB 518. *Worcester Works Finance Ltd.* v. *Cooden Engineering Co. Ltd.* (1972) 1 QB 210.
[135] (1977) 1 QB 529.   [136] (1979) 1 Lloyds Rep. 481.
[137] (1988) Ch. 317, 325–6.   [138] (1990) AC 876, 879.
[139] (1990) AC 876, 883–4.   [140] (1990) AC 876, 894.
[141] *R.* v. *Ewing* (1983) QB 1039. *R.* v. *Spencer* (1985) QB 771.

Three further exceptions, not applicable to the Court of Appeal when exercising its civil jurisdiction, need to be considered.

First, in *R. v. Newsome and Browne*,[142] it was held that a full court has power to overrule previous sentencing decisions in circumstances in which none of the exceptions to *stare decisis* on which the Civil Division acts was in point. Principles of sentencing are not viewed in the same light as substantive rules of law.

Secondly, section 36 of the Criminal Justice Act 1972 empowers the Attorney-General to refer a point of law to the Criminal Division of the Court of Appeal in a case in which, following a ruling by the trial judge, an accused has been acquitted. There is some authority for the view that, in such a case, the court may refuse to follow one of its own decisions.[143] If so, this would be an example of prospective overruling (not otherwise practised by English courts) since, although the acquittal in the instant case would stand, courts below the House of Lords would, presumably, be expected to follow the ruling given on the reference for the future.

Thirdly (and most importantly), a full court of the Criminal Division of the Court of Appeal may depart from a decision in the interests of the liberty of the accused. This power was exercised in *R. v. Taylor*, where Lord Goddard CJ said:

This Court has to deal with questions involving the liberty of the subject, and if it finds, on reconsideration, that, in the opinion of a full court assembled for that purpose, the law has been either misapplied or misunderstood in a decision which it has previously given, and that, on the strength of that decision, an accused person has been sentenced and imprisoned it is the bounden duty of the court to reconsider the earlier decision with a view to seeing whether that person has been properly convicted.[144]

That was a decision of the court of Criminal Appeal, but it has been assumed that Lord Goddard's proposition applies equally to its successor, the Criminal Division of the Court of Appeal.[145] Arguably, this exception ought also to apply when the Court is exercising its civil jurisdiction if the case involves the liberty of the subject, such as cases concerned with deportation or detention in

---

[142] (1970) 2 QB 711.
[143] *Attorney-General's reference (no. 1 of 1981)* (1982) 75 Cr. App. Rep. 45.
[144] (1950) 2 KB 368, 371.
[145] *R. v. Newsome and Browne* (1970) 2 QB 711. *Hoskyn v. Metropolitan Police Commissioner* (1978) 67 Cr. App. Rep. 88. *R. v. Spencer* (1985) QB 771.

mental hospitals.[146] It is to be noted that the exception exists only when an accused person has been sentenced 'and imprisoned', not when a mere fine has been imposed. Even when a sentence of imprisonment has been passed on the basis of previous decisions which the court now believes merit reconsideration, it may prefer to uphold the conviction and leave it to the House of Lords to reverse its decision on appeal rather than adjourn the case to a hearing of the full court.[147]

The first exception in *Young*'s case states that the court 'is entitled and bound to decide which of two conflicting decisions of its own it will follow'. In *R.* v. *Jenkins*, Purchas LJ said that in such circumstances the criminal division of the Court of Appeal *must* opt in favour of that decision which is most favourable to the accused.[148] However, in three subsequent cases where the court was faced with just such a conflict it chose to follow the decision which was adverse to the accused.[149] Purchas LJ's opinion is out of line with the current view that, apart from the exceptions considered above, the doctrine in *Young*'s case applies in the same way to the Criminal Division as to the Civil Division of the Court of Appeal.

5. OTHER COURTS

Prior to the decision in *Tal*'s case,[150] divisional courts regarded themselves as free to choose between conflicting divisional court decisions.[151] Since *Tal*, as we saw in the last chapter, divisional courts no longer consider themselves bound by previous decisions in matters involving the exercise of a supervisory, as distinct from an appellate, jurisdiction.

Even in the context of appellate jurisdiction, *Tal* introduced a further exception so far as criminal appeals are concerned. It had been held in *Younghusband* v. *Luftig*[152] that divisional courts are

[146] See Paul Jackson, 'Precedent and the Liberty of the Subject', *LQR* 101 (1985), 323.
[147] *R.* v. *Sheppard* (1980) 70 Cr. App. Rep. 210 CA, reversed (1981) AC 394 HL.
[148] (1983) 76 Cr. App. Rep. 313, 318.
[149] *R.* v. *Spencer* (1985) QB 771. *R.* v. *Martindale* (1986) 2 All ER 928. *R.* v. *Slack* (1989) QB 775.
[150] *R.* v. *Manchester Coroner, ex parte Tal* (1985) QB 67.
[151] *Nicholas* v. *Penny* (1950) 2 KB 466. *R.* v. *Tottenham Juvenile Court, ex parte ARC* (1982) 74 Cr. App. Rep. 267.
[152] (1949) 2 KB 354.

absolutely bound by their own decisions when hearing criminal appeals. Robert Goff LJ, in *Tal*, pointed out that two earlier cases,[153] which stated the opposite view, had not been cited in *Younghusband* and that Lord Goddard CJ, who delivered the leading judgment in that case, himself subsequently decided in *R. v. Taylor*[154] that the Court of Criminal Appeal was not bound by its own decisions where the liberty of the subject is concerned. Furthermore, appeals from divisional courts to the House of Lords had subsequently been introduced. Goff LJ concluded:

No material distinction can now be drawn between a divisional court exercising its appellate jurisdiction in criminal cases on appeals from justices by way of case stated and the Court of Appeal (Criminal Division) exercising its appellate jurisdiction in criminal cases, appeals now lying from both courts to the House of Lords under the same conditions.[155]

It therefore seems that a divisional court may not be bound by a decision of another divisional court relating to a criminal appeal where the liberty of the subject is involved.[156] On the other hand, it has never been suggested that the decision of a two-judge divisional court is any less binding than that of a court constituted by more than two judges. The practice of sitting with only two judges is very common in divisional courts.

It is unclear what room for manœuvre is conferred on divisional courts and first instance judges as regards prima-facie binding decisions of the Court of Appeal. Clearly such a decision will not be binding if it has been unambiguously overruled by a subsequent decision of the House of Lords; and, even when there has been no such explicit overruling, a judge may feel free to disregard a decision of the Court of Appeal which, in his view, cannot stand with the principles underlying a subsequent decision of the House.[157] Where there are conflicting decisions of the Court of Appeal, it seems that a first instance judge will normally regard himself as

---

[153] *Fortescue v. Vestry of St Matthew, Bethnal Green* (1891) 1 QB 170. *Kruse v. Johnson* (1898) 2 QB 91.

[154] (1950) 2 KB 368.   [155] (1985) QB 67, 79.

[156] In *Rogers v. Essex County Council* (1985) 2 All ER 39, a divisional court, on the authority of *Tal's* case, regarded itself as bound by a decision of an earlier divisional court exercising appellate jurisdiction, and went on to advance elaborate arguments for distinguishing the decision. No suggestion was made that, since the earlier decision was unfavourable to the accused, the court might not be bound. However, the liberty of the accused was not at stake since they had been granted an absolute discharge. The decision was reversed by the House of Lords but without comment on precedent (1986) 3 All ER 321.

[157] *Midland Bank Trust Co. Ltd. v. Hett Stubbs and Kemp* (1979) Ch. 384 Oliver J.

bound by the later decision,[158] unless he considers the precendential force of the later decision to be undermined by the fact that it itself misunderstood the doctrine of precedent.[159] The position is most obscure in regard to the *per incuriam* exception.

In *R.* v. *Northumberland Compensation Appeal Tribunal*,[160] a divisional court declined to follow a decision of the Court of Appeal on the ground that it was inconsistent with earlier decisions of the House of Lords which had not been cited. In *Cassell and Co. Ltd.* v. *Broome*,[161] the House of Lords took the view that no inferior court could treat one of its own decisions as having been reached *per incuriam*; and Lord Diplock, delivering the opinion of the Privy Council in *Baker* v. *The Queen*,[162] stated that, in the light of *Cassell*, the *per incuriam* rule does not apply to decisions of any appellate court superior to that in which it is sought to be invoked—an opinion apparently approved by Lord Simon in *Miliangos* v. *George Frank (Textiles) Ltd.*[163] Despite these assertions, judges at first instance appear to regard *per incuriam*, along with the other exceptions set out in *Young*'s case, as valid grounds on which the authority of Court of Appeal decisions may be questioned.[164]

6. DECISIONS WITHOUT ARGUMENT

It was said as long ago as 1661 that 'precedents *sub silentio* and without argument are of no moment'.[165] It seems always to have been accepted that if a proposition of law, though implicit in a decision, was never expressly stated either in argument or in the

[158] See e.g. *CCC Films (London) Ltd.* v. *Impact Quadrant Films Ltd.* (1985) QB 16. *Manor Electronics Ltd.* v. *Dickson*, *The Times*, 8 Feb. 1990.
[159] *Uganda Co. (Holdings) Ltd.* v. *Government of Uganda* (1979) 1 Lloyds Rep. 481, 486–7 Donaldson J.
[160] (1951) 1 KB 711.   [161] (1972) AC 1027.
[162] (1975) AC 774, 788.   [163] (1976) AC 443, 479.
[164] *The Alexandros P* (1986) 1 All ER 278 Webster J. On the question of what can constitute a purpose 'beneficial to the community' in the field of charity law, there is sometimes said to be a conflict between the decision of the House of Lords in *Williams' Trustees* v. *Inland Revenue Commissioners* (1947) AC 447 and the subsequent decision of the Court of Appeal in *Incorporated Council of Law Reporting for England and Wales* v. *Attorney-General* (1972) Ch. 73. On that assumption, Stamp LJ stated in *Inland Revenue Commissioners* v. *McMullen* (1979) 1 All ER 588, 592, that the later decision should be followed; whereas the opposite view was expressed by Dillon J in *Barralet* v. *Attorney-General* (1980) 3 All ER 918, 926.
[165] *R.* v. *Warner*, 1 Keb. 66.

judgment, the decision constitutes no binding authority for it,[166] whether on the ground that there is here an exception to *stare decisis*, or for the reason that such a proposition is not truly part of the ratio. The last fifteen years have seen a tendency to regard decisions as not binding at any level of the judicial hierarchy as to propositions expressly affirmed by them if, owing to the absence of any argument on the point, it can be inferred that the deciding court merely assumed their correctness. In this light, decisions without argument must be viewed as a general exception to *stare decisis*.

In *Baker* v. *The Queen*,[167] the Privy Council held that, although inferior courts were bound by decisions of the Board even if they were *per incuriam*, they were not bound by propositions of law incorporated into the *ratio decidendi* which had merely been assumed to be correct without argument. The issue related to the construction of a Jamaican statute which provided that 'sentence of death shall not be pronounced on . . . a person under the age of eighteen . . .'. The question was whether this exemption applied to persons who were under 18 at the date when they committed murder, or only to those who had not attained that age at the date sentence was passed. An earlier decision of the Board was clear authority for the former construction; but in that case the first-instance judge had adopted this interpretation and the only question considered on appeal was whether he had been entitled, on the evidence, to conclude that the accused had attained 18 at the time of the offence. The Board had allowed the appeal on the ground that the evidence did not support this finding. The construction which exempts all those who were under age at the date of the crime therefore formed an essential part of the *ratio decidendi* of the earlier decision of the Board, as was recognized in *Baker*'s case. Nevertheless, in *Baker* the majority of the Board held that the Court of Appeal for Jamaica had been entitled to adopt the other construction, as prohibiting the death penalty only for those who had attained 18 at the time of sentence. It was the practice of the Board not to allow parties to raise points of law which had not been argued below, and from this it could be

---

[166] See e.g. the treatment by the House of Lords in *Read* v. *Lyons* (1947) AC 156 of its decision in *Rainham Chemical Works Ltd.* v. *Belvedere Fish Guano Co. Ltd.* (1921) 2 AC 11, on the issue of whether manufacturing explosives in time of war is a non-natural user of land within the rule in *Rylands* v. *Fletcher*.

[167] (1975) AC 774.

inferred that the correctness of the wider construction had been merely assumed rather than decided.

A consequence of this practice is that in its opinions delivered on an appeal the Board may have assumed, without itself deciding, that a proposition of law which was not disputed by the parties in the court from which the appeal is brought is correct. The proposition of law so assumed to be correct may be incorporated, whether expressly or by implication, in the *ratio decidendi* of a particular appeal; but because it does not bear the authority of an opinion reached by the Board itself it does not create a precedent for use in the decision of other cases.[168]

A similar stance towards *rationes decidendi* without argument was adopted by the Court of Appeal in *National Enterprises Ltd. v. Racal Communications Ltd.*[169] The issue there was whether the Arbitration Act 1950 should be construed as conferring jurisdiction on the court to appoint an arbitrator in the case of an arbitration agreement which provided for an arbitrator to be appointed by a third party but where the third party had declined to do so. An earlier decision of the Court of Appeal had ruled that it should. However, in that case the only question taken on appeal was whether, as a matter of construction of the particular contract, there had been an arbitration agreement at all. From this it could be inferred that the Court of Appeal had merely assumed that the Act conferred jurisdiction in these circumstances—even though it had not expressly stated that it was acting on an assumption. This inference was strengthened by the personal recollections of Russell LJ, who sat in the Court of Appeal in both cases, that the jurisdiction question had not been effectively raised in argument so that the Court did not address its mind to the point nor pronounce upon it. Accordingly, it was not bound by its previous decision.[170]

In *Barrs* v. *Bethel*,[171] *Baker*'s case and the *National Enterprises* case were treated as authority warranting a first instance judge in declining to follow the *ratio decidendi* of a decision of the Court of Appeal where a point had not been argued. The issue was whether ratepayers have an unfettered *locus standi* to challenge decisions of local authorities. The Court of Appeal had ruled that they did, but, in *Barrs* v. *Bethel*, Warner J found that the only question canvassed had related to the scope of a particular power and that

[168] (1975) AC 774, 788.   [169] (1975) Ch. 397.
[170] (1975) Ch. 397, 405–6.   [171] (1982) 1 All ER 106.

the Court of Appeal had not addressed its mind to the general question of *locus standi*. He was accordingly not bound by the decision:

Undoubtedly, the Court of Appeal, in that case, held that the plaintiff was entitled to the declaration he sought on the ground that a local authority owed to its ratepayers, in the application of the general rate fund, a fiduciary duty analogous to that of a trustee. But the report of Counsel's argument, both before Vaisey J. and before the Court of Appeal, and the summary of it in the Court of Appeal's judgment, show that no point was taken as to the plaintiff's *locus standi*.[172]

Baker's case and *Barrs* v. *Bethel* were subsequently treated as authority entitling a first instance judge to decline to follow even a decision of the House of Lords. In *re Hetherington Decd.*,[173] Browne-Wilkinson VC held that trusts for the saying of masses for the dead are charitable trusts. However, he rejected the contention that he was bound to come to this conclusion by the decision of the House of Lords in *Bourne* v. *Keane*,[174] even on the assumption that the point had formed part of the *ratio decidendi* of that case, since it had not been argued on both sides and had not been pronounced upon in their Lordships' speeches:

In my judgment the authorities therefore clearly establish that even where a decision of a point of law in a particular sense was essential to an earlier decision of a superior court, but that superior court merely assumed the correctness of the law on a particular issue, a judge in a later case is not bound to hold that the law is decided in that sense. So therefore, in my judgment, *Bourne* v. *Keane* . . . is not decisive of the case before me.[175]

The upshot of these decisions is a loosening in the doctrine of *stare decisis*. It does not encompass *rationes decidendi* where it can be inferred that the deciding court did not address its mind to a proposition of law, even if that proposition was essential to its decision; and that inference can be easily drawn from the absence of any (or even any adequate) argument on the point in question.

---

[172] (1982) 1 All ER 106, 116.   [173] (1990) Ch. 1.
[174] (1919) AC 815.   [175] (1990) Ch. 1, 10.

7. OBSOLETE DECISIONS

In Scotland it is accepted that:

> If it is manifest that the *ratio decidendi* upon which a previous decision has rested has been superseded and invalidated by subsequent legislation or from other like causes, that *ratio decidendi* ceases to be binding.[176]

A recent decision of the Court of Appeal suggests that there is a similar doctrine of obsolescence in England. In *Pittalis* v. *Grant*,[177] landlords appealed against a county court judgment which had dismissed their claim for possession. They sought to raise a question concerning the construction of the Rent Act 1977 which had not been argued before the county court. In 1891 the House of Lords had laid down that no appeal lies from the county court to the Court of Appeal on a question of law which has not been raised before the county court.[178] That rule had been accepted ever since, although exceptions had been recognized. Nevertheless, the Court concluded that the rule was obsolete and should not be followed. The basis of the rule had been the restriction of appeals from the county court to the Court of Appeal to questions of law. That restriction having been removed by subsequent legislation, the foundation of the rule had disappeared. Nourse LJ stated:

> We are conscious that it may seem a strong thing for this court to hold thus of a rule established by the House of Lords, albeit one enfeebled by exceptions, the statutory support which gave it life at last turned off. But where it can see that the decision of the higher court has become obsolete, the lower court, if it is not to deny justice to the parties in the suit, is bound to say so and to act accordingly.[179]

On its face this statement asserts the existence of an exception to *stare decisis* of general application at any level of the judicial hierarchy. No reference was made, however, to any other case in which a similar course had been taken, and it is open to question whether an isolated decision can be regarded as firmly grounding such a qualification to the *stare decisis* principle. It will be recalled that the House of Lords has forthrightly repudiated other grounds on which the Court of Appeal has claimed that it is not bound by decisions of the House.[180] Furthermore, the point of law in issue

---

[176] *Beith's Trustees* v. *Beith* (1950) SC 66, 70.
[178] *Smith* v. *Baker and Sons* (1891) AC 325.
[180] See p. 99 *supra*.

[177] (1989) QB 605.
[179] (1989) QB 605, 618.

went to jurisdiction, and we have seen, in other contexts, that English courts take a more relaxed view of the binding force of precedent in the fields of procedure and jurisdiction than they do when substantive questions of law are involved.[181] It remains to be seen whether *Pittalis* v. *Grant* is as revolutionary as it appears.

8. SUMMARY OF EXCEPTIONS TO *STARE DECISIS*

(1) The House of Lords is not bound by its own decisions. But it will not overrule a decision, unless (i) the law, as a whole, would be improved by so doing; (ii) (save where fundamental principles are at stake) contentions are advanced in the present case which were not considered in the former case; (iii) overruling would not upset justified reliance on the earlier decision; (iv) the overruling would not conflict with parliamentary confirmation of the earlier decision; and (v) (in civil cases) overruling will affect the outcome of the present appeal.

(2) The Court of Appeal (Civil Division) is bound by its own decisions, unless the case falls within one of the three exceptions set out in *Young* v. *Bristol Aeroplane Co. Ltd.*, viz. (i) there are conflicting decisions of the Court of Appeal; (ii) a decision of the Court of Appeal cannot stand with a subsequent (or, exceptionally, a prior) decision of the House of Lords; (iii) a decision of the Court of Appeal was given *per incuriam*. Further, it is probably not bound by a decision given in interlocutory proceedings, or one which has been disapproved by the Privy Council, or where the Court of Appeal is the final appellate court. It may not be bound by a decision of a two-judge court, or by a decision which was taken on appeal to the House of Lords and the House decided that the point on which the Court of Appeal had ruled did not arise for decision. It is possible (but unlikely) that the Court is not bound by a decision which has been affected by changes in public international law.

(3) The Court of Appeal (Criminal Division) is bound by its own decisions, save for the exceptions in (2) above (where applicable); except that a full Court is not bound by sentencing decisions and those affecting the liberty of the accused, and it may be that it can depart from an earlier decision where it makes a ruling pursuant to a reference by the Attorney-General.

---

[181] p. 150 *supra*.

(4) Divisional courts are bound by previous divisional court decisions only where the latter involved the exercise of an appellate, as distinct from a supervisory, jurisdiction. The exceptions in *Young*'s case apply and, further, on the hearing of a criminal appeal, a divisional court is not bound by a decision which affects the liberty of the accused.

(5) Divisional courts and judges of the High Court do not regard themselves as bound by decisions of the Court of Appeal which cannot stand with subsequent decisions of the House of Lords. Where there are conflicting decisions of the Court of Appeal, they will normally follow the later decision. It is an unsettled question whether they are free to disregard decisions of the Court of Appeal on the ground that they were given *per incuriam*.

(6) *Rationes decidendi* of decisions, at any level of the judicial hierarchy, are not binding on inferior courts as to propositions incorporated within them whose correctness was assumed without argument. The same may be true of *rationes decidendi* which have become obsolete.

V

PRECEDENT AS A SOURCE OF LAW

Case-law and jurisprudential problems

We have now completed the account of the operation of the rules of precedent summarized on p. 6. These rules generate what may not ineptly be described as 'jurisprudential' problems of their own. Are they rules of law? Can the rules of precedent be based on precedent? Why does the idea of the prospective overruling of a judicial decision tend to be anathema to an English lawyer when retrospective legislation is equally abhorrent to him? Brief discussions of these questions will be found in Chapters VII and VIII. This chapter and Chapter VI are primarily concerned with problems posed by case-law generally. They would arise even if the English rules of precedent were very different from what they are. They stem from the older and more important rule that judges must have regard to case-law.

In what sense is a judicial decision, i.e. a precedent, a source of law? Do decided cases throw any light on the question, raised by Austin, whether a custom is law before it is enforced by the courts? In what sense is custom subordinate to precedent and precedent to legislation? What is the nature of the joint operation of statute and precedent as sources of English law? These are the types of problem with which this chapter is concerned.

Chapter VI considers problems more directly connected with the judicial process. What is the nature of judicial reasoning? What is meant by the charge that our judges are sometimes guilty of conceptualism? How are cases of first impression dealt with, and how is the law developed by the judges?

Chapter VII is by no means confined to jurisprudential questions raised by the rules of precedent for it touches upon, albeit very briefly, the major jurisprudential problem raised by case-law, namely, the compatibility of the common law with a number of definitions of law or elucidations of the working of a legal system. It is, however, necessary to stress that, whereas Chapters I to IV can claim to be a comparatively thorough account of the working of the rules of precedent, Chapters V to VIII are not intended to do more than draw attention to jurisprudential problems raised by case-law generally and by the rules of precedent in particular.

1. THE DIFFERENT SOURCES OF LAW

The phrase 'source of law' is used in several different senses. First, there is the literary source, the original documentary source of our information concerning the existence of a rule of law. In this sense the law reports are a source of law, whereas a textbook on tort or contract, or a digest of cases falls into the category of legal literature. Next there are the historical sources of law, the sources—original, mediate, or immediate—from which rules of law derive their content as a matter of legal history. In this sense the writings of Bracton and Coke and the works of other great exponents of English law are sources of law, for they enunciate rules which are now embodied in judicial decisions and Acts of Parliament. In this sense, too, Roman law and medieval custom are sources of English law, for parts of our law which are now immediately attributable to decisions in particular cases or specific statutory provisions can be traced to a rule of Roman law, and a great deal of the English land law originated in feudal custom. This sense of the phrase 'source of law' can be extended to anything which accounts for the existence of a legal rule from the causal point of view. On the one hand, it may be applied to the Queen in Parliament and Her Majesty's judges as the immediate authors of rules of law; on the other hand, it may be used to cover public opinion, moral principles, and even those judicial idiosyncrasies which some American realists insist should be the true subject-matter of a mature study of law.[1]

Although the historical sources of law are of the greatest importance and interest, they are not considered at length in

---

[1] 'If the law consists of the decisions of the judges and if those decisions are based on the judge's hunches, then the way in which the judge gets his hunches is the key to the judicial process. Whatever produces the judge's hunches makes the law' (Frank, *Law and the Modern Mind* (1st English edn., 1949), 104). The author canvasses a study of the personality of the judge by reference to his biography and background, etc. For a brief account of the views of the realists, see Ch. II, section 2, *supra*.

books on analytical jurisprudence. These works contain elaborate discussions of legislation, precedent, custom, and juristic writings, but they are mainly concerned with sources of law in a third and entirely different sense of the word from that denoted by literary and historical sources. In this sense, 'source' means, not a causal origin, direct or remote, but that from which a rule derives its validity as a rule of law. The enquiry is not 'How do you account for the content of a particular legal rule?' but 'Why do you say that certain rules are rules of law?' This approach colours the discussion of sources and gives a meaning to such questions as 'Are there more sources of law than one?' 'Is custom a source of law?' and 'Is European Community legislation an ultimate or derivative source of law?'

The criteria of validity vary. Every legal system is based on fundamental rules or ultimate principles by means of which it is possible to ascertain whether a particular rule is a rule of law. There is, of course, plenty of scope for controversy concerning the best way of formulating these basic rules. In the case of the English system it is at least generally agreed that legislation (direct or subordinate) and the *rationes decidendi* of cases coming before the superior courts have the force of law. Other legal systems are based on different ultimate principles. Whatever may be the truth with regard to the French system, that system is not based on the rule that decided cases make law for the future. Sir John Salmond referred to sources from which legal rules derive their validity as 'legal' sources as distinct from 'historical' sources, since the former are 'those which are recognised as such by the law itself'.[2] Precedent, legislation, and custom are legal sources of English law because:

It is itself a principle of English law that any principle involved in a judicial decision has the force of law. Similar legal recognition is extended to the law producing effect of statutes and immemorial custom. Rules such as these establish the sources of law.[3]

2. PRECEDENT AND CUSTOM

The following extract from Blackstone epitomizes the approach of English law to customary practices:

The municipal law of England, or the civil conduct prescribed for the inhabitants of this Kingdom, may with sufficient propriety be divided into

---

[2] *Jurisprudence* (11th edn.), 133.   [3] Ibid. 136.

two kinds: the *lex non scripta*, the unwritten or common law; and the *lex scripta*, the written or statute law. The *lex non scripta*, or unwritten law, includes not only general customs, or the common law properly so called, but also the particular customs of certain parts of the Kingdom; and likewise those particular laws that are by custom observed only in certain courts and jurisdictions.[4]

The idea that the common law consists of general customs is the declaratory theory in another guise. We have already seen that it died hard, and was not dead in Blackstone's day. No doubt there was an element of truth in it at least during the early Middle Ages, for the common law was composed of the customs generally observed among Englishmen, hence the name 'common'. In a great many instances the judges must have had recourse to these customs of the existence and nature of which they were probably well aware; but all general customs must long since have been embodied in judicial decisions which are the only important source of the modern common law as distinct from statute law.

The particular customs of certain parts of the kingdom are occasionally considered by contemporary courts. An example of such a custom is the practice of the fishermen in a certain locality to spread their nets on a particular stretch of sand. Customs of this nature usually, if not invariably, operate in derogation of the common law. They generally permit what the common law prohibits. The spreading of the nets would be a trespass to the foreshore were it not for the local practice. The courts allow a local custom to be effective provided it complies with certain tests which have been laid down in four or five centuries of case-law.

The tests are variously stated. For present purposes it is sufficient to say that the custom must be reasonable, it must not contradict a statute, it must have been observed as of right (i.e. not by force or permission), and it must have existed since time immemorial.[5] This last requirement has the curious technical meaning that the custom must have existed since 1189, the last occasion on which a specific date was fixed for the barring of certain actions for the recovery of land (this matter is now covered by statutes providing for fixed periods of limitation of six or twelve years). The situation is redeemed from complete absurdity by the fact that the proponent of the custom does not have to prove its existence since 1189, for he will succeed unless his opponent can

---

[4] *Commentaries* (1813 edn.), i. 81.
[5] These are the tests enumerated in Salmond's *Jurisprudence* (12th edn.), 199.

show that the custom must have come into being since that date by establishing, for example, that it is based on practices consequent on the Statutes of Labourers of the fourteenth century.[6]

The requirement that the custom must be reasonable is of some interest in the present context. In some legal contexts, reasonableness is a question of fact to be determined by a jury when there is one. For example, civil negligence is by definition a failure to comply with the standard of a reasonable man, and the question whether this standard was reached by the defendant in a particular case must be left to the jury. In other legal contexts reasonableness is a question of fact, but, even where there is a jury, it is a fact which must be determined by the judge. For example, in order to succeed on a claim for damages for malicious prosecution, the plaintiff must show that the defendant had not got reasonable and probable cause for prosecuting. Even if the case is tried with a jury, the existence of reasonable cause must be determined by the judge. This reservation of certain questions of fact for the judge no doubt originated as one of the methods by which our judges secured some degree of control over the jury after it had become impossible for them to influence the verdict by less desirable means.

Decisions on questions of fact do not constitute a precedent, for every case is considered to be unique. In order to constitute a precedent, a decision must concern a point of law. The question whether a local custom is reasonable is a question of law in this sense. Previous cases are cited and analysed when an issue is raised concerning the reasonableness of a custom. The test was once formulated in very broad terms by Parker J who said the custom

must be such that, in the opinion of a trained lawyer, it is consistent, or at any rate not inconsistent, with those general principles which, quite apart from particular rules or maxims, lie at the very root of our legal system.[7]

Obviously there is plenty of scope for controversy here, and the matter is one on which guidance from precedent may sometimes be most welcome.

The following brief discussion of the relation between precedent and custom as sources of law is confined to local custom. Two questions must be distinguished. First, the question whether a local custom is to be regarded as law before it is enforced by the

[6] *Simpson* v. *Wells* (1872) LR 7 QB 214.
[7] *Johnson* v. *Clarke* [1908] 1 Ch. 303 at 311.

courts, and second the sense in which custom can be said to be subordinate to precedent as a source of law.

When does a custom become law?

To revert to an example which has already been mentioned, it was held in 1905 that the fishermen of Walmer were entitled by a local custom to dry their nets on a particular stretch of sand.[8] Would it have been correct for someone speaking in 1900 to say that the fishermen of Walmer were legally entitled to act in that way, although such conduct would elsewhere amount to trespass? John Austin's answer to this question would have been an emphatic negative because a custom is a 'moral rule' before it has been made the ground of a judicial decision, after which it is law established by judicial decision.[9] The opposite view is taken by a number of other writers, notably Sir Carleton Allen.[10] According to this view, the correct description of the position of the fishermen of Walmer in 1900 would be the same as that applicable to a situation mentioned in a statute which had not been construed by the courts. If a statute of 1890 had empowered the fishermen to dry their nets on the foreshore, only someone who was guilty of an error similar to Gray's would have said, in 1900, that it was not the law that they might do so, although, under the common law, such conduct was trespass.

John Chipman Gray was a distinguished American jurist of the early twentieth century, but his suggestion that a statute is not law until it has been interpreted by the courts is commonly regarded as eccentric.[11] It was the outcome of his view that the judges are the creators of all law,[12] but an English judge invariably acts and talks as though a statute had been law from the moment when it came into effect. Statutes are always held to have governed the rights of citizens long before those rights are questioned in a court. The vast majority of statutes never come before the courts, but no one denies that their contents constitute the greater part of English law.

---

[8] *Mercer v. Denne* [1905] 2 Ch. 538.
[9] *Jurisprudence* (5th edn.), ii. 523.
[10] *Law in the Making* (7th edn.), ch. 2, and see esp. excursus B.
[11] *Nature and Sources of Law* (2nd edn.), 123–5 and 283.
[12] 'The law of the state or of any organised body of men is composed of the rules which the courts, that is, the judicial organs of that body lay down for the determination of legal rights and duties' (ibid. 84).

Which of the above views about custom is correct so far as English law is concerned? The answer depends on the manner in which the tests by which the validity of a local custom is determined are applied by the courts. Those requiring immemorial antiquity and observance as of right are questions of fact. If disputed, they must, like any other factual dispute, be decided by the courts, but this does not mean that a custom is not law before it is upheld by a judicial decision. The requirement of consistency with statute need not trouble us, because it simply means that a statute can abrogate any custom, just as a statute can abrogate a judicial decision or an earlier statutory provision. The crucial point concerns the approach of our courts to the test of reasonableness. If the courts took the view that this gives them a complete discretion to reject or uphold a custom according to their opinion of what was reasonable, there would be something to be said for the view that a custom is not law before its enforcement, but this is not the approach of our courts. Reasonableness is treated by them as a question of law, and, to a certain extent, what is reasonable is something which can be ascertained by reference to past cases. So far as reported decisions go, it is believed that it has not yet been held that the manufacturer of ginger ale, as opposed to ginger beer, owes a duty of care to the ultimate consumer if he supplies it in opaque bottles, but no English lawyer would hesitate to say that this is the case, having regard to *Donoghue* v. *Stevenson*. Of course, there can be but few local customs concerning which it is possible to speak with such certainty, but the principle remains the same. Accordingly it seems that, in contemporary England, a local custom is law before it is upheld by the courts.

The subordination of custom to precedent as a source of law

Although it may be correct to speak of custom as a distinct source of law because local customs can truly be said to be law before they are enforced, custom must be regarded as subordinate to precedent. Suppose a lawyer advises a client that a particular custom is valid before it has been judicially enforced. If he were asked for the grounds of his opinion, he would say that the custom appeared to him to comply with the tests of validity laid down by the cases. This is a type of derivation or subordination in a different sense from that in which precedent is subordinate to legislation. It is a type of derivation because the courts exercise a certain control over customary rules as the question whether those rules are reasonable is dependent on case-law.[13] If our hypothetical lawyer were asked why he based his opinion that a particular custom is law on the tests laid down in the cases, he would say that that was because the principles on which cases have been decided represent English law. He could not justify his respect for the cases by derivation from the sovereignty of Parliament in the same way as that in which he could justify his regard for the tests of validity of a local custom by direct derivation from the cases. If he did refer to the sovereignty of Parliament at all, it would only be to say that the principles on which cases are decided represent English law, subject to legislation to the contrary. The subordination of precedent to legislation is based on the fact that a statute can always alter the effect of a judicial decision. A particular custom is also subordinate to legislation in this sense because it can be rendered of no effect by a statute, but it is very doubtful whether a particular custom is subordinate to precedent in this sense. Even if they have not all been embodied in the *rationes decidendi* of cases coming before the House of Lords, and although there is some difference of opinion about the manner in which they should be formulated, the tests of the validity of a local custom are too deeply rooted in our law to be changed by judicial as opposed to parliamentary action.

The distinction between subordination by derivation and subordination due to the power of abrogation has an important bearing on the formulation of the ultimate principles of a legal system. So far as the English system is concerned, as precedent is subordinate to legislation by reason only of the fact that the effect of a judicial decision can be abrogated by legislation, the rule concerning the efficacy of precedent must be treated as ultimate. It is not necessary to treat the rules concerning the validity of a local custom in the same way, because these rules are derived from precedent although they probably cannot be abrogated by judicial decision. It is true that, in places, Salmond equated the law-producing effect of statute, judicial decision, and immemorial custom, but his subsequent treatment of the ultimate principles of the English legal system makes it plain that he considered these to be the rules that Acts of Parliament and judicial decisions have the force of law, and no other rules.

[13] The courts never apply tests such as that of reasonableness to determine the validity of the contents of a statute, once satisfied that it was duly enacted, and that is why statute law is not said to be derived from case-law.

3. THE RELATION OF PRECEDENT TO LEGISLATION

Precedent is, as we have seen, subordinate to legislation as a source of law in the sense that a statute can always abrogate the effect of a judicial decision, and the courts regard themselves as bound to give effect to legislation once they are satisfied that it was duly enacted. In this context the word 'bound' bears the same meaning as that which it bears in such sentences as 'A judge of first instance is bound by the *ratio decidendi* of cases decided by the Court of Appeal', and this was discussed at the beginning of Chapter III. The subordination was not always as complete as it is today, but it was clearly recognized by the beginning of the nineteenth century at the latest.

All that a court of justice can do is to look to the Parliamentary roll. If from that it should appear that a bill has passed both Houses and received the Royal Assent, no court of justice can inquire into the mode in which it was introduced into Parliament, or into what was done previous to its introduction, or what passed in Parliament during its progress in its various stages through both Houses.[14]

The courts' reaction to a suggestion that a bill which had received the Royal Assent and been placed as an Act on the Parliament roll did not contain amendments made in the Lords must remain as much a matter of speculation as it was when Maitland raised the question some sixty years ago.[15]

Joint operation of legislation and case-law

English precedent rules are derived from judicial practice not from statute. No doubt Parliament could enact legislation abrogating or altering any of them, but it has not done so. Consequently, precedent and legislation are ultimate as distinct from derivative sources of law, neither owes its validity to the other or to any other legal source,[16] but precedent is of course subordinate to legislation in the sense that legislation can abrogate it. The relationship is of interest from the point of view of the joint operation of case-law

---

[14] *Edinburgh Railway Co.* v. *Wauchope* (1842) 8 Cl. and F. 710 at 724–5. See *British Railways Board* v. *Pickin* [1974] AC 765. For discussion of the scope of the doctrine of parliamentary sovereignty, see Winterton *LQR* 92 (1976), 591; Allott *CLJ* 38 (1979), 79; Allan *OJLS* 3 (1983), 22.

[15] *Constitutional History of England*, 381–2.

[16] See p. 167 *supra* for this terminology.

and statute law. Dean Roscoe Pound said in a famous article[17] that four ways may be conceived of in which courts in such a legal system as ours might deal with a legislative innovation.

1. They might receive it fully into the body of the law as affording not only a rule to be applied but a principle from which to reason, and hold it, as a later and more direct expression of the general will; as superior authority to judge-made rules on the same general subject; and so reason from it by analogy in preference to them.

2. They might receive it fully into the body of the law to be reasoned from by analogy the same as any other rule of law, regarding it, however, as of equal or coordinate authority in this respect with judge-made rules upon the same subject.

3. They might refuse to receive it into the body of the law and give effect to it directly only; refusing to reason from it by analogy but giving it, nevertheless, a liberal interpretation to cover the whole field it was intended to cover.

4. They might not only refuse to reason from it by analogy and apply it directly only, but also give to it a strict and narrow interpretation, holding it down rigidly to those cases which it covers expressly.

Pound said that the fourth hypothesis represents the orthodox common-law attitude towards legislative innovation although he thought we were tending towards the third. Of the second and first hypotheses he said that he thought they would

doubtless appear to the common lawyer as absurd. He can hardly conceive that a rule of statutory origin may be treated as a permanent part of the general body of the law.

But Pound submitted that the course of legal development upon which we had already entered must lead us to adopt the method of the second, and eventually the method of the first, hypothesis.

Pound's article was written as long ago as 1907 and it was primarily concerned with the United States. So far as the English legal system is concerned, it is open to question whether the second, or even perhaps the first hypothesis, has not been accepted for a considerable time. The common-law presumption that a person is dead if he has been absent from and unheard of by those likely to have heard of him for a continuous period of seven

---

[17] 'Common Law and Legislation', *HLR* 21 (1907), 383.

years or more was established early in the nineteenth century and is generally supposed to have been evolved by analogy with statutes of the seventeenth century.[18] Courts of equity applied the Statute of Limitations analogically, laying down a time-limit within which actions must be begun. More recently, statutory provisions to the effect that, when corroborative evidence is required in a criminal case, it should 'implicate the accused in a material particular', have been applied by analogy to the evidence of accomplices with regard to which the jury must be warned of the danger of convicting without corroboration.

Analogical application of statutes

The terms of one statutory provision may be used as the ground of a conclusion concerning the construction of another statutory provision. In R. v. *Bourne*,[19] for instance, a doctor was charged with abortion. He had operated on a young girl who was the victim of a rape with a view to procuring her miscarriage. He had come to the conclusion, after consulting another doctor, that the operation was necessary for the preservation of the girl's health. The offence of abortion is defined by s. 58 of the Offences against the Person Act 1861 in the following terms:

Any person who, with the intent to procure the miscarriage of any woman . . . unlawfully administers to her or causes to be taken by her any poison or noxious thing or unlawfully uses any instrument or other means is guilty of abortion.

Macnaghten J treated the case as one which turned on the effect to be given to the word 'unlawfully', and he found guidance in the Infant Life Preservation Act 1929, which created the offence of child destruction. This crime is committed by someone who, with intent to destroy the life of a child capable of being born alive, by any wilful act, causes it to die before it has an existence independent of its mother.[20] Under a proviso in the Infant Life Preservation Act, no one is guilty of child destruction unless it is proved that the act which caused the death of the child was not done in good faith for the purpose only of preserving the life of the

---

[18] Thayer, *A Preliminary Treatise on Evidence*, 319.

[19] [1939] 1 KB 687.

[20] A foetus must be 28 weeks or more old before it is deemed to have an existence independent of its mother. That is one reason why the offence differs from that of abortion. A further distinction between the two offences lies in the fact that child destruction may be committed in the course of a natural birth.

mother. Macnaghten J directed the jury in *Bourne*'s case that the accused was not guilty if they thought that he might have been acting to preserve the life of the mother, and that the term 'life' could be broadly construed so as to include a healthy existence. The doctor was acquitted; such conduct would now be protected by the express wording of the Abortion Act 1967.

The foregoing examples show that legislative innovations are sometimes received fully into the body of the law to be reasoned from by analogy. It is, however, possible to point to many instances in which this has not been done.[21] There is no convincing reason why superiority in analogical force should always be attributed to legislation. Pound spoke of it as a later and more direct expression of the general will, and hence as something to be reasoned from by analogy in preference to judge-made rules on the same subject. But this fails to take account of the fact that the force of analogy is something which varies very greatly. Legislation should surely only be regarded as the superior of case-law in this respect when there are competing analogies of equal force from each of these sources, and that is a situation which arises so infrequently that the fact that our judges do not appear to have considered it can hardly be the occasion of any surprise.

Where some part of the common law is abrogated by statute, the effect on subsequent judicial reasoning varies according to how deeply the reform is understood to have dug. When the unpopular common-law doctrine of common employment was abolished by the Law Reform (Personal Injuries) Act 1948, it was held that arguments derived from it should no longer be advanced.[22] On the other hand, general statements of principle about the characteristics of interests in land contained in *National Provincial Bank Ltd.* v. *Ainsworth*[23] are frequently invoked even though the particular ruling which they were used to support in that case—that deserted wives have no interest in a matrimonial home capable of binding successors to their husbands—was abrogated by the Matrimonial Homes Act 1967. In this context, it is necessary to bear in mind a distinction between 'the present law', which it is the court's duty to apply as a consistent whole, and the historic 'common law', which is an evolving source of principles to be invoked in the way of analogical and doctrinal reasoning when the present law is open to

---

[21] See P. S. Atiyah, 'Common Law and Statute Law', *MLR* 48 [1985], 1; J. Bell and G. Engel (eds.), *Cross, Statutory Interpretation* (2nd edn.), 41–4.
[22] *Broom* v. *Morgan* (1953) 1 QB 597.   [23] (1965) AC 1175.

more than one interpretation. So far as the law presently in force is concerned, if some proposition of the common law is in direct conflict with a proposition emanating from Parliament, it is no longer valid. Broader statements of principle contained within the historic common law—whether conceptual definitions or wide formulations of individual responsibilities or rights—have a more timeless quality. They grow, flourish, and sometimes wither away. Legislation may play a role in this evolutionary process, to the extent that it is clearly premissed on normative assumptions inconsistent with those embodied in a particular principle. But the mere fact that the ruling in a certain case has been abrogated does not necessarily rob general principles enunciated in that decision of continuing doctrinal force.[24]

Statute law and case-law are directly integrated in our system so far as the legal meaning of certain words is concerned. Most words have not got a specifically legal meaning. In the absence of good reason to the contrary, the courts give effect to the ordinary meaning whether the words are used in a statute, a private document, or an oral transaction. In any event, the courts are more often than not concerned with the effect of whole phrases and sentences in a particular context rather than with that of a single word. There are, however, certain instances in which a word has acquired a legal meaning.

When this is the case, the influence of the doctrine of precedent on the construction of a statute must be as great as its influence on the construction of private documents. There are, however, some special problems concerning precedent and the interpretation of statutes which must now be considered.

4. PRECEDENT AND THE INTERPRETATION OF STATUTES

The two points calling for discussion are the question whether it is necessary to make any modification in the usual method of determining the *ratio decidendi* when the case under consideration turns on the interpretation of a statute, and the suggestion, derived from *Ex parte Campbell*,[25] that once statutory words have been interpreted by a superior court, the re-enactment of those words in substantially the same statute invests that interpretation with parliamentary authority.

[24] See J. W. Harris, *Law and Legal Science*, 111–22.
[25] (1869) LR 5 Ch. 773.

The ratio decidendi *of a case interpreting a statute*

According to the view taken in Chapter II, the *ratio decidendi* is, generally speaking, any rule of law expressedly or impliedly treated by the judge as a necessary step in reaching his conclusion. It was recognized that due regard must be had to the facts of the particular case and the *rationes decidendi* of other cases. Reference was also made in Chapter II to the opinion of Lord Halsbury in *Quinn* v. *Leathem*[26] according to which a case is only authority for what it actually decides. On this view, every case has certain facts which all lawyers would recognize to be material, and the *ratio decidendi* is all the material facts plus the conclusion, i.e. the major premiss which would warrant the order of the court if the material facts were made to constitute the minor premiss of a syllogism. We also saw that there are certain circumstances in which it becomes necessary to take this view of the proposition of law for which a case is authority. Examples are decisions for which no reason is given, and decisions which have been distinguished in subsequent cases. Must such a view be taken of all decisions concerning the interpretation of a statute? Two dissenting judgments of Lord Denning appear to give an affirmative answer to this question. As Denning LJ he said, in *Paisner* v. *Goodrich*:[27]

When the judges of this court (the Court of Appeal) give a decision on the interpretation of an act of Parliament that decision itself is binding on them and their successors. But the words which the judges used in giving a decision are not binding. This is often a very fine distinction, because the decision can only be expressed in words. Nevertheless, it is a real distinction which will best be appreciated by remembering that, when interpreting a statute, the sole function of the court is to apply the words of the statute to a given situation. Once a decision has been reached on that situation, the doctrine of precedent requires us to apply the statute in the same way in any similar situation; but not in a different situation. Whenever a new situation emerges, not covered by previous decisions, the court must be governed by the statute and not by the words of the judges.

This passage was intended as a protest against applying the tests laid down by previous cases to determine whether part of a house was 'let as a separate dwelling' within the meaning of the Rent and Mortgage Interest Restriction Act 1920, when the case before the court concerned an agreement by which the landlord, who

[26] [1901] AC 495 at 506, p. 57 *supra*.   [27] [1955] 2 QB 343 at 358.

retained part of the house, was to share the use of a spare bedroom with the tenant, while the previous cases concerned agreements to share the use of bathrooms or sitting-rooms or kitchens. Denning LJ was clearly of the opinion that the question whether the situation before the court differs in a material respect from that covered by the previous decision must be decided by the court dealing with the new case, and that that court is in no way bound by the principle which the judge in the previous case appeared to consider necessary for his decision.

Lord Denning repeated this view concerning the authority of past decisions on the interpretation of a statute in *London Transport Executive* v. *Betts*.[28] In that case the House of Lords was concerned with the question whether a depot in which vehicles might be reconditioned was used for their 'maintenance' so as to take it outside the statutory provisions concerning the rating of industrial hereditaments. A previous decision of the House[29] had treated a paint shop as used for the 'maintenance' of vehicles within the meaning of the relevant legislation, and, in *Betts*'s case, the majority concluded that this previous decision applied to the depot. In the course of his dissenting speech Lord Denning said:

That is, to my mind, a decision on the particular facts of the paint shop and nothing else. The decision may be binding on your Lordships if there is another such paint shop anywhere, but it is not, in my opinion, binding for anything else. If your Lordships were to elevate that particular precedent into a binding decision on the meaning of 'maintenance', you would, I believe, carry the doctrine of precedent farther than it has ever been carried before.

When *Paisner* v. *Goodrich* reached the House of Lords, the decision of the majority of the Court of Appeal on the construction of the Rent Act was reversed. Lord Reid alluded to the observations of Denning LJ but he does not appear to have agreed with them. Lord Reid said:

No court is entitled to substitute its words for the words of the act. A court, however, can, and must, decide the appropriate test in a particular case and, when the Court of Appeal has laid down a test, that test ought to be followed in all cases which do not present substantial relevant differences. . . . That does not mean that the words used by the Court of Appeal are to be treated as if they were words in an act of Parliament. In

[28] [1959] AC 211 at 246.
[29] *Potteries Electric Traction Co. Ltd.* v. *Bailey* [1931] AC 151.

substantially different circumstances they are only a guide, and not a rule.[30]

The *ratio decidendi* of any case is only a guide in substantially different circumstances, but Lord Reid, unlike Lord Denning, would evidently consider that the judge in a subsequent case should have regard to the words used by the previous judge in order to determine whether there are relevant differences between the facts of the two cases. This conclusion is borne out by the fact that in *London Transport Executive* v. *Betts*,[31] Lord Reid asserted in effect that there is no difference, so far as the binding force of the *ratio decidendi* is concerned, between a decision on the construction of a statute and a decision on any other point of law.

While it would plainly be going too far to say that there is anything in the nature of a fixed practice according to which decisions on the interpretation of a statute are only authoritative in subsequent cases in which all the material facts are the same, without regard to the rule of law which the judge considered necessary for those decisions, there is at least one reason why the *ratio decidendi* of cases concerned with statutory interpretation may have to be given a restricted effect. It is generally recognized that differing decisions on the meaning of the same words need never be treated as conflicting if the words are used in different statutes.

It is possible to point to several cases in which, when a court has been called on to construe certain words in a statute, a decision on the meaning of the same words in a different statute has been disregarded for no other reason than that the case was concerned with a different statute.[32] When this practice is followed, the *ratio decidendi* of the previous case may be restrictively interpreted because the court responsible for it may have thought it was acting on a more general principle of construction. The practice is no doubt a desirable one in many instances, but it is to be regretted that the judges sometimes say no more than that the case cited turned on a different statute from that with which they are concerned. There may be the best of reasons for construing different statutes in different ways, even if they do contain the same words, but the grounds of a decision to do so ought always to be clearly expressed.

---

[30] *Goodrich* v. *Paisner* [1957] AC 65 at 88.   [31] [1959] AC 211 at 232.
[32] See *R.* v. *Evans-Jones and Jenkins* (1923) 17 Cr. App. Rep. 121.

Ex parte Campbell

If the doctrine of precedent has something less than its usual force when the same words are used in different statutes, it may be more rigid than ever when applied to the re-enactment of a statute which has already been construed by the courts. In *Ex parte Campbell*[33] James LJ said:

Where once certain words in an Act of Parliament have received a judicial construction in one of the Superior Courts, and the Legislature has repeated them without alteration in a subsequent statute, I conceive that the Legislature must be taken to have used them according to the meaning which a Court of competent jurisdiction has given to them.

Taken literally, this rule of statutory construction would mean that, if a first instance judge construed a statute in a particular way and that statute were re-enacted in the same form, it would not be open to the Court of Appeal or the House of Lords to give it a different interpretation. That this was the inference to be drawn was asserted by Lord Buckmaster in *Barras* v. *Aberdeen Steam Trawling and Fishing Co. Ltd.*[34] This view has, however, been decisively rejected by two decisions of the House of Lords, in each of which their Lordships refused to give to a re-enacting statute the meaning attributed to its terms by decisions of the Court of Appeal prior to the re-enactment. In *Farrell* v. *Alexander*, Lord Wilberforce expressed scepticism about the doctrine of parliamentary endorsement of decided cases, on the ground that it might often be fictional to suppose that the draftsman had them in mind.[35] In the same case, Lord Simon rejected the doctrine on a different ground: the draftsman could indeed be presumed to know the relevant case-law, but he must also be presumed to know that any decision interpreting the words he uses carries only as much authority as it bears under the general doctrine of precedent.[36] *Farrell* v. *Alexander* was not cited in *R.* v. *Chard*,[37] but in the latter case the House again repudiated Lord Buckmaster's view. They preferred the opinion expressed by Lord Macmillan in the *Barras* case,[38] that the presumption in favour of parliamentary endorsement applied only where judicial interpretation was well settled and well recognized, and even then it must yield to the rule that

[33] (1869) LR 5 Ch. 703 at 706.   [34] (1933) AC 402, 412.
[35] (1977) AC 59, 74–5.   [36] (1977) AC 59, 89–91.
[37] (1984) AC 279.   [38] (1933) AC 402, 446–7.

statutory language is to be given its plain meaning where that can be clearly ascertained. It may be concluded that the doctrine derived from James LJ's principle now retains very little force.

5. PRECEDENT AND EUROPEAN COMMUNITY LAW

Since 1 January 1973, those revisions of European Community law which are directly applicable within member states have been sources of English law. The historical causes of this development include the accession of the United Kingdom to the Treaty of Rome and other treaties and the enactment of The European Communities Act 1972. Section 2 (4) of that Act provides that 'any enactment passed or to be passed' shall be construed and have effect subject to the provisions of the section, which incorporate Community law into domestic law. There are two views as to the juridical consequences of this incorporation. The first, which has some support in the Court of Appeal, is that parliamentary sovereignty has been limited: any rule of domestic law which prevented courts from giving effect to directly enforceable rights established in Community law would be bad. 'To that extent', in the words of Bingham LJ, 'a United Kingdom statute is no longer inviolable as it once was'.[39] The second view, which to date appears to be prevalent in the House of Lords, is that the incorporation of European law has resulted in a radically new doctrine of statutory interpretation, according to which every act of Parliament is to be construed in such a way as to avoid conflict with directly enforceable rights: section 2 (4) of the 1972 Act 'has', in the words of Lord Bridge, 'precisely the same effect as if a section were incorporated' in any later enactment which in terms laid down that its provisions are to be without prejudice to directly enforceable Community rights.[40] On the former view, the Treaty of Rome and other treaties establishing the various communities are ultimate sources of English law. On the latter view, they are derivative sources owing their status as parts of English law to the enactment of the 1972 Act. On either view, directly enforceable Community law will be applied. It would only be necessary to

[39] *R. v. Secretary of State for Transport, ex parte Factortame Ltd.* (1989) 2 CMLR 353, 403. See also the decision of the Court of Appeal in *Pickstone* v. *Freemans plc* (1989) AC 66, 73.
[40] *R. v. Secretary of State for Transport, ex parte Factortame Ltd.* (1990) 2 AC 85, 140. See also the decision of the House of Lords in *Pickstone* v. *Freemans plc* (1989) AC 66, 109.

make a definitive choice between them if, without abrogation of the treaties by mutual consent of the participating states, the United Kingdom Parliament were to enact legislation which could not be construed in the way suggested by Lord Bridge, for example, if it purported to repeal the 1972 Act or to enact expressly that some provision was to take effect notwithstanding its infringement of Community law.

English courts loyally accept as conclusive the pronouncements of the European Court of Justice on European Community law. They also accept the jurisprudence of the Court which has established that, in the event of conflict between a rule of European law and a rule of domestic law, the former must prevail.[41] No such conflict has yet emerged so far as English rules of precedent are concerned. As we saw in Chapter III, the Court of Appeal in *Duke* v. *Reliance Systems Ltd.* refused to regard an earlier decision of its own as *per incuriam* merely because an EEC directive, which might have influenced its construction of a statute, had not been cited to it.[42] In that case, Sir John Donaldson MR said that he did not believe that section 2 (4) of the 1972 Act 'has the effect of abrogating the doctrine of *stare decisis* in this court, even when European law is involved'.[43] However, the case did not concern directly enforceable rights but merely a directive binding national governments, and in any event the directive had not been issued until after the passing of the statute whose construction was in question. No doubt, if an earlier Court of Appeal decision overlooked some directly enforceable provision of Community law the *per incuriam* exception would apply.

To conceive of a direct conflict between the provisions of Community law and the English rules of precedent is to imagine a situation in which something has gone awry with the procedure laid down by Art. 177 of the Treaty of Rome. That article provides that where a question of Community law is raised before any court or tribunal of a member state, and that court or tribunal considers that a decision on the question is necessary to enable it to give a judgment, it may request the European Court of Justice to give a preliminary ruling. The article further provides that where any

[41] *Costa* v. *Enel* (6/64) (1964) ECR 585, 593–4 judgment of ECJ. *Amministrazione delle Finanze dello Stato* v. *Simmenthal SpA* (106/77) (1978) ECR 629, 643–4 judgment of ECJ. *The Siskina* (1979) AC 210, 262 Lord Hailsham LC. *Macarthys Ltd.* v. *Smith* (1981) QB 180, 200 Lord Denning MR. *R.* v. *Secretary of State for Transport, ex parte Factortame Ltd.* (No. 2), (1991) 1 All ER 70 ECJ and HL.
[42] See p. 151 *supra*.   [43] (1988) QB 108, 113.

such question is raised in a case pending before a court or tribunal against whose decisions there is no judicial remedy under national law, 'that court or tribunal shall bring the matter before the Court of Justice'. Thus, a discretion to refer questions is conferred on all courts and tribunals, and an obligation to refer is imposed on final appellate courts.[44]

Where a reference is made, the ruling obtained is clearly binding on the referring court. For a direct clash with English precedent rules to occur, something like the following sequence of events would have to come about. In case A, a superior English court rules on a question of Community law which, by virtue of direct applicability, is also a question of English law. (Section 3 of the 1972 Act provides that questions of Community law are questions of law not fact, so that they differ in this respect from questions of foreign law.) In case B, an inferior court or tribunal has the following alternatives: (i) to follow the *ratio decidendi* of case A; (ii) in the exercise of its discretion under Art. 177, to refer the matter to the European Court for a preliminary ruling; (iii) if satisfied, in the light perhaps of a subsequent judgment of the European Court, that the decision in case A was mistaken, itself to make a ruling in a contrary sense. Alternatives (ii) and (iii) would represent a departure from English rules of precedent. It seems clear that the jurisprudence of the European court itself supports at least the second alternative.[45] It was held in the *Rheinmühlen* cases[46] that no hierarchical rule of bindingness within a national court structure could exclude the discretion of an inferior court to refer a question under Art. 177 for a preliminary ruling.

For the foregoing situation to have come about, the superior English court in case A would have had to have given a ruling either without making a reference or one which went beyond the terms of a ruling made pursuant to a reference. That might occur if, say, the Court of Appeal took the view that European law on a point was so clear that it need not exercise its discretion to refer the matter—always assuming that it also decided that, as to the issue before it, it was not the final court of appeal so that it had a

---

[44] For a general discussion of Art. 177 and the preliminary rulings procedure, see T. C. Hartley, *The Foundations of European Community Law* (2nd edn.), ch. 9; N. Brown and F. G. Jacobs, *The Court of Justice of the European Communities* (3rd edn.), ch. 10.

[45] Brown and Jacobs, *Court of Justice*, 318–22.

[46] *Rheinmühlen v. Einfuhr -und Vorratsstelle fur Getreide und Futtermittel* (146/73) (166/73) (1974) ECR 33 and 139.

discretion not to refer. Or it might arise where the House of Lords took the view that the duty of the final appellate court to refer questions did not apply because some ruling of the European Court already covered the issue, or where the House simply overlooked the fact that a decision on a question of Community law was a necessary step in reaching its judgment. In the latter context, it may be surmised that the view that the *per incuriam* doctrine does not apply, as between *rationes* of the House and the decisions of inferior courts,[47] would not be decisive. Should any of these scenarios arise, an English court or tribunal might be forced to choose between English rules of precedent and the jurisprudence of the European Court of Justice, and current trends suggest that it would prefer the latter. Indeed, an argument might be advanced that it was statutorily bound to do so by the terms of section 3 (1) of the European Communities Act. That subsection provides that 'any question as to the meaning or effect of any of the treaties' shall be for determination 'in accordance with the principles laid down' by the European Court. It might be contended that the issue whether English precedent rules have been partially abrogated is a question as to the effect of the Treaty of Rome.

[47] *Cassell and Co. Ltd.* v. *Broome* (1972) AC 1027, 1054 Lord Hailsham LC. *Baker* v. *R.* (1975) AC 774, 788 Lord Diplock. *Miliangos* v. *George Frank (Textiles) Ltd.* (1976) AC 443, 479 Lord Simon.

VI

PRECEDENT AND
JUDICIAL REASONING

1. INTRODUCTORY

This chapter begins with a consideration of the extent to which judicial reasoning about law may be properly described as either 'deductive' or 'inductive'. The question is probably less significant than the frequency with which it is raised suggests, but the discussion makes it possible to bring into relief certain features of English case-law which have a bearing on the application of precedent. The rest of the chapter is primarily concerned with reasoning by analogy. A few remarks were made on this topic in Chapter I, and it is now proposed to consider this feature of the English doctrine of precedent in greater detail. The subject is an important one because it is principally by means of such reasoning that the judges have developed a coherent body of law. Having ascertained the *ratio decidendi* of a previous case, and having, where necessary, interpreted that case in the light of other decisions, they must decide whether to apply it to the facts before them. Sometimes the judge has no choice in this matter because he is bound by the previous case according to the rules of precedent. On other occasions he has a high degree of choice on the question whether the previous case should be applied. At its best this procedure is an excellent means of developing the law and it is illustrated in section 3. It is none the less attended by certain dangers. The consideration of past cases with a view to ascertaining their *rationes decidendi* is not conducive to a thorough examination of the social consequences of the decisions, and important social factors are sometimes ignored when the question whether previous cases are distinguishable from that before the court is approached. This type of danger which is, to some extent, the product of reasoning by analogy is discussed in section 4. In section 5 reference is made to cases where there is nothing in the nature of a binding precedent in order to point to a contrast with those in which precedent predominates. Cases of the former kind are often said to be 'cases of first impression'.

The reader must be on his guard against concluding that the procedure discussed in connection with reasoning by analogy is in any sense one which the judge is obliged to follow according to the doctrine of precedent. Decisions in perfect compliance with that doctrine and of indubitable excellence so far as their social consequences are concerned are no doubt often reached intuitively, and to this extent the realists have drawn attention to an important feature of the judicial process. All that can be done in a work of this nature is to outline what is believed to be a fairly normal type of judicial reasoning.

The discussion is confined to reasoning about law. No attempt is made to consider judicial reasoning about fact. The question whether a person's conduct complies with a certain standard, such as the degree of care to be expected of a reasonable man by which issues of civil negligence are decided, is sometimes said to be one of law,[1] but judicial reasoning on the subject is not considered in this chapter because decisions with regard to it do not constitute a precedent.[2] The relevant cases are frequently compared, but a judge is in no way obliged to compare them.

2. DEDUCTION AND INDUCTION IN JUDICIAL REASONING[3]

The main justification for describing any aspect of judicial reasoning as deductive is the appropriateness of one type of syllogism at a certain stage of the argument. This is best illustrated by the application of a statute to the facts of a case.

Suppose A is charged with abortion by using an instrument to procure a miscarriage. The argument in support of a conviction can be set out as follows: According to s. 58 of the Offences against the Person Act 1861, whosoever, with intent to procure the miscarriage of any woman, shall unlawfully use any instrument, shall be guilty of an offence and, being convicted thereof, shall be liable to imprisonment for life. A unlawfully used an instrument to procure the miscarriage of a woman, therefore A is guilty of the

---

[1] O. C. Jensen, *The Nature of Legal Argument*.

[2] *Qualcast (Wolverhampton) Ltd.* v. *Haynes* [1959] AC 743.

[3] For discussions of this subject see Allen, *Law in the Making* (7th edn.), 161; Jensen, *The Nature of Legal Argument*, ch. 1; MacCormick, *Legal Reasoning and Legal Theory*, ch. 2; Stone, *Precedent and Law*, 22–31; Alexy, *A Theory of Legal Argumentation*, 221–30.

offence charged. So far as its verbal form is concerned this is exactly the same kind of syllogism as that which runs 'All men are mortal, Socrates is a man, therefore Socrates is mortal.' Is there such a substantial difference between the two statements as to justify the description of the second, but not the first, as an example of deductive reasoning? Those who deny that this type of judicial reasoning is deductive would point to the difference in kind between the two conclusions. They would urge that the implications of the statement 'A is guilty of the offence charged' differ fundamentally from the implications of Socrates' mortality. This latter is a factual conclusion. Socrates is certain to die. By contrast, the statement that A is guilty of the offence charged can only be rendered fully intelligible by reference to a number of legal rules, including those under which the judge is empowered to punish someone found guilty by a jury. Due allowance must certainly be made for this distinction, but it may yet be the case that there is a sufficient resemblance between the methods by which the conclusion is reached to justify the description of each of them as an example of deductive reasoning.

Those who object to the use of this description might also point to the difficulty there is in applying some of the tests of valid deduction to the conclusions following from the application of legal rules. However definitely these rules may be stated, they must always be read in conjunction with others. There is thus some difficulty in testing the validity of a syllogism based on a legal rule by enquiring whether a denial of the conclusion entails the denial of one or other of the premises. For example, s. 178 (b) of the Licensing Act 1964 provides that a publican who supplies liquor to a constable on duty shall be liable to a fine. There is no reference to the accused's state of mind, and it would appear to follow from the fact that A, a publican, supplied B, a constable on duty, with a glass of beer, that A is guilty of an offence against s. 178 (b). But this would not necessarily be the case because the courts have construed the section in the light of a rule applied in a number of other contexts to the effect that a reasonable mistake of fact is a defence to a criminal charge.[4] Therefore, if A believed on reasonable grounds that B was off duty when the beer was supplied, he would not be guilty of the offence charged although the words of the statute would suggest that A's guilt is the only

---

[4] *Sherras* v. *De Rutzen* [1895] 1 QB 918.

possible conclusion. One of the standard tests of the validity of deductive reasoning about fact is certainly to enquire whether a denial of the conclusion entails a denial of one or other of the premisses. If it does not do so, the reasoning must be faulty. But the objection that the test cannot easily be applied to the kind of legal reasoning under consideration can be met by making allowance for the defeasible[5] nature of legal rules when formulating the appropriate premiss. In the example which has been given, the major premiss could read 'A publican who supplies liquor to a constable on duty is liable to a fine unless the circumstances bring him within the ambit of certain defences.' The list of possible defences would not be a long one. It would include the defences of insanity, duress, and mistake.

Allowance must also be made for the fact that the precise scope of most legal rules is uncertain. There is usually a hard core of cases to which they undoubtedly apply, but there is a penumbra with regard to which a certain amount of doubt is inevitable. The hard core is seldom if ever the subject of judicial reasoning about law, for it only gives rise to cases turning on questions of fact. Cases on the penumbra do call for judicial reasoning about law, but there is an element of triviality in describing the reasoning to which they give rise as deductive. This is because the crucial decision is made before the reasoning can be cast into syllogistic form. Not only is the syllogism constructed after the facts have been found, but it is also constructed after any legal problems concerning the scope of the rule have been solved.[6]

This may be illustrated by a further reference to *R. v. Bourne*.[7] The result of this case can be expressed in syllogistic form as follows: s. 58 of the Offences against the Person Act 1861 only penalizes those who unlawfully use an instrument with intent to procure a woman's miscarriage. Dr Bourne did not use an instrument unlawfully because he acted in order to prevent a young girl from becoming a physical wreck, therefore Dr Bourne was not guilty of an offence against s. 58. The conclusion only

[5] The description is that of Professor Hart, see *Proceedings of the Aristotelian Society*, NS 49. 171.

[6] A division of the judicial process into two independent types of inquiry, viz. (a) what is the relevant rule (question of law)? and (b) did the party in fact do what the rule requires (question of fact)? may mislead; it conceals the fact that until the meaning of the legal rule is settled it is impossible to refer to the facts of the case in its terms' (H. L. A. Hart, *Proceedings of the Aristotelian Society*, suppl. 29. 260).

[7] [1939] 1 KB 687, p. 175 *supra*.

follows syllogistically from the terms of the statute and the facts of the case after a difficult point concerning the meaning of 'unlawfully' has been settled. Macnaghten J did not have recourse to any syllogism in order to settle this point. He reasoned analogically from the provisions of the Infant Life Preservation Act 1929. That statute deals with the crime of child destruction and says that, for the purpose of the definition of this offence, it is not unlawful to take the life of a child before it has an existence independent of its mother, provided the accused acted in order to preserve the mother's life. Although there is no similar provision in the Act of 1861 Macnaghten J considered himself entitled to interpret the word 'unlawfully' as used in that Act in a similar sense. He also interpreted the conception of the conservation of life with reference to that of a normal healthy life as opposed to the life of a physical wreck. He might have chosen one of the many statements concerning the indefensibility of taking life as an analogy pointing to a different conclusion from that at which he arrived. Having chosen the analogy of child destruction, he might have distinguished it from abortion either on the ground that the statutory definition of the former offence expressly refers to the defence of conserving the mother's life and thus suggests that it cannot be implied in the statutory definition of another offence, or else on the ground that Dr Bourne was protecting the health, not the life, of the girl upon whom he operated. Excellent reasons can be given in support of the course adopted by Macnaghten J, but they must be taken to have determined his choice before his conclusion can be presented in the form of a syllogism.

When a judicial decision is based on case-law without any reference to any statute, the reasoning can be cast into syllogistic form at the final stage of the argument. Once the judge has decided upon the relevant rule, its scope, and the facts, the validity of his conclusions can be established by deduction in the approved way. Once again the syllogism is trivial, but, whether we are concerned with the application of statutes or cases, the triviality of the reasoning involved at the stage when it is applied does not alter the fact that it is essentially deductive. Deductive reasoning might be far from trivial if used at an earlier stage in a legal argument. It could be employed to expose the logical fallacies in the arguments of counsel, or even the judicial reasoning in a previous case, but a discussion of these possibilities would not have much to do with the effect of case law generally and the doctrine of precedent in particular on legal reasoning.

The idea that judicial reasoning about law can be properly described as inductive stems from the fact that a judge often extracts a rule for the decision of the case before him from one or more previous decisions. Alternatively, he sometimes formulates a rule and then tests it by reference to past cases. The first procedure may be likened to the induction of the scientist who formulates a general proposition of fact from particular instances, and the second procedure may be likened to what has been termed 'secondary induction'[8] by which particular instances are examined with a view to establishing or disproving the validity of a general proposition which has already been formulated. Although the analogy between judicial reasoning with regard to case-law and these inductive processes is clear enough, the differences are sufficiently striking to cast the gravest doubts upon the propriety of describing judicial reasoning as inductive. The most important reason is that, for the scientist, the instant case is relevant either to his formulation of the general proposition from particular instances because it is one of the instances, or else to the testing of the rule which he had already formulated because it is part of the material by which that rule is tested. For the judge, on the other hand, the purpose of the rule is to aid in the decision of the instant case. To quote an American writer:

The judge does not employ the case before him as a means of testing the validity of the rules which he employs in reasoning towards his decision. The whole theory of decision according to law is that the rules are to govern the case, and not, like scientific laws, to be governed by it.[9]

The question whether judicial reasoning about law is deductive or inductive is not susceptible of an answer in general terms because everything depends on the stage of the argument with reference to which the question is raised. When an answer in general terms is attempted it is usually that the reasoning is deductive when concerned with the application of a statute because it proceeds from the general to the particular, but inductive when concerned with the application of case-law because it proceeds from the particular to the general. The foregoing discussion suggests that the usual answer is open to two objections.

[8] Kneale, *Probability and Induction*, 104.
[9] Dickinson, 79 *University of Pennsylvania Law Review* 833.

In the first place, there are considerably more analogies between law cases in which a statute is applied and a typical instance of deductive reasoning about fact than there are between the application of case-law and inductive reasoning about factual matters. Secondly, reasoning which supporters of the usual answer describe as deductive plays the same part in the application of case-law as it does in the application of a statute.

3. REASONING BY ANALOGY[10]

When a single precedent is concerned it is possible to point to three stages in judicial reasoning by analogy although it is not suggested that they are always separated in practice. First comes the perception of relevant likenesses between the previous case and the one before the court. Next there is the determination of the *ratio decidendi* of the previous case and finally there is the decision to apply that *ratio* to the instant case. Analogy may be said to be employed at the first stage, it plays no part at the second stage but it is frequently decisive at the third where the judge has to consider whether the facts of the case before him resemble those of the previous case sufficiently to necessitate the application of its *ratio decidendi*, or to justify him in applying it if he wishes to do so.

Some of the leading cases in which *Donoghue* v. *Stevenson* has been considered furnish good examples of this kind of reasoning. As we have seen, the generally accepted view of the *ratio decidendi* of *Donoghue*'s case is that:

a manufacturer of products, which he sells in such a form as to show that he intends them to reach the ultimate consumer in the form in which they left him with no reasonable possibility of intermediate examination and with the knowledge that the absence of reasonable care in the preparation or putting up of the products will result in an injury to the consumer's life or property, owes a duty to the consumer to take that reasonable care.[11]

Four years later, it was argued, *faute de mieux*, in *Grant* v. *The Australian Knitting Mills*[12] that the principle of *Donoghue* v. *Stevenson* was confined to cases in which food or drink was put into circulation without the possibility that anyone other than the

---

[10] For discussion of this subject, see Levi, *An Introduction to Legal Reasoning*; McCormick, *Legal Reasoning and Legal Theory*, 161–5, 180–94; Alexy, *A Theory of Legal Argumentation*, 281–4.

[11] pp. 44 *supra*.   [12] [1936] AC 85.

consumer would touch it. The plaintiff had contracted dermatitis in consequence of wearing pants containing an excess of sulphites, the presence of which was due to the negligence of the defendant manufacturers. The pants were purchased from a retailer and there was therefore no contractual relationship between the plaintiff and the manufacturers. When giving the advice of the Judicial Committee of the Privy Council Lord Wright expressed himself as follows with regard to this aspect of the case:

Counsel . . . sought to distinguish *Donoghue*'s case from the present on the ground that in the former the makers of the ginger beer had retained 'control' over it in the sense that they had placed it in stoppered and sealed bottles, so that it would not be tampered with until it was opened to be drunk, whereas the garments in question were merely put into paper packets, each containing six sets, which in the ordinary course would be taken down by the shopkeeper and opened and the contents handled and disposed of separately. . . . Their Lordships do not accept that contention. The decision in *Donoghue*'s case did not depend on the bottle being stoppered and sealed. The essential point in this regard was that the article should reach the consumer or user subject to the same defect as it had when it left the manufacturer. That this was true of the garment is, in their Lordships' opinion, beyond question.[13]

In *Haseldine* v. *Daw*,[14] the plaintiff sustained injuries in consequence of the collapse of a lift in which he was ascending on his way to the flat of one of the tenants of a large block. The landlord had employed a firm of engineers to repair the lift and the collapse occurred in consequence of their negligence. The question before the Court of Appeal was whether the Court was bound to give judgment for the plaintiff against the engineers. The majority took the view that they were for, to quote Goddard LJ:

Where the facts show that no intermediate inspection is practicable or is contemplated, a repairer of a chattel stands in no different position from that of a manufacturer, and owes such a duty of care to a person who, in the ordinary course, may be expected to make use of the thing repaired.[15]

The principle of *Donoghue*'s case was thus analogically extended in spite of the existence of two features by which *Haseldine* v. *Daw* might have been distinguished. In the first place the defendants were repairers and not manufacturers. Earlier authorities had suggested that a repairer was not liable on such facts. In *Donoghue* v. *Stevenson* these authorities were said to have turned on the way

<hr/>

[13] Ibid. 106–7.   [14] [1941] 2 KB 343.   [15] At 379.

in which the cases were pleaded.[16] Nevertheless, Lord Atkin's statement of the effect of *Donoghue*'s case was in terms confined to manufacturers and this was stressed in the dissenting judgment in *Haseldine* v. *Daw*. The second feature which might have been held sufficient to distinguish the two cases was the fact that the lift could have been inspected after the repairs had been completed, whereas the manufacturers had rendered an examination of the ginger beer before consumption impossible because noxious matter would not necessarily come from the bottle when the first glass was poured out. Did Lord Atkin's reference to 'no reasonable possibility of intermediate examination' mean that which was in fact possible, or an examination which the defendant might reasonably have anticipated? *Haseldine* v. *Daw* answers this question in the second sense.

The type of judicial reasoning with which we are at present concerned may lead to the instant case being decided by a rule different from that constituting the *ratio decidendi* of the previous one. Dissimilarities as well as resemblances between the two cases having been perceived, and the *ratio decidendi* of the previous case having been ascertained, the court may decide that this *ratio decidendi* does not apply to the instant situation, and ought not to be extended to cover it. Such a decision may be prompted by the terms of the rule itself or by the necessity of paying attention to some other rule. The terms of the rule itself accounted for the refusal of the Court of Appeal to apply *Donoghue* v. *Stevenson* in *Farr* v. *Butters*.[17] In that case the manufacturers of a crane sold it in parts to the employers of a workman, and the manufacturers were held not liable for that workman's death. He had had an ample opportunity to examine the crane for defects as he was the man who put it together, and he was in fact aware of the existence of such defects. A competing analogy caused Atkinson J, with reluctance, to abstain from applying *Donoghue* v. *Stevenson* in *Otto and Otto* v. *Bolton & Norris*.[18] The builders of a house were held not to be liable for injuries sustained by the purchaser's mother in consequence of the collapse of a defective ceiling.[19] Whether one speaks of 'reasoning by analogy' when the reasoning

---

[16] [1932] AC 562 at 591.   [17] [1932] 2 KB 606.
[18] [1936] 2 KB 46.
[19] The rule in *Donoghue* v. *Stevenson* would be applied to these facts today (*D. and F. Estates Ltd.* v. *Church Commissioners for England* [1989] AC 187). (*Murphy* v. *Brentwood DC* (1990) 2 All ER 908).

leads to the differentiation of a previous case is of course a purely verbal question.

To revert to the three main stages of reasoning by analogy, the perception of relevant resemblances or distinctions between the previous case and the one before the court is largely dependent on the context. Quite apart from the fact that there are bound to be a number of differences which any lawyer would at once recognize as immaterial, the way in which the instant case is argued and pleaded will frequently be of the utmost importance. The discovery of the *ratio decidendi* of the previous case is primarily a psychological problem. The determination by judge A of the principle according to which judge B decided case C is likely to be greatly influenced by the language used by judge B, but the very words ought not to be, and usually are not, decisive. The literal interpretation of a statute may have something to be said for it, but there is nothing to be said for such an interpretation of previous judgments. Our case-law has fared badly on the rare occasions when this approach has been adopted.[20]

There remains the question of the decision to apply the *ratio decidendi* of the former to the instant case. Sometimes there is no real choice in this matter. Granted that the Privy Council was bound by *Donoghue* v. *Stevenson* on the hearing of an Australian appeal, it would have been difficult not to apply that decision to the facts of *Grant* v. *The Australian Knitting Mills* (the case concerned with the sulphurated pants).[21] On other occasions there is undoubtedly room for choice because lawyers might well take different views concerning the legal significance of some distinction between the previous case and the one before the court. In that event everything will depend on whether the judge considers that the rule by which the previous case was decided is one that should be extended or restricted. Different views could have been, and were, taken on each of the questions with which *Haseldine* v. *Daw* (the case of the defective lift) was concerned. Did the principle of *Donoghue* v. *Stevenson* apply to a repairer as well as a manufacturer? And did it apply when there was a possibility, but

[20] See the interpretation of the words of Willes J in *Indermaur* v. *Dames* (1866) LR 1 CP 274.

[21] The question whether there is a real choice in the matter of following a case must, of course, be to some extent a matter of opinion. For example, it was argued that the fact that the pants might have been washed before they were worn provided a satisfactory reason for distinguishing *Grant*'s case from *Donoghue* v. *Stevenson*.

nothing in the nature of a probability, of intermediate inspection? The reason why each of these questions was answered in the affirmative had already been stated by Goddard LJ in an earlier case:

The legal conception of duty due to proximity has been authoritatively laid down by ,the House of Lords in *Donoghue* v. *Stevenson* and the modern tendency is to enlarge, and not to restrict, the ambit of that duty. The common law must expand to keep abreast of modern life.[22]

This tendency has not manifested itself in all the judgments in which *Donoghue* v. *Stevenson* has been considered,[23] and no doubt it was the fear of an undue extension of tortious liability which lay at the root of the dissenting judgment in *Haseldine* v. *Daw*.

The foregoing account of judicial reasoning by analogy is incomplete. The facts mentioned in a *dictum* rather than those of a previous case are frequently the starting-point, and the reasoning is usually concerned with more than one past decision. When several decisions are involved the reasoning consists of four stages: the perception of analogies (which may frequently conflict) between the instant case and a number of previous ones, the determination of the *rationes decidendi* of the previous cases, the construction of a rule or rules from those *rationes* and the decision to apply the rule, or one of the rules, to the instant case.[24] Notwithstanding the inadequacy of the foregoing discussion, it is hoped that enough has been said to enable the reader to realize that there is a danger that this kind of analogical reasoning may occasionally become too narrow and thus degenerate into conceptualism.

4. CONCEPTUALISM AND REASONING BY ANALOGY

Judicial reasoning by analogy leads to conceptualism when the factors of which account is taken at the third stage of the reasoning are unduly restricted. For example, the judge may fail to count the social consequences of his decision among the factors to be

---

[22] *Hanson* v. *Wearmouth Coal Co. Ltd. & Sunderland Gas Co.* [1939] 3 All ER 47 at 54.
[23] See e.g. *Barnett* v. *Packer* [1940] 3 All ER 575.
[24] For an illustration see the speech of Lord Diplock in *Dorset Yacht Co. Ltd.* v. *Home Office* [1970] AC 1004 *infra.* pp. 205–6.

reckoned with in deciding whether to apply the *ratio decidendi* of a past case.

In a famous passage in his *Interpretations of Legal History*[25] Dean Roscoe Pound of Harvard complained of an attitude of the courts in the nineteenth century according to which

a historically derived conception was the whole measure of judicial action. The conception was not to be fitted to the case so as to bring about a result in that particular case by which the law might be given effect with reference to its end. The result in the particular case was immaterial. The case was to be fitted to the conception after the manner of Procrustes.

So far as the United States is concerned, the twentieth-century case of *Hynes* v. *New York Central Railway Co.*[26] is said to have been a welcome sign of the times because of the denunciation of 'the jurisprudence of conceptions'[27] by the New York Court of Appeals. The defendants' electric railway ran beside the Harlem River. From one of their bulkheads a diving board projected 8½ feet beyond the line of the defendants' property. A boy who, while bathing in the river, was lawfully exercising the rights of a member of the public, climbed on to the bulkhead and proceeded to the end of the diving board where he was struck and killed by wires which fell from one of the defendants' poles in consequence of the negligence of the defendants' servants. It was held that the boy's personal representative could recover damages from the railway company although the boy was technically a trespasser on its property. In the course of his judgment Cardozo J said that the case was a striking illustration of the dangers of 'a jurisprudence of conceptions', the extension of a maxim or definition with relentless disregard of consequence to 'drily logical extreme'.[28]

In one sense, and that a highly technical and artificial one, the diver at the end of the spring board is an intruder on the adjoining lands. In another sense, and one that realists would accept more readily, he is still on public waters in the exercise of public rights. The law must say whether it will subject him to the rule of the one field or of the other, of this sphere or of that.

It did not follow from the fact that the springboard was part of the land for the purposes of the law of property that it should be treated similarly for the purposes of the law of tort.

---

[25] At p. 119.   [26] (1921) 231 NY 229.
[27] This expression seems to have originated with Ihering.   [28] At 235–6.

Another way of describing the vice against which Pound and Cardozo were protesting is to say that it is that of arguing on the following lines: 'In the instant case the deceased was a trespasser. Previous cases show that no duty of care is owed to trespassers, therefore no duty of care was owed to the deceased although his trespass was incidental to the exercise of his rights as a bather in a public river in which capacity a duty of care was owed to him. A person cannot be in one legal category for the purpose of one branch of the law, e.g. that relating to the defendants' power to exclude trespassers, and in another category for the purpose of another branch of the law, e.g. that relating to the defendants' duty of care.' This fallacy, if it is a fallacy, is one to which reasoning by analogy is prone because, if the instant case is compared first with previous cases concerning landowners' duties towards those exercising public rights, and next with those relating to landowners' duties to trespassers, the instant case must appear to bear a closer resemblance to cases of the second class than to those of the first. It is only when the consequences of the decision are considered that doubts about the wisdom of following cases of the second class are likely to arise. There would, for instance, be something quite unrealistic about a situation in which two bathers were struck by the same wire falling through the negligence of the occupier of land and one could recover because he was in the water at the time, while the other must fail because he was in the act of diving back into the water.[29]

The danger of reasoning by analogy which is under consideration is brought into further relief by cases concerned with the meaning of words and phrases. It is fatally easy to adopt some such line of reasoning as the following: the instant case is concerned with the meaning of such and such an expression. That expression was interpreted in such and such a way in a previous case, therefore that interpretation should be applied in the instant case. It is unnecessary to enlarge upon the evils of such an approach. They can all be summed up in the remark 'It is wrong to ignore the context in which phrases are used.'

The vice under consideration is one from which English judges are generally immune. We have already seen how Lord Halsbury denied that a case can be quoted for a proposition that may seem to flow logically from it. Lord Halsbury continued:

[29] A rational decision could now be reached in English law thanks to *British Railways Board* v. *Herrington* [1972] AC 879.

such a mode of reasoning assumes that the law is necessarily a logical code, whereas every lawyer must acknowledge that the law is not always logical at all.[30]

'Logic' in this context appears to be synonymous with consistency. The vice at which Lord Halsbury's remarks were aimed seems to have been the extension of the rule according to which the previous case was decided, to a case which could not reasonably be distinguished on its facts without pausing to consider whether the rule was one which ought to be extended. No doubt courts have occasionally acted in this way, but, in the main, they act on the view that an unreasonable distinction between cases coming from different epochs is better than the extension of an old rule to modern circumstances in which it would not operate satisfactorily. A husband has a right of action for the loss of his wife's consortium due to the defendant's negligence. Consistency might seem to have required that the House of Lords should have conferred a similar right on a wife when the problem was presented to them in 1951, but the action for loss of consortium is now thought to be anomalous and its scope was not extended by the House of Lords.[31] The House was not technically bound by decisions concerning the husband's action, but it could hardly have contemplated overruling them.

The recognition that rules need to be qualified and that anomalies ought not to be extended must not be allowed to obscure the general utility of arguments based on the need for consistency. Lord Halsbury was simply protesting against the assumption that the law is necessarily a logical code. Large portions of our law have evolved precisely because cases have been quoted for propositions that follow logically from them.

The common law is tolerant of much illogicality, especially on the surface, but no system of law can be workable if it has not got logic at the root of it.[32]

[30] [1901] AC 495 at 506, p. 57 *supra*.
[31] *Best* v. *Fox* [1952] AC 716.
[32] Lord Devlin in *Hedley Byrne and Co. Ltd.* v. *Heller and Partners Ltd.* [1964] AC 464 at 516.

5. CASES OF FIRST IMPRESSION[33]

It will be recollected that Willes J once said:

> Private justice, moral fitness and public convenience when applied to a new subject make common law without a precedent.[34]

This does not mean that, when the case is one of first impression, it is the normal function of the judge to give judgment according to his personal views on these matters without doing something more. A judgment which merely sets out the facts and arguments and concludes with the observation that justice, moral fitness, or public convenience indicates that one or other of the parties should succeed would be little better than a decision without reasons, and it is not customary for the modern English judge to give such a decision when confronted with a novel point of law. The normal procedure is for him to state the pros and cons of each party's case, and formulate the principle upon which his decision is based.

It goes without saying that a judge does not ordinarily disregard one side of a case, but this is what happened in *Priestley* v. *Fowler*,[35] the decision which served as the foundation of the doctrine of common employment according to which a servant could not recover damages from his master for injuries caused by the negligence of a fellow servant. A butcher's servant was injured by the overturning of a van which was overloaded in consequence of the negligence of one of his fellows. He claimed damages from his employer and, recognizing that there was no precedent, Lord Abinger CB decided the case by considering the possible consequences of a judgment in favour of the plaintiff.

> The master, e.g., would be liable to the servant for the negligence of the chambermaid for putting him into a damp bed; for that of the upholsterer for sending a crazy bedstead whereby he was made to fall down while asleep and injure himself; for the negligence of the cook in not properly cleaning the copper vessels used in the kitchen; of the butcher, in supplying the family with meat of a quality injurious to health; of the builder for a defect in the foundation of the house whereby it fell, and injured both the master and the servant by the ruins.

---

[33] See Le Froy, 'Judge-Made Law', *LQR* 20 (1904), 399, and 'The Basis of Case-Law', *LQR* 22 (1906), 293.

[34] p. 28 *supra*.   [35] (1838) 3 M. and W. 1.

Admittedly these utterances were delivered with reference to a servant who was one of the family, but the industrial era was sufficiently far advanced in 1838, when *Priestley* v. *Fowler* was decided, for the injustice of a general rule that a master is not liable to his servant in respect of the negligence of another servant to be patently obvious, and, if Lord Abinger had paused to consider this injustice, he might at least have attached reservations to his opinion which would have prevented *Priestley* v. *Fowler* from becoming the basis of the doctrine of common employment. His allusion to the disastrous consequences of a contrary decision was far fetched. The distinction between a servant and an independent contractor may not have been as clear in 1838 as it was to become later, but it is doubtful whether, even then, a master would have been liable to anyone for the negligence of his upholsterer, butcher, or builder.

When a judge does consider the pros and cons of each party's case, there is no recognized name for the reasoning, but it has characteristics of its own which distinguish it from deduction and induction. It has been well described by Professor Wisdom as:

a matter of weighing the cumulative effects of one group of severally inconclusive items against the cumulative effects of another group of severally inconclusive items.[36]

It is not the same as reasoning about questions of fact. The judge sometimes has to consider the probable social consequences of his decision, but he is also concerned with such matters as the manner in which his decision can be justified in the light of existing legal principles, the kinds of legal argument which it may be used to support in the future and the force of conflicting analogies.

An example is provided by the method by which the House of Lords reached its decision in *Lister* v. *Romford Ice & Cold Storage Co. Ltd.*[37] by a majority of 3 to 2. The appellant was a lorry-driver employed by the respondents. He had driven negligently in the course of his employment, and caused personal injuries to a fellow servant to whom the respondents had been held vicariously liable to pay damages, the doctrine of common employment having been previously abolished by statute. The respondents claimed an indemnity from the appellant. It was not seriously disputed that he

[36] *Philosophy and Psycho-analysis*, 157.
[37] [1957] AC 555. See also the analysis of the judgment in *re Makein* [1955] Ch. 194 by Professor Hart in *Proceedings of the Aristotelian Society*, suppl., 29. 262.

owed them a contractual duty to drive with due care or that his breach of that duty had caused the damage in respect of which the respondents claimed to be indemnified, but it was contended that there was an implied term in the contract of employment that the respondents would insure themselves against liability to third parties in respect of the appellant's negligence and that they would not claim to be indemnified by him. The respondents were in fact covered by insurance, and the claim was made at the instigation of their insurance company. If allowance is made for the difficulty of collating five separate judgments, the reasons for and against the decision of the majority of the House of Lords in favour of the respondents may be summarized as follows:

(1) The suggested implied term could not be precisely formulated. Was it that the respondents would insure against all claims in respect of the appellant's negligence, or in all cases where it was customary to do so or was the implied term simply that the respondents would allow the appellant to have the benefit of any insurance actually taken out by them in respect of the liability in question? In favour of the appellant it was urged that the last of these implications was sufficiently precise.

(2) Where should the line be drawn in implying terms in a contract of employment with regard to the employer's duty to insure? Should an implication corresponding to that for which the appellant contended be included in a contract to employ a crane-driver, builder, or even a domestic servant? In favour of the appellant it was urged that the answer depended on the question whether it was customary for the employer to insure against the damage in question.

(3) If such an implication should be made in a contract to employ a lorry-driver today, when did it become the law that it should be made? Should it have been made before the Road Traffic Act 1930, when insurance against third-party risks was common, but not compulsory? Or did the Act of 1930 alter the law with regard to the terms to be implied in a lorry-driver's contract of employment? Against this it was urged that it was sufficient that the implication should be made today. The common law changes from time to time when there is no binding precedent, although it may be difficult to say how and when the change takes place.

(4) An insurer has a right of subrogation, i.e. if he pays money to the assured in respect of a claim, he is placed in the shoes of the assured so far as the latter's rights against others in relation to the

same claim are concerned. To allow the appeal in the instant case would be to deprive the respondents' insurers of their right of subrogation. In favour of the appellant it was urged that, if this were a hardship, it was one against which the insurers could protect themselves.

(5) To make the implication for which the appellant contended would be to encourage laxity on his part with regard to his duty to drive with due care. In favour of the appellant it was urged that a similar objection could be made against all contracts to insure against third-party risks even when the employer's personal liability was concerned.

Three points emerge from the foregoing analysis. In the first place, the arguments are general in their terms. If there is any sense in which they can be said to have been based on private justice, moral fitness, or public convenience, it is with reference to a number of possible cases, and not solely to that before the court.[38] If it is true to say that the average judgment in a case of first impression reflects the personal views of the court, those views refer more to the possible repercussions of the case than to its particular facts. Secondly, even when judicial reasoning is based on the cumulative effect of several independent premises, a time inevitably comes when all that the judge can say is 'I have weighed the pros and cons which I have stated and I now give judgment for so and so in accordance with the principle I have formulated after weighing the stated pros and cons.' The important thing is that it is of the essence of the judicial process that the pros and cons should first be weighed. Finally, with regard to the fifth point concerning the danger of removing one of the sanctions against careless driving, it is to be observed that the Law Lords acted on guesswork. No enquiry was made concerning the average lorry-driver's reactions, if any, to his master's vicarious liability and its consequences. It is not the practice of the English courts to collect general evidence of this nature. American courts have been known to do so since Brandeis J, when at the Bar, induced the Supreme Court to consider evidence of the effect of long working hours in a case concerned with labour legislation.[39] The 'Brandeis

---

[38] This feature of judicial reasoning is nowadays commonly called 'universalizing', see, e.g. MacCormick, *Legal Reasoning and Legal Theory*, ch. 4.

[39] See Cardozo, *Growth of the Law*, 124. The effect of the decision in *Lister*'s case was in fact considered by an interdepartmental committee at the instance of the Minister of Labour (22 MLR 652). Although it made various suggestions, the

brief' has much to be said for it, but to an Englishman it may well seem that a court would be considering matters that are best considered as a prelude to parliamentary legislation if it were to do much more than act on the personal notion of its members with regard to such questions.

Although reasoning by analogy is typical of cases where there are precedents, and reasoning with reference to the cumulative effect of independent premisses is characteristic of cases in which there is no precedent, they are not mutually exclusive. If the term 'precedent' is construed sufficiently broadly, there are very few cases in which there is literally none to serve as an analogy, however remote. In some cases weighty *dicta* and previous decisions do much to clarify the issues, although the ultimate answer can only be provided with the aid of reasoning with reference to the cumulative effect of independent premisses, which often consists of balancing various policy considerations.

Dorset Yacht Co. Ltd. v. *Home Office*[40] was just such a case. The issue was whether, assuming negligence by their custodians could be proved, the Home Office was liable for damage done to a yacht moored in Poole harbour by Borstal trainees who had escaped from a camp on Brownsea Island. By a majority of 4 to 1 the answer given by the House of Lords was in the affirmative. It was not disputed that, if the custodians were liable in negligence, the Home Office was vicariously liable, but there was no direct authority to the effect that there could be liability for negligently permitting the escape from custody of mentally normal adults who commit torts against third parties. The 'neighbour' principle enunciated by Lord Atkin in *Donoghue* v. *Stevenson* was plainly in point:

You must take reasonable care to avoid acts or omissions which you can reasonably foresee would be likely to injure your neighbour. Who then in law is my neighbour? The answer seems to be persons who are so closely and directly affected by my act that I ought reasonably to have them in contemplation as being so affected when I am directing my mind to the acts or omissions which are called in question.[41]

But the neighbour principle is not of universal application in English law, and this is particularly true of cases in which the

committee did not press for legislation. No court could have heard all the evidence heard by the committee.

40 [1970] AC 1004.   41 The full statement is set out on p. 44 *supra*.

activities of third parties are concerned. No one has yet suggested that A is liable for failing to prevent damage to the person or property of B by persons over whom A has no legal right of control, however easy it might have been for him to prevent the damage. Nevertheless three members of the majority placed the neighbour principle in the forefront of their reasoning and concluded that there was nothing in the case to justify a refusal to act upon that principle.

Lord Diplock, the fourth member of the majority, analysed the reasoning of judges in some of the rare cases in which they ultimately act on policy considerations and perform a function which they hesitate to call legislative. He described the reasoning at the first stage at which the authorities were considered as 'inductive':

In all the decisions which have been analysed a duty of care has been found to exist wherever the conduct and relationship possessed each of the characteristics A, B, C, D etc. and has not so far been found to exist when any of these characteristics were absent.

Then comes a stage at which the reasoning is described by Lord Diplock as 'deductive':

In all cases where the conduct and relationship possessed each of the characteristics A, B, C, D etc. a duty of care arises.[42]

Lord Diplock then stressed the point that, in formulating a principle on the basis of the relevant authorities, allowance must be made for features which were absent from as well as present in the cases included in the analysis:

In all cases where the conduct and relationship possess each of the characteristics A, B, C and D etc., but do not possess any of the characteristics Z, Y or X, etc., which were present in the cases eliminated from the analysis, a duty of care arises.

After an exhaustive examination of the authorities which included *Ellis* v. *The Home Office*,[43] a case in which it was assumed that the Home Office would be liable for a prison officer's negligence in allowing a violent prisoner to injure another inmate, Lord Diplock concluded:

A is responsible for damage caused to the person or property of B by the tortious act of C (a person responsible in law for his own acts) where the

---

[42] [1970] AC at 1059.   [43] [1953] 2 QB 135.

relationship between A and C has the characteristics (1) that A has the legal right to detain C in penal custody and to control his acts while in custody; (2) that A is actually exercising his legal right of custody of C at the time of C's tortious act and (3) that A if he had taken reasonable care in the exercise of his right of custody could have prevented C from doing the tortious act which caused damage to the person or property of B; and where also the relationship between A and B has the characteristics (4) that at the time of C's tortious act A has the legal right to control the situation of B or his property as respects physical proximity to C and (5) that A can reasonably foresee that B is likely to sustain damage to his person or property if A does not take reasonable care to prevent C from doing tortious acts of the kind which he did.[44]

Characteristics (2) and (4), present in the *Ellis* case, were absent from the case under consideration but Lord Diplock decided that the fact that Ellis was in custody of his assailant's custodians when he sustained his damage was not essential to the duty of care owed by the custodians to those whose person or property would be directly at risk in consequence of their negligence. The final decision could only be reached by balancing the public interest in the rehabilitation of criminals by Borstal training, training known to have frequent failures, against the interest of the private individual in the integrity of his person or property.

6. CONCLUSIONS

Reasoning by analogy is the characteristic product of *stare decisis* and our doctrine of precedent. It leads to decisions which create rules and thus limits the range to be covered by reasoning with reference to the cumulative effect of independent premises. There will inevitably tend to be fewer relevant premises when the question is whether the instant case falls within a particular rule, than when the question is at large. The main dangers of reasoning by analogy have already been considered. They are certainly not sufficiently pronounced to cast doubt upon the merits of *stare decisis*.

Two further dangers to which the doctrine of precedent gives rise should be mentioned at the end of a discussion of its effect upon legal reasoning. The first is that it may disguise the fact that no reasons have in reality been given for a particular judgment. We have already seen that judgments based on the mere assertion

[44] [1970] AC at 1063.

that such and such a decision would be just or convenient are not substantially different from those without reasons. A judgment is also no better than an unreasoned decision when it refers to conflicting cases and does no more than state that some will be followed and others not followed or, where this is possible, overruled, without any indication why such a course is being adopted. Needless to say such judgments are exceptional[45] but they occur more frequently than most English lawyers would care to admit.

The second danger to which the doctrine of precedent gives rise springs from the improbability that all relevant cases will be cited. If it is subsequently discovered that conflicting decisions were overlooked, there is a risk that over-subtle distinctions will be drawn in order to conceal the conflict. The risk of oversight is less today because of the availability of computerized retrieval systems. But these in their turn carry with them the danger of excessive citation of unreported decisions which do not illustrate additional principles, a practice recently frowned on by English courts.[46]

---

[45] But see *R.* v. *Podola* [1960] 1 QB 325. So far as the decision concerned the onus of proof, the judgment of the Court of Criminal Appeal does no more than express disagreement with the argument of the appellant's counsel and enumerate previous cases, stating that some are overruled. No reasons are given for the adoption of either course.

[46] *Stanley* v. *International Harvester Co. of Great Britain Ltd.*, *The Times*, 7 Feb. 1983 CA; *Roberts Petroleum Ltd.* v. *Bernard Kennedy Ltd.* (1983) 2 AC 192 HL.

VII
PRECEDENT AND LEGAL THEORY

1. PRECEDENT AND THE DEFINITION OF LAW

The English doctrine of precedent raises problems in relation to any proposed definition of law. For the purposes of the present discussion, these problems can, in the main, be reduced to two questions; (i) Does the proposed definition include the *rationes decidendi* of cases as well as the contents of legislation? (ii) Does the proposed definition include the rules which confer authority on the *ratio decidendi* of a case, i.e. the rules by virtue of which a particular *ratio* has the force of law? If the answer to the first question is in the negative, the definition must be rejected in so far as it purports to be applicable to the English legal system. No lawyer would hesitate to say that the rule in *Rylands* v. *Fletcher* is just as much a rule of English law as the statutory requirement that a will must be signed by two witnesses. It is perhaps more doubtful whether the proposed definition of law would have to be rejected if the answer to the second question were in the negative. There is a difference between a rule which constitutes or is derived from a *ratio decidendi* and a rule conferring authority on that *ratio decidendi*, just as there is a difference between a rule based on the contents of a statute and a rule conferring authority on that statute. It could be maintained that the difference is sufficiently great to justify the exclusion of the second type of rule from the definition of law.

Salmond
According to Salmond 'the law consists of the rules recognized and acted on by courts of justice'.[1] Standing alone this would be too wide a definition if only because it includes the ordinary rules of reasoning upon which courts, like the rest of us, base their factual

---

[1] *Jurisprudence* (11th edn.), 41.

PRECEDENT AND LEGAL THEORY 209

conclusions. The definition must be related to the following important passage in Salmond's book:

> It is requisite that the law should postulate one or more first causes, whose operation is ultimate, and whose authority is underived. In other words there must be found in every legal system certain ultimate principles, from which all others are derived, but which are themselves self-existent. . . . The rule that a man may not ride a bicycle on the footpath may have its source in the bye-laws of a municipal council. The rule that these bye-laws have the force of law has its source in an act of Parliament, but whence comes the rule that acts of Parliament have the force of law? This is legally ultimate; its source is historical only, not legal. The historians of the constitution may know its origin, but lawyers must accept it as self-existent. . . . No statute can confer this power upon Parliament, for this would be to assume and act on the power that is to be conferred. So also the rule that judicial decisions have the force of law is legally ultimate and underived. No statute lays it down. It is certainly recognized by many precedents, but no precedent can confer authority upon precedent. You must first possess authority before you can confer it. If we inquire into the number of these ultimate principles, the answer is that a legal system is free to recognize any number of them, but is not bound to recognize more than one. From any one ultimate legal source it is possible for the whole law to be derived, but one such there must be. A statute, for example, may at any time give statutory authority to the operation of precedent, and so reduce it from an ultimate to a derivative source of law.[2]

This passage suggests that, for Salmond, law consists of the rules recognized and acted upon by courts of justice, provided the court recognizes such rules to be binding (i) because they are derived from the principles accepted as ultimate in the legal system in which the court operates, or (assuming it is thought desirable to include the ultimate principles themselves in the definition of law) (ii) because the rules are ultimate in such a system. In the case of the English legal system, this certainly means that the contents of legislation and the *rationes decidendi* of cases decided in superior courts are law.

So far as the first suggestion is concerned, there are two types of rule in any legal system, those by means of which the rules of the system may be identified (Salmond's ultimate principles) and those constituting the substantive and adjective law. If it is thought to be confusing or inelegant to use the same word 'law' to cover rules of law and the rules which tell us what, within a given system, is law,

---

[2] Ibid. 137. The passage has been slightly altered in the 12th edition at 111.

some other word can be coined for rules of the second type, but to do so would be to run counter to the ordinary language of the practising lawyer according to which the rules that acts of Parliament and judicial decisions have the force of law are themselves rules of English law. They are so described by the practitioner precisely because they are recognized by the courts. This is the feature which distinguishes them from conventions such as that according to which the Queen assents to bills passed by both Houses of Parliament. Although many of these conventions are acted on as regularly as rules of law, and although they play just as important a part in the working of the constitution, they are not recognized by the courts.

Kelsen[3]

There is a superficial similarity between Salmond's approach and the concept of the basic norm which constitutes so important a feature of Hans Kelsen's pure theory of law. For Kelsen, the law of the modern state consists of a hierarchy of norms addressed to officials,[4] stipulating that, under certain conditions, coercive measures 'ought'[5] to be applied. Such norms are all posited by human acts of will. They may include judge-made general norms, as well as statutory or customary norms, so that the theory can encompass the *rationes decidendi* of cases, provided that these can be cast in the canonical sanction-stipulating form. At the top of this pyramid of positive norms come those contained within the historically first constitution. These are the norms from which authority is ultimately derived to issue all the other norms of the system. A by-law is empowered by a statute, a statute by the current constitution, the current constitution by some earlier constitution, and so on. Eventually, one arrives at the historically first constitution, whose validity is assumed in legal thought. This means, according to Kelsen, that the theorist must postulate a basic norm which is presupposed by all juristic statements.[6] The

---

[3] For a summary of Kelsen's theory, see Harris, *Legal Philosophies*, ch. 6.

[4] Kelsen, *General Theory of Law and State*, 124–62; *Pure Theory of Law*, 145–50, 221–78.

[5] Kelsen employs 'ought' stipulatively to stand for 'shall', 'may', and 'can' (*Pure Theory of Law*, 6, 10, 77, 119).

[6] *General Theory of Law and State*, 116–17, 395–6, 437. *What is Justice*, 219–22, 262. *Pure Theory of Law*, 9–10, 46, 50, 194–5, 198–205. (1965) 17 SLR 1128, 1141–51. In essays published during the last decade of his life, Kelsen characterized the basic norm as a 'fiction' in the technical sense of Vaihinger's *Philosophy of 'as if'*,

basic norm confers norm-creating power on those who promul-
gated or, in the case of a customary constitution, created the
historically first constitution.

Kelsen writes:

> If the historically first constitution was laid down by a resolution of an
> assembly, the basic norm authorizes the individuals forming that
> assembly; if the historically first constitution arose by way of custom, the
> basic norm authorizes this custom—or, more correctly, it authorizes the
> individuals whose conduct forms the custom giving rise to the historically
> first constitution.[7]

Salmond's 'ultimate principles' are not mere postulates. They
are consciously appealed to in judicial practice. They may
constitute part of what Kelsen calls 'the historically first constitution'. The basic norm, in contrast, is presupposed by lawyers
'mostly unconsciously'.[8] The theorist postulates it because only so
can he explain the basis on which objective validity can be
attributed to the *oughts* of positive law, without asserting some
natural law foundation for their bindingness.

Kelsen's highly abstract validity-derivation thesis is one which it
is not easy to apply to the concrete instances of any system. In the
case of legal systems with an unwritten constitution, special
problems arise from the fact that the emergence of ultimate
constitutional empowering rules can often not be dated, as the
notion of 'historically first constitution' seems to require. Nevertheless, one aspect of the theory has been invoked as a tool for the
understanding of certain kinds of change in fundamentals. This is
his technical concept of 'revolution'. If validity-assertions about
the effective law are related at time $T1$ to one constellation of
ultimate sources, and then at time $T2$ they are related to a
different set, and the change was not authorized by anything
contained within the first constellation, then there has occurred a
'change in the basic norm', or 'revolution'.[9] We saw in Chapter II
that a technical revolution of this sort is one way of explaining the
juridical basis of the 1966 Practice Statement of the House of

Isr. LR 1 (1966), 1. 'The Function of a Constitution', in Tur and Twining (eds.),
Essays on Kelsen.

[7] 'The Function of a Constitution', in Tur and Twining (eds.), *Essays on Kelsen*,
at 114.

[8] *General Theory of Law and State*, 116.

[9] *General Theory of Law and State*, 118. *What is Justice*, 224. *Pure Theory of
Law*, 49–50, 208–11. *Isr. LR* 1 (1966), 1, 2.

Lords. At the end of Chapter V, we distinguished one view of the significance of the incorporation into English law of EEC law as being that a 'United Kingdom statute is no longer inviolable as it once was'.[10] If it comes to be accepted that Parliament cannot derogate from directly applicable Community law, and also that the constitution prior to 1973 did not empower Parliament to impose such a limitation on its successors, then another Kelsenian revolution will have taken place.

It should be stressed that this conception of revolution has no more than explanatory power. It cannot prescribe whether changes brought about in a way not provided for in the previous constitution should be accepted. Furthermore, in the many instances where judicial practice is ambiguous so that details of precedent rules are unsettled, Kelsen's theory can neither prescribe nor describe the process of incremental evolution. Nevertheless, where it can be seen, as a matter of history, that one fundamental rule has been replaced by another, his conception of 'revolution' provides an explanation which is an alternative to contrived theories of constitutional continuity.

Hart[11]

H. L. A. Hart's book, *The Concept of Law*, published in 1961, has claims to be considered among the most original as well as the most important contributions to jurisprudence of the twentieth century. It treats law as a union of primary and secondary rules. Primary rules impose duties. Secondary rules indicate how primary rules may be created, changed, or extinguished.

According to Hart law may also be regarded as a hierarchy of rules. The pedigree of each rule, primary or secondary, may be traced back to the 'rule of recognition', the Hartian equivalent of Salmond's ultimate principles. It specifies some feature or features possession of which by a suggested rule is taken as a conclusive affirmative indication that it is a rule of law.[12] It may be simple or complex, and it may be in separate parts, one subordinate to, but not derived from the other, like precedent and legislation in English law. The rule of recognition does not owe its validity to

[10] *R. v. Secretary of State for Transport, ex parte Factortame Ltd.* (1989) 2 CMLR 353, 403 Bingham LJ.

[11] For a summary of Hart's theory, see Harris, *Legal Philosophies*, ch. 9.

[12] *The Concept of Law*, 92.

another rule, but to the fact that it is accepted and acted upon by the appropriate officials.

When we move from saying that a particular enactment is valid, because it satisfies the rule that what the Queen in Parliament enacts is law, to saying that in England this last rule is used by courts, officials and private persons, as the ultimate rule of recognition, we have moved from an internal statement of law asserting the validity of a rule of the system to an external statement of fact which an observer of the system might make even if he did not accept it.[13]

Unlike Kelsen's basic norm, the rule of recognition is not a mere postulate of theory. It is a social rule whose existence can be empirically recorded.

Hart also makes helpful and realistic observations specifically directed to the subject of this book:

Any honest description of the use of precedent in English law must allow a place for the following pairs of contrasting facts. *First*, there is no single method of determining the rule for which a given authoritative precedent is an authority. Notwithstanding this, in the vast majority of decided cases there is very little doubt. The headnote is usually correct enough. *Secondly*, there is no authoritative or uniquely correct formulation of any rule to be extracted from cases. On the other hand, there is often very general agreement, when the bearing of a precedent on a later case is in issue, that a given formulation is adequate. *Thirdly*, whatever authoritative status a rule extracted from precedent may have, it is compatible with the exercise by courts that are bound by it with the following two types of creative or legislative activity. On the one hand courts deciding a later case may reach an opposite decision to that in a precedent by narrowing the rule extracted from the precedent, and admitting some exception to it not before considered, or, if considered, left open. This process of 'distinguishing' the earlier case involves finding some legally relevant difference between it and the present case, and the class of such differences can never be exhaustively determined. On the other hand, in following an earlier precedent, the courts may discard a restriction found in the rule as formulated from the earlier case on the ground that it is not required by any rule established by statute or earlier precedent.[14]

Dworkin[15]

In short, Hart's *Concept of Law* represents law as a system of rules and recognizes that, at certain points, the courts play a creative or

---

[13] Ibid. 104.   [14] Ibid. 131.
[15] For a summary of Dworkin's theory, see Harris, *Legal Philosophies*, ch. 14.

legislative role. Dworkin disagrees on both points. The conception of law as a system or rules, he contends, fails to make allowance for principles and the attribution of anything in the nature of a legislative power to the judges suggests that they exercise a discretion which they do not in fact possess.[16]

Principles are to be distinguished from rules. Rules are propositions like 'the maximum speed on the turnpike is sixty miles an hour'.

Rules are applicable in an all-or-nothing fashion. If the facts a rule stipulates are given, then either the rule is valid, in which case the answer it supplies must be accepted, or it is not, in which case it contributes nothing to the decision:[17]

Of course rules have exceptions, but, according to Dworkin, there is no reason in theory why they should not all be added on, and the more that are, the more accurate the statement of the rule. Principles are exemplified by the judgment of a New Jersey court in *Heningsen* v. *Bloomfield Motors Inc.*[18] Heningsen bought a car, signing a standard order form limiting the manufacturers' liability for defects to making good defective parts—'this warranty being in lieu of all other warranties, obligations or liabilities'. None the less it was held that the manufacturers were liable for medical and other expenses incurred in consequence of an accident due to the car's defective steering mechanism by Heningsen and his wife, the donee of the car. In the course of the judgment reference was made to the general principle that 'one who does not choose to read a contract before signing it cannot later relieve himself of its burdens', and to the 'basic tenet of freedom of parties to contract'; but they were outweighed by the 'basic doctrine that the courts will not permit themselves to be used as instruments of inequity and injustice'. More specifically, the exemption clause being virtually uniform among motor manufacturers, 'The courts generally refuse to lend themselves to the enforcement of a "bargain" in which one party has unjustly taken advantage of the economic necessities of the other.' Unlike rules, relevant principles may, and frequently do, conflict; it is the judge's duty to weigh them and a decision that one or more predominate may be the foundation of a rule binding in subsequent cases. Conversely, a consideration of one or more

[16] See R. M. Dworkin, *Taking Rights Seriously*, ch. 2.
[17] Ibid. 24.   [18] 32 NJ 358, 161 A (2nd) 69, 1960.

relevant rules may lead to the formulation by a judge of a principle to be weighed against other principles.

All that is meant, when we say that a particular principle is a principle of our law, is that the principle is one which officials must take into account, if it is relevant, as a consideration inclining in one direction or another.[19]

Principles and the rule of recognition

We may pass over much that is controversial in the foregoing paragraph and proceed at once to Dworkin's major point against the view that law is a system of rules—his contention that the reliance by courts on principles cannot be accounted for by reference to a rule of recognition:

We argue for a particular principle by grappling·with a whole set of shifting, developing and interacting standards (themselves principles rather than rules) about institutional responsibility, statutory interpretation, the persuasive force of various sorts of precedent, the relation of all these to contemporary moral practices, and hosts of other such standards. We could not bolt all these together into a single 'rule', even a complex one, and if we could the result would bear little relation to Hart's picture of a rule of recognition, which is the picture of a fairly stable master rule specifying 'some feature or features possession of which by a suggested rule is taken as a conclusive affirmative indication that it is a rule . . .[20]

It is, however, not particularly difficult to formulate a master rule by which principles as well as rules of English law may be identified. It could read: 'Where relevant, all courts must apply statutory provisions, the rules of precedent, and the *rationes decidendi* of cases. In a case to which no statutory provision or *ratio decidendi* applies, all courts must, before deciding it, take into account principles derived from legislation, from the *rationes decidendi* of relevant cases and from relevant *dicta*.' All the principles mentioned in *Heningsen* v. *Bloomfield Motors Inc.*, like all the considerations itemized in the quotation from Geldart's *Elements of Law* on p. 33, are supported by masses of *dicta* if not by *rationes decidendi*. In a system in which legislation and binding precedent are the major legal sources of law, the only ultimate sources, and the major coercive sources, it is but right that the persuasive sources should be related to them. In any event, for what it is worth, it is possible to find *dicta* in support of more or

---

[19] *Taking Rights Seriously*, 26.   [20] Ibid. 40–1.

less any principle. The following piece of rhetoric can always be called in aid in the absence of better 'authority':

> But there are certain principles of law, which, though not expressed either in the common law, or in the judgments of any judges, or in the language of acts of Parliament, nevertheless must be held to qualify all that falls from judges in expounding the common law, and all that is to be found throughout the Statute Book in the various acts of Parliament.[21]

The answer to the question whether the principles as distinct from the rules of law should be included in the definition of law is that there is something to be said on both sides. Their exclusion might be thought to imply that they are only of minor significance. Such a conclusion would of course be absurd, if only because the principles play a considerable part in the solution of legal problems to which no rule is directly applicable, and enable the practitioner or legal writer to predict how law will develop. They are essential to a coherent view of the law. On the other hand it is important to preserve the distinction between a lawyer's statement 'this is the law' and the same lawyer's statement 'this is probably the law'. There is a far higher degree of certainty in the first than in the second statement. The merit of the approach adopted by Salmond and Hart is that it enables us to say that the rules under which statutes and judicial decisions have the force of law (the one being subordinate to, but not derived from the other), the contents of United Kingdom and directly applicable EEC legislation, and the *rationes decidendi* of cases, together with local customary rules which owe their legal validity (but not their existence) to judicial decisions concerning the tests to which their contents must conform, and nothing else, are law in England. The utility of this approach in certain contexts must not blind us to the fact that, in other contexts, the word 'law' is frequently and properly used in a more comprehensive sense.

Courts as legislators

We have already had occasion to suggest that the expression 'judicial legislation' is highly metaphorical,[22] but it, or its equivalent, is not uncommonly used by judges although usually with the accompanying observation that it is a rare phenomenon. Metaphorical language is, however, also employed to preserve the

---

[21] Kelly CB in *River Wear Commissioners* v. *Adamson* (1876) 1 QBD at 551.
[22] p. 34 *supra*.

notion, derived from the declaratory theory of judicial decision, that judges never make law. What appear to be new rules are sometimes said to be 'imminent in the law as a whole', or the result of the 'internal logic of the law'. Professor Dworkin has made this feature of legal discourse the focal point of a theory which denies that judges 'legislate'. His 'rights thesis' was first put forward in his celebrated essay on 'hard cases', originally published in 1975,[23] and has been elaborated in his book *Law's Empire* published in 1986. He distinguishes between arguments of policy which justify a political decision by showing that it advances some collective goal of the community and arguments of principle which justify a political decision by showing that it respects or secures some individual or group right. Litigants are entitled to the decision which is most consistent with the relevant principles to be deduced from the rest of the law. Dworkin imagines a superhuman judge, Hercules, who constructs 'a scheme of abstract and concrete principles that provides a coherent justification for all common law precedents and, so far as these are to be justified on principle, constitutional and statutory provisions as well'.[24] Hercules supposes that there is always a right answer to any question of law. He will find it by taking into account the entire body of authoritative legal materials (the dimension of 'fit'), on the one hand, and, on the other hand, considerations of justice, fairness, and procedural due process (the 'substantive' dimension).[25]

So far as precedents are concerned, Dworkin draws an important distinction between their 'enactment force'—which appears to correspond with the notion of *ratio decidendi*—and their 'gravitational force'. We have seen that precedents may influence the development of the law in subsequent cases in ways that go far beyond those coercive rules which dictate that, within the judicial hierarchy, courts are sometimes bound by the *rationes decidendi* of earlier decisions. Dworkin contends that analogical reasoning from precedents can only be explained and justified if we recognize that judicial reasoning, at least in common-law civil cases, is guided by arguments of principle rather than policy. 'Fairness' requires background rights to be treated consistently. There is no similar requirement of consistency so far as public goals are concerned. Therefore, the perceived judicial obligation to aim for a coherent interpretation of precedents must presuppose

---

[23] (1975) 88 HLR 1057, reprinted in *Taking Rights Seriously*, ch. 4.
[24] *Taking Rights Seriously*, 116–17.   [25] *Law's Empire*, chs. 7–10.

that they were supported by propositions about rights, 'principles', not propositions about goals, 'policies'.[26]

Dworkin's principle–policy dichotomy has been the subject of a wealth of critical literature, for and against. So much turns on how we read the cases. As Dworkin tell us, 'in the end all my arguments are hostage to each reader's sense of what does and can happen in court'.[27] It is clear that the mere use by judges of the words 'principle' or 'policy' is not decisive, since Dworkin employs these terms stipulatively. Everything depends on the distributional character of the arguments we understand the court to have invoked. Did they relate exclusively to some outcome to which the parties, or persons similarly situated, are entitled (principle)? Or did they include considerations of the public good (policy)? Judicial reasoning can often be interpreted either way.

The only English decision which receives detailed discussion in *Law's Empire* is *McLoughlin* v. *O'Brian*.[28] In that case, the plaintiff's family was involved in a road accident caused by the negligence of the defendants. She was informed of the accident and taken to hospital, where she learned that her youngest daughter had been killed and witnessed the injuries to other members of her family. She alleged that what she heard and saw caused her severe shock resulting in psychiatric illness. Previous case-law had gone no further than allowing recovery of damages for nervous shock to persons who suffered it at or near the scene of an accident, so the question was whether it should be extended to apply to Mrs McLoughlin. The Court of Appeal, though they considered her psychological injury to be reasonably foreseeable, none the less concluded that there were sound policy considerations against such an extension, especially the argument that to allow her claim would be to open the floodgates to speculative and costly litigation. The House of Lords unanimously reversed the Court of Appeal.

Dworkin maintains that such an adjudication should be understood in the following way. The court takes the existing precedents as recognizing moral rights of persons suffering foreseeable damage to be compensated and concludes that, consistently, the plaintiff must also have such a right. It eschews considerations of the overall public good. He singles out for approval the speech of

---

[26] *Taking Rights Seriously*, 110–15.
[27] *Law's Empire*, 15.   [28] (1983) 1 AC 410.

Lord Scarman,[29] which may itself have been influenced by Dworkin's principle–policy distinction. Lord Scarman said:

The appeal raises directly a question as to the balance in our law between the functions of judge and legislature. . . . The function of the court is to decide the case before it, even though the decision may require the extension or adaption of a principle or in some cases the creation of new law to meet the justice of the case. But, whatever the court decides to do, it starts from a base-line of existing principle and seeks a solution consistent with or analogous to a principle or principles already recognised.

The distinguishing feature of the common law is this judicial development and formation of principle. Policy considerations will have to be weighed: but the objective of the judges is the formulation of principle. And, if principle inexorably requires a decision which entails a degree of policy risk, the court's function is to adjudicate according to principle, leaving policy curtailment to the judgment of Parliament. Here lies the true role of the two lawmaking institutions in our constitution. . . . If principle leads to results which are thought to be socially unacceptable, Parliament can legislate to draw a line or map out a new path. . . .

Why then should not the courts draw the line, as the Court of Appeal manfully tried to do in this case? Simply, because the policy issue as to where to draw the line is not justiciable.[30]

However, as Professor Simon Lee has pointed out,[31] none of the other members of the House in *McLoughlin* expressed themselves in quite this way. They considered the policy arguments which had swayed the Court of Appeal, and found them insufficient. Lord Edmund-Davies was forthright in his rejection of Lord Scarman's approach:

In my judgment, the proposition that 'the policy issue . . . is not justiciable' is as novel as it is startling. So novel is it in relation to this appeal that it was never mentioned during the hearing before your Lordships. And it is startling because in my respectful judgment it runs counter to well-established and wholly acceptable law.[32]

Dworkin has less to say about those coercive rules which require judges to give effect to the 'enactment force' of precedents. They are, as we saw in Chapter I, of less significance in the United States

[29] *Law's Empire*, 28.   [30] (1983) 1 AC 410, 429–31.
[31] (1988) *OJLS* 8 (1988), 278.
[32] (1983) 1 AC 410, 427. Lord Edmund-Davies gave as recent instances in which the House of Lords had considered policy arguments: *Rondel* v. *Worsley* (1969) 1 AC 191; *Dorset Yacht Co. Ltd.* v. *Home Office* (1970) AC 1004; *British Railways Board* v. *Herrington* (1972) AC 877.

than in England, and the bulk of Dworkin's examples are American. Furthermore, Dworkin situates his ideal judge, Hercules, in the ultimate court of appeal. Consequently, Hercules need pay attention, on the dimension of fit, only to those precedents which he does not recant. 'If the courts propose to overrule the decision, no substantive argument of fairness, fixing on the actual decision in the case, survives . . .'.[33] Thus, even if he can be taken as the ideal model for Lord Hercules, his portrait must be modified to fit Hercules J, or Hercules LJ.

It has been questioned whether Dworkin's rights thesis can, consistently, make any allowance for the authoritative status of precedents: if a precedent has correctly weighed background rights, appeal to it is superfluous; if it has not, it should be discarded.[34] However, Dworkin does put forward a theory of 'embedded mistakes' in accordance with which a court might grant continuing validity to a rule laid down in a decision it believes to have been wrong.[35] If citizens had justifiably relied on the decision, considerations of procedural due process might tell against overruling it because of the unfair surprise that would ensue.[36] That there might be circumstances in which a court could not overrule a wrong decision may also be catered for by Dworkin's passing reference to the part a doctrine of precedent might play at the constitutional level of Hercules' holistic theory.[37] This point merits elaboration in the English context. We have seen that the details of many of our coercive precedent rules are unsettled because judicial practice is not fixed, and others, though settled, are controversial. Normative arguments in these contexts do and should reflect the role binding precedent ought to play within our unwritten constitution.

Our conclusions on such questions are likely to be affected by whether or not we can agree with Dworkin that our law should not be interpreted as conferring discretion on judges to create rights in hard cases. If judges only legislate when they make mistakes, their power to bind successors should be narrowly circumscribed. If, on the other hand, there are cases in which the law provides no uniquely right answer so that a judge must choose the answer he

---

[33] *Taking Rights Seriously*, 118.

[34] David Pannick, 'A Note on Dworkin and Precedent', *MLR* 43 (1980), 36.

[35] *Taking Rights Seriously*, 118–23. See S. L. Hurley, 'Coherence, Hypothetical Cases and Precedent', *OJLS* 10 (1990), 221.

[36] *Law's Empire*, 403.   [37] *Taking Rights Seriously*, 121–2.

thinks best, there is something to be said for deferring to that choice for the future unless subsequent developments render it out of date. Rejection of Dworkin's right-answer thesis would lend support to the constitutional propriety of rules according to which inferior courts are bound by the decisions of higher courts and appellate courts below the House of Lords are generally bound by their own decisions. The less we believe in legal truth, the more we will value legal finality.

There are features of judicial discourse which it is particularly difficult to fit to the contention that judges do not make law. When, in the *Miliangos* case,[38] the House of Lords overruled its decision in *re United Railways of Havana*,[39] it also castigated the Court of Appeal for failing to follow the *Havana Railways* case. The House took the view that, until its present judgment, its earlier decision represented the law which it was the duty of all inferior courts to apply. In the view of the majority of its members, it was not necessary to conclude that the earlier decision had been mistaken when it was laid down. The point was that subsequent events, especially modern fluctuations in exchange rates, warranted the House in now abrogating the previous rule and promulgating a new one. 'Judicial legislation' seems an apt enough description of such a proceeding.

When the House of Lords decides not to overrule a decision of its own, this may, as we saw in Chapter IV, be because it considers the issue one as to which there are two 'tenable' views, the choice between them being one of 'impression'. Professor Dworkin invites testing of his arguments by our sense of what 'does and can happen in court'. References to 'impression' appear more compatible with Hart's concept of 'discretion' than with Dworkin's right-answer thesis. It should be stressed that Hart denies that discretion entails arbitrariness. He says that the discretion left to a judge by the 'open texture' of a legal rule means that 'the conclusion, even though it may not be arbitrary or irrational, is in effect a choice'.[40] If the judge invokes morality (Dworkin's 'substantive' dimension), choice may still remain:

judicial decision, especially on matters of high constitutional import, often involves a choice between moral values, and not merely the application of some single outstanding moral principle; for it is folly to believe that

---

[38] *Miliangos* v. *George Frank (Textiles) Ltd.* (1976) AC 443.
[39] (1961) AC 1007.   [40] *The Concept of Law*, 124.

where the meaning of the law is in doubt, morality always has a clear answer to offer. At this point judges may again make a choice which is neither arbitrary nor mechanical; and here often display characteristic judicial virtues, the special appropriateness of which to legal decision explains why some feel reluctant to call such judicial activity 'legislative'. These virtues are, impartiality and neutrality in surveying the alternatives; consideration of the interest of all who will be affected; and a concern to deploy some acceptable general principle as a reasoned basis for decision. No doubt because a plurality of such principles is always possible it cannot be *demonstrated* that a decision is uniquely correct: but it may be made acceptable as the reasoned product of informed impartial choice. In all this we have the 'weighing' and 'balancing' characteristic of the effort to do justice between competing interests.[41]

2. LAW AND FACT

It has been emphasized at different points in this book that decisions on questions of fact do not constitute a precedent. A few words must now be added with regard to the distinction between propositions of law and propositions of fact. The distinction merits prolonged discussion, but we are here only concerned with its relevance to the doctrine of precedent.

The distinction between law and fact is one that has to be drawn in several different contexts. Three of them are germane to the present discussion. First, there is the general rule that, when a case is tried with a jury, questions of fact must be decided by that body, questions of law being reserved for the judge. Next, there is the rule that there is no appeal on a question of fact from certain classes of decisions of a County Court judge, and finally, there is the doctrine which has already been mentioned that decisions on questions of fact do not constitute a precedent. In the third sense, but not in the first two, questions of construction may sometimes be treated as questions of fact. For example, the Court of Appeal has recently ruled that prior decisions construing the terms of a common-form arbitration clause did not constitute precedents binding on it or on lower courts, since the true meaning of the clause depended in every case on the circumstances of the particular contract.[42]

A conspicuous example of the confusion which can be caused by classifying questions of fact or law independently of their context is

[41] *The Concept of Law*, 200.
[42] *Ashville Investments Ltd.* v. *Elmer Contractors Ltd.* (1989) QB 488.

provided by a series of cases in which a motorist or motor-cyclist claiming damages for personal injuries had collided with an unlighted object during the night.[43] At one time it seemed to be the view of the Court of Appeal that the plaintiff must necessarily have been guilty of contributory negligence because he was either going at a pace at which he could not stop within the limits of his vision, or if he could stop within those limits, he was not keeping a proper look-out. It came to be recognized, however, that no one case of negligence is sufficiently like another to constitute a precedent, and that the so-called 'dilemma principle' which has just been mentioned was only applicable to certain sets of facts. The cases in which it had been enunciated must therefore be taken to have turned on questions of fact. But there is another context in which they must be said to have turned on a question of law. The whole point of some of these cases was that there was insufficient evidence to warrant a finding in the County Court that the plaintiff had not been guilty of contributory negligence. Accordingly, in the context of the rules that questions of law are for the judge, not the jury, and that there is no appeal on fact from a County Court, the cases in question must be said to have turned on a point of law. There is no reason why the distinction should be the same in every context. Questions of the sufficiency of evidence must be treated as questions of law where there is a jury,· but they are hardly a suitable subject-matter for a precedent.[44]

In the context of the doctrine of precedent, the question whether a particular matter is one of law or fact is itself a question of law. Is there anything in the nature of a test for determining which is which? Salmond would have made the distinction turn on whether the question was one which could be answered according to a general principle. If it was such a question, and if it was so answered, then, although it was a question of fact, Salmond would have considered that a decision with regard to it constituted a precedent. He gave the question whether the defendant made a certain statement as an example of one which cannot be answered on principle. With this was to be contrasted the question whether, in making the statement, the defendant was guilty of fraud or

---

[43] *Baker* v. *E. Longhurst Ltd.* [1933] 2 KB 461; *Tidy* v. *Battmann* [1934] 1 KB 319; *Morris* v. *Luton Corporation* [1946] KB 114.

[44] The point that the distinction between law and fact is relevant in varying contexts is sometimes overlooked in discussions of the cases mentioned in the last footnote, see e.g. 62 *LQR* 110 and 9 *CLJ* 361.

negligence. Though the second question is, like the first, one of fact, Salmond considered that it could be answered on principle and that, if this were done, the decision would constitute a precedent 'and the question together with every other essentially resembling it, will become for the future a question of law predetermined by the rule thus established'.[45] It has become difficult, if not impossible, to rely on the distinction taken by Salmond after the decision of the House of Lords in *Qualcast (Wolverhampton) Ltd.* v. *Haynes*.[46] A master owes a duty of care to his servant to provide him with a safe system of work. When the work involves dangers against which the servant could guard by wearing protective spats, is the question whether, in order to escape liability for negligence, the master should have instructed the plaintiff, one of his servants, to wear the spats, one of fact or law? There were several previous cases which appeared to the County Court judge to have been decided on the general principle that a master is guilty of negligence if he fails to give instructions with regard to the use of protective clothing when that might guard against dangers to which the servant is exposed by his work. Nevertheless, the House of Lords held that these cases did not constitute a precedent. Reversing the County Court judge and the Court of Appeal, the House decided in favour of the defendant on the particular facts. Several of the Law Lords made a point that the judge's reasons for his conclusion on an issue which would be decided by a jury if there were one could not be treated as a precedent. It seems, therefore, safe to assume that, within the context of the rules of precedent, any question which would be left to a jury if there were one, must be treated as a matter of fact. Beyond this, it is impossible to provide a test for distinguishing between law and fact. The problem will remain so long as cases dealing with questions of fact continue to be reported and such cases will almost inevitably continue to be reported, if only because the question whether a case will be treated as a precedent depends on the way in which future courts treat that case.

[45] *Jurisprudence* (11th edn.), 222.   [46] [1959] AC 743.

VIII
THE FUTURE

Changes in practice

Precedent rules are based on the practice of the judges. The basic rules set out on page 6 seem firmly established. In particular, the rule that intermediate appellate courts are generally bound by their own decisions has not been questioned since the decision of the House of Lords in *Davis* v. *Johnson*.[1] Nevertheless, the view has been expressed in the Privy Council that opinions of the supreme tribunal on such a question cannot constitute the *ratio decidendi* of any case and are not therefore strictly binding.[2] One cannot rule out the possibility that, at some future date, a full court of the Court of Appeal will decide to abrogate or modify the rule in *Young* v. *Bristol Aeroplane Co. Ltd*. What the reaction of the House of Lords would be to such a move, and what the final upshot, must remain matters of mere conjecture. All one can say is that most commentators believe that such a step would be desirable, but it is judicial practice which counts.

However, precedent rules, like other features of judicial practice, are the subject of constant incremental evolution. We have seen how existing exceptions to *stare decisis* have been recently widened. Future developments may throw light on many of the unsettled questions mentioned in Chapter IV. In particular, it is to be hoped that a definite rule will emerge as to whether the Court of Appeal is bound by decisions of two-judge courts, as to the scope and applicability of the *per incuriam* exception, and as to whether there is or is not a general exception of obsolescence.

As to more radical developments, it is possible that the increasing importance of European Community law will, eventually, bring about changes in the English doctrine of precedent. We saw in Chapter V that this has not so far occurred, but we envisaged

---

[1] (1979) AC 264.
[2] *Attorney-General of St Christopher Nevis and Anguilla* v. *Reynolds* (1980) AC 637, 659.

circumstances in which new exceptions to *stare decisis* might result from the European dimension. A more remote possibility is that the jurisprudence of the European Court itself might affect the way English judges see their role. It could give greater impetus to the tendency to adopt a purposive, rather than a literal, approach to the interpretation of statutes which was apparent even before the entry of the United Kingdom into the European Community;[3] and that in turn may affect the style in which *rationes decidendi* are articulated. On the other hand, however European we become, it is unthinkable that judges in a common-law jurisdiction should ever abandon the notion that a single decision of a superior court can authoritatively lay down a rule of law in favour of the French view that only an accumulation of precedents can have this effect. United Kingdom domestic law must give way before directly applicable Community law; but the way in which the content of domestic case-law will be identified will continue to be governed— for any future that one can foresee—by something like our existing doctrine of precedent.

Legislative innovations

It has never been doubted that Parliament could alter or abrogate any aspect of the doctrine of precedent. Indeed, the view has occasionally been expressed that some precedent rule is so firmly established that only Parliament could change it.[4] In other jurisdictions, such measures have been passed. For example, the legislature of Zimbabwe has enacted legislation laying down that the Zimbabwean Supreme Court shall not be bound by any of its own decisions.[5] The United Kingdom Parliament has never sought to intervene in this direct way; and if it did, results might not match expectations. It is one thing to enact that courts are not obliged to follow other courts' rulings. It is another to prevent a practice of treating like cases alike from crystallizing once again into quasi-rules.

Indirectly, legislation has frequently affected the content of precedent rules. This occurs every time Parliament abolishes an old court or establishes a new one. However, the tendency has been for newly created courts to be slotted in to the precedent

---

[3] *Carter* v. *Bradbeer* (1975) 3 All ER 158, 161 Lord Diplock.
[4] *Miliangos* v. *George Frank (Textiles) Ltd.* (1976) AC 443, 470 Lord Simon.
[5] (1981) ASAL 205–6. For this example, I am indebted to Professor Edwin Cameron of the South African Bar (ed.).

rules which governed the practice of their predecessors, as the Criminal Division of the Court of Appeal has assumed that rules applicable to the Court of Criminal Appeal apply equally to it. There is a perennial debate about whether we need the present structure of two tiers of appeal. Were the judicial function of the House of Lords to be abolished, so that the Court of Appeal became the ultimate court for England, there can be little doubt that it would inherit the same attitude to its past decisions as the House of Lords now adopts towards past decisions of the House.

Constitutional developments

Another perennial debate concerns the question of whether a bill of rights, especially the European Convention on Human Rights and Fundamental Freedoms, should be incorporated into United Kingdom domestic law. If this were done, it might, eventually, have implications for the English doctrine of precedent similar to those which may emerge in relation to European Community Law. That is, it might come about that an English court would not regard itself as bound by a decision of the Court of Appeal or the House of Lords if that decision could not stand with a subsequent ruling of the European Court of Human Rights. Furthermore, if it came to be accepted that Parliament could not derogate from the bill of rights as, on one view, it cannot derogate from European Community law, additional modifications could result. If the courts acquired a power of constitutional review over primary legislation so that Parliament could not overturn their decisions, the rule that intermediate appellate courts are bound by their own decisions might well be abandoned in the constitutional context and the House of Lords could be expected to use its power to overrule its own decisions more freely.

Precedent under a code

Parts of English law may be codified in the not too distant future. Is there any reason why the rules of precedent applicable to subjects governed exclusively or primarily by case-law should not apply to the construction of the codes? If a rigid doctrine of precedent like ours is desirable where there is no code, but quite a number of codifying statutes, it may well be equally desirable when there is a detailed code consisting of a greater number of codifying sections. If it transpires that there are defects, they ought to be remediable by legislation. If, on the other hand, we have a code in general terms, a rigid doctrine of precedent would probably be most undesirable. General provisions are not readily susceptible of amendment in anything but equally general terms. They must be adapted by the courts to changing times and conditions as, for example, the provisions of the constitution of the United States have been reinterpreted from time to time. The generality of a lot of the French codes may have more than a little to do with the differences between the doctrines of precedent in England and France.

Several of the codifiers of the past have prohibited courts from considering the law as it stood before the introduction of their code. Provisions of this nature have turned out to be fruitless. It seems that the best a codifier can do is to hope that his words will meet with the approach canvassed by Lord Herschell in *Vagliano* v. *Bank of England*:

I think the proper course is in the first instance to examine the language of the statute and to ask what is its natural meaning, uninfluenced by any considerations derived from the previous state of the law, and not to start with inquiring how the law previously stood, and then, assuming that it was probably intended to leave it unaltered, to see if the words of the enactment can bear an interpretation in conformity with this view. If a statute intended to embody in a code a particular branch of the law is to be treated in this fashion, it appears to me that its utility will be almost entirely destroyed, and the very object with which it was enacted will be frustrated.[6]

This would mean that pre-code cases would cease to be binding upon the construction of the code, although they might continue to be of considerable value as examples of its application. When a provision of a code is intended to alter the previous law, previous cases should only be cited when there is uncertainty concerning the pre-existing law.

Prospective overruling

What many people regard as the last relict of the declaratory theory is the current invariable English practice of retrospective overruling.

And if it be found that the former decision is manifestly absurd, or unjust, it is declared, not that such a sentence was bad law, but that it was not law.[7]

---

[6] [1891] AC at 144. Lord Herschell was speaking of the Bills of Exchange Act 1882.   [7] *Blackstone's Commentaries*, i. 69–70.

This practice could be productive of great hardship and might operate as an undesirable curb on the exercise by a court of its overruling powers. For example, if the House of Lords were to overrule the decisions which most lawyers consider to have set the seal on the doctrine of privity of contract, settlements of property based on the assumption of the validity of that doctrine would lose much of their point, and the intentions of the settlor together with the legitimate expectations of others would be defeated. Such injustices could be avoided if the decision in question could be overruled with purely prospective effect. The old law would apply to events occurring before the date of the overruling (including those of the instant case), but it would cease to be applicable to transactions entered into after that date.

Considerations of this nature have led to the abandonment in the United States of the principle that overruling must necessarily be retrospective. Such a conclusion is hardly to be wondered at in a country where judicial decision can invalidate statutes under which divorces have been granted or bonds issued. It has come to be recognized in the United States that a State appellate court may choose whether to overrule a previous decision retrospectively or prospectively.[8] The United States' Supreme Court has been held to have similar powers, whether the case be civil or criminal,[9] and criteria for the decision whether the overruling should be prospective or retrospective have been laid down.[10] In the circumstances, it is hardly surprising that a fairly large amount of American legal literature has accumulated on the subject.[11]

Prospective overruling is not invariably the most just course. This point can be made most clearly apparent in relation to criminal proceedings. Suppose that A's conviction is affirmed by the Criminal Division of the Court of Appeal on the strength of one of its past decisions which the House of Lords holds, on A's appeal, to have been erroneous. If the overruling of the decision of the Court of Appeal is to be entirely prospective, A's conviction ought to be affirmed.[12] Let it be assumed that the House of Lords

[8] *Great Northern Railway* v. *Sunburst Oil and Refining Company*, 288 US 350 (1932).
[9] *Linkletter* v. *Walker*, 381 US 618 (1965).
[10] *Johnson* v. *New Jersey*, 394 US 619 (1966).
[11] See Andrew G. Nicol, 'Prospective Overruling: A New Device for English Courts', 39 *MLR* 542.
[12] A point frequently made against prospective overruling is that the practice deprives litigants of an incentive to appeal.

none the less hold that A is to be acquitted though stating that the decision of the Court of Appeal is only overruled from the date of their speeches. Persons who had conducted themselves in the same way as A, maybe at a later date, would continue to be criminally liable. The retrospective overruling of a criminal case can be as unjust as the prospective overruling to those who are already undergoing a sentence of imprisonment in consequence of a final conviction, but, in the case of prospective overruling, there is the added injustice to those who have not yet been prosecuted or whose prosecutions were pending at the date of the decision by which the earlier case was overruled prospectively. The American Supreme Court has had to grapple with especially difficult problems because it entertains proceedings for habeas corpus by those who have been detained pursuant to a conviction based on a decision which the court has subsequently overruled.

Time alone will show whether the House of Lords will assume the power already assumed by the American Supreme Court and declare that it can, when overruling a case, state the moment at which and the terms on which the overruling shall take effect. To date the House has done no more than overrule with purely prospective effect a decision of the Court of Criminal Appeal laying down a rule of practice prohibiting the addition of counts for other offences in an indictment for murder. The House did this notwithstanding the fact that, had the accused been prosecuted under the practice which it held should prevail in the future, the Court of Criminal Appeal would have acquitted him of both murder and robbery. The House confirmed his conviction for the latter offence at a trial which took place after his appeal against his conviction for murder had been allowed by the Court of Criminal Appeal on the ground of misdirection concerning his alibi. The House was, however, most careful to emphasize that it was a rule of practice, not a rule of law, which was being overruled.[13]

It is sometimes said that the House of Lords in effect overruled *Candler* v. *Crane Christmas and Co.*[14] prospectively in *Hedley Byrne and Partners Ltd.* v. *Heller and Partners Ltd.*[15] In the former case the Court of Appeal held that, at common law, there was no liability in tort for a negligent misrepresentation. In the *Hedley Byrne* case the defendants had negligently made a false statement concerning the solvency of the company, but they had

---

[13] *Connelly* v. *Director of Public Prosecutions* [1964] AC 1254.
[14] [1951] 2 KB 164.   [15] [1964] AC 465.

also used words exempting themselves from liability for such a statement. The House of Lords held that *Candler's* case had been wrongly decided, but affirmed the judgments of the lower Courts in favour of the defendants in the *Hedley Byrne* case on the ground that the exempting provision applied. The overruling of *Candler's* case was no less retrospective than any other overruling. Someone who made a negligent mistatement long before the *Hedley Byrne* decision could have been successfully sued the day after that decision, whereas he was previously under no tortious liability.[16]

It is sometimes said that prospective overruling is an impossibility because anything said by the court concerning the date at which its decision should become effective is unnecessary for the disposal of the legal issue in dispute, and therefore a mere *dictum*; but it is open to question whether the *obiter–ratio* distinction has any more relevance in this context than it has in that of the rules of precedent.[17] In any event, we have seen that the typical judicial approach to such a situation is to treat anything in the nature of an insistence on the distinction as unrealistic,[18] and, if it were thought proper to insist upon it, the trial could be treated as bifurcated. First there is the issue whether a particular case should be overruled, and then there is the issue concerning the date at which the overruling should become effective. Normally this would be a crucial question so far as the parties are concerned, because if, instead of allowing the overruling to be completely retrospective in the ordinary way, the court decrees that the new rule shall only apply to facts occurring from and after the date of its decision, the party who procured an affirmative answer to the question whether a case should be overruled might still be the ultimate loser.[19]

The appropriate 'cut-off' date is a matter which might present great difficulty if the practice of prospective overruling were introduced into English law. For example, in *Miliangos* v. *George Frank (Textiles) Ltd.*,[20] the House of Lords overruled a previous decision of its own according to which, on claims for a liquidated debt payable in foreign currency, judgment had to be given for the appropriate amount of English currency as at the date when

---

[16] 39 *MLR* 555.   [17] p. 105 *supra*.

[18] *W. B. Anderson and Sons Ltd.* v. *Rhodes* [1967] 2 All ER 850, at 857, *per* Cairns J, p. 80 *supra*.

[19] Traynor, 'Quo Vadis: Prospective Overruling', lecture at the University of Birmingham, 7 May 1974.

[20] [1976] AC 443.

payment was due.[21] If the overruling had been prospective, a possibility suggested by Lord Simon of Glaisdale in a dissenting speech, the cut-off date would not necessarily have been that of the *Miliangos* decision *tout court*. The new rule might have been made applicable to debts incurred after that date, to debts falling due after that date, and it is by no means clear that the House of Lords would have been in agreement on these matters simply because there is no obviously just solution.

Lord Simon of Glaisdale also canvassed the possibility of prospective overruling in a dissenting speech in an earlier case and, in this instance, Lord Diplock too thought that the possibility should be examined.[22] Other judges have pronounced against the practice extra-judicially. To quote Lord Devlin:

I do not like it. It crosses the Rubicon that divides the judicial and the legislative powers. It turns judges into undisguised legislators.[23]

Thoughts of this nature provide the answer to the question why retrospective parliamentary legislation is anathema whereas, although it amounts to legislation, retrospective overruling has been accepted for upwards of 500 years. This is surely due to the fact that adjudication is thought of as something that related to past events. It is true that the English judge is to a limited extent a developer of the law, even a legislator, but his other function, that of administering justice according to law between the parties who are concerned with past events, is unquestionably the more important of the two.

[21] *Re United Railways of Havana and Regla Warehouses Ltd*, [1961] AC 1007.
[22] *R. v. National Insurance Commissioner* ex parte Hudson [1972] AC 944.
[23] 39 *MLR* at 11.

TABLE OF CASES

INDEX